For Lavinia Cohn-Sherbok and Nicholas Grey

Debating Palestine and Israel

Attempts to contrive political routes out of the long and frustrating impasse in Israel have failed so far, perhaps in part because the problem isn't just political, but also moral, and the moral dimensions seem genuinely irresoluble, poised between two tragedies: the extinction of Jewish hopes of a secure Israel, and the frustration of Palestinian hopes of a sovereign Palestine. The privilege of reading the serious, sensitive, searching, well informed, and impressively candid debate between Mary Grey and Dan Cohn-Sherbok can help us touch the contending fears and hopes at their heart, and grasp both the difficulty and, perhaps, the possibility of doing justice to both sides.

Felipe Fernandez-Armesto

A Christian theologian, Mary Grey, and Rabbi Dan Cohn Sherbok have created a dialogue on the struggle between Israel and Palestine which is respectful of both sides, deep and intellectually sophisticated, and discusses both the history and the contemporary reality with the compassion and urgency so badly needed. No matter how much you think you know about this tragic struggle, you'll learn a lot more, and have a better ability to contribute to its resolution, after you read this book!

Michael Lerner

An interesting and valuable debate between well-informed partisans on both sides of the Israel–Palestine conflict. This may be a unique attempt to provide a rational discussion of this most intractable and interminable of international disputes.

W. D. Rubenstein

In the Israeli–Palestinian conflict there have been two mutually exclusive discourses. In this book by Catholic feminist theologian Mary Grey and Jewish theologian Rabbi Dan Cohn-Sherbok, there is a courageous attempt to bring these two discourses together in one conversation.

Rosemary Radford-Ruether

Debating Palestine and Israel

Dan Cohn-Sherbok
and Mary Grey

First Published 2014
by Impress Books Ltd

Innovation Centre, Rennes Drive, University of Exeter Campus,
Exeter EX4 4RN

© Dan Cohn-Sherbok and Mary Grey 2014

Typeset in Sabon by Swales & Willis Ltd, Exeter, Devon

Printed and bound in England by Short Run Press, Exeter, Devon

All rights reserved. No part of this book may be reprinted or
reproduced or utilised in any form or by any electronic,
mechanical, or other means, now known or hereafter invented,
including photocopying and recording, or in any information
storage or retrieval system, without permission in writing from
the publishers.

British Library Cataloguing in Publication Data
A catalogue record for this book is available from the British Library

ISBN 13: 978-1-907-60549-9 (paperback)
ISBN 13: 978-1-907-60550-5 (ebook)

Maps reproduced by permission of Routledge

Contents

About the authors	xii
Preface	xv
Foreword	xx
The Palestine–Israeli Conflict (Timeline)	xxii
Maps	xxix

Chapter 1: Nineteenth-Century Anti-Semitism — 1

The Problem of Anti-Semitism	1
Anti-Semitism – A Christian Counter-Current	3
A Jewish State?	6
A Separate Homeland Is Not the Only Solution	8
The Question of a Jewish Homeland	10
Assimilation Can Never Be the Answer!	12

Chapter 2: Zionism — 15

The Many Faces of Zionism	15
The Zionist Quest	17
The Bible is Our Mandate!	19
An Historic Mandate	22
The *Eretz Israel* Has a History for Palestinians Too!	24
The Bible and History	26

Chapter 3: The Balfour Declaration — 29

The Road to Balfour	29
The Road to Balfour – Contradictory Promises	31

CONTENTS

British Betrayal   34
Balfour – A Web of Deceit   37
Settlers and Incomers   39
There Were Other Ways!   41

Chapter 4: The Aftermath of the Balfour Declaration   45

The Unravelling of Deceit   45
The Problem of Anti-Semitism   48
Aftermath of Balfour – Buying Up Arab Land   50
The Jewish Problem   53
You Cannot Solve One Injustice with Another!   55
A Clear View of History   57

Chapter 5: The British Mandate   61

Arab Resistance   61
The Impact of Balfour in Palestine   63
Delegitimizing the State of Israel   65
Was This Conflict Avoidable?   68
Jews and Arabs   70
A Failure of Empathy   72

Chapter 6: Palestine before the Second World War   75

The Contribution of Women in the Struggle   75
The Liberation of Women   78
Palestinian Women and the Arab Rebellion   79
Arab Intransigence   82
Gandhi and the Issue of Justice for Palestine   84
Misunderstanding Zionism   86

Chapter 7: Between the First and Second World War   89

Jewish Extremism   89
Seeking Justice for Both Sides   91
The Grand Mufti and the Jews   94
Increasing Radicalisation on All Sides –
   Revolt against the British   96
Nazism and the Zionist Cause   98
Anti-Palestinian Propaganda   100

CONTENTS

Chapter 8: Post War Developments 1946–1948 — 103

Zionist Systematic Planning — 103
Plan Dalet: The Controversy — 105
Al Nakba – The Catastrophe — 107
The War of Independence — 110
Let the Truth Be Known! — 112
Delegitimizing Israel — 115

Chapter 9: The War of Independence and Aftermath — 117

The War of Independence — 117
A Crucial Moment in Our Story — 119
The Nakba — 122
Seeking the Truth about al Nakba — 123
Revisionist History — 126
Revisionist History and Misinterpretations — 128

Chapter 10: Suez and Beyond — 131

Aftermath of 1948 — 131
Obstacles to Reconciliation — 133
The Right to Return – Still a Burning Issue — 135
The Palestinian Struggle — 137
The Persistence of Non-violence — 141
The Plight of the Refugees — 143

Chapter 11: The Six-Day War and Its Aftermath — 144

Continuing Aggression — 144
Triumph and Tragedy — 146
Arab Aggression against Israel — 148
Palestinian Refugees and Their Host Arab Countries — 151
The PLO and the Jews — 153
Ben-Gurion and 'Peaceful Coexistence' –
  Confronting the Truth — 154

Chapter 12: Renewed Conflict between Israel and the Arabs — 158

Yasser Arafat and the Battle of Karameh — 158
Mounting Aggression — 161

CONTENTS

You Cannot Kill a People's Memory! ... 163
Justifying Horror ... 166
Mounting Violence – Yet a Chink of Hope ... 167
The Road to Peace ... 170

Chapter 13: The Palestinian Problem ... 173

Obstacles to Peace ... 173
Camp David – A Failed Peace Initiative and Its Aftermath ... 176
The Death of the Camp David Accords ... 178
The Massacres of Sabra–Shatila ... 181
Arabs and the Peace Initiative ... 183
Admit the Picture Is More Ambiguous! ... 185

Chapter 14: The Uprising ... 188

The Non-violent Intifada of 1987 ... 188
An Alternative View ... 190
Another Alternative – Palestinian Christian Non-violence ... 193
Palestinians and Armed Struggle ... 195
The Enduring Spirit of the First Intifada ... 198
The Possibility of Peace ... 200

Chapter 15: Arab–Israeli Negotiations ... 203

The Road to Peace ... 203
Obstacles to Peace ... 205
Undermining the Peace Process ... 208
Were the Oslo Accords Just? ... 209
The Danger of Intransigence ... 211
This Elusive Peace – Another Significant Dimension ... 213

Chapter 16: Before and after September 11 – The Second Intifada 2000 and the Attack on the Twin Towers ... 216

A New Wave of Violence – Sharon Lights the Match! ... 216
Reviving the Peace Process ... 219
The Horrific Impact of 'The Wall' ... 221
The Separation Barrier ... 223
The Imperative of Truth ... 226
The Security Fence (or Wall) ... 228

CONTENTS

Chapter 17: Continuing Conflict — 231

- Towards Peace — 231
- Operation Defensive Shield — 234
- Defensive Shield — 237
- The Need for a Reconciling Stance — 239
- Palestinians and Violence — 241
- The Many Types of Violence and the Many Faces of Resistance — 243

Chapter 18: Gaza and Beyond — 246

- Gaza – A Crucible of Suffering — 246
- Continuing Violence — 249
- Who Started It? — 252
- Gaza — 255
- Goldstone Report — 256
- The Return of the Exiles — 259

Chapter 19: Beyond the Gaza War — 262

- Faltering Steps toward Peace — 262
- The Complexities of the One- or Two-State Solutions — 265
- The Two-State Solution — 268
- What Solution is Viable? — 271
- The Right of Return — 274
- What to Do about Settlements? — 276

Chapter 20: The Future — 280

- What Chance for Peace? — 280
- The Settlements — 283
- The Struggle for Jerusalem — 284
- Jerusalem and Borders — 287
- A *Kairos* Moment for Peace? — 289
- Towards Peace — 292

Bibliography — 295
Index — 301

About the authors

Dan Cohn-Sherbok

My great grandfathers were immigrants to the United States from Hungary at the end of the nineteenth century. Initially the family lived on the East Side of New York City; one of my grandfathers was a kosher butcher, and I have a photograph of him standing in front of his shop. After my maternal grandmother married my grandfather, who worked initially as a cigar-roller, they moved to Denver, Colorado. My mother grew up in a modern Orthodox synagogue where she was confirmed. My father who was an orthopaedic surgeon came to do medical research at the National Jewish Hospital in Denver and met and married my mother. They joined the large Reform Temple where I had a bar mitzvah and was confirmed. I went to a typical American high school; at the same time I attended religion school once a week and on the weekends. After high school I studied philosophy at a small all-male liberal arts college – Williams College – in Massachusetts. From a young age I wanted to be a rabbi – my aim was to serve congregations in the United States. I never had a desire to settle in Israel, although I visited there during my junior year abroad in Athens. From 1966 to 1971 I was a student at the Hebrew Union College-Jewish Institute of Religion in Cincinnati, Ohio – the largest Reform Jewish seminary in the world. During my studies I served as a student rabbi in various congregations throughout the United States. I then was a rabbi in Australia, England and South Africa. Although I tried very hard, these experiences helped me to see that that the rabbinate was not for me, and I enrolled as a PhD student at Cambridge University. Several years later I taught Jewish theology at the University of Kent. Subsequently I became Professor of Judaism at the University of Wales where I am now Emeritus Professor. Over the years I have been particularly interested in the Israel–Palestinian conflict, and I have written a number of books dealing with modern Israel: *Israel: The History of an Idea*; *The Palestine-Israeli Conflict* (with Dawoud El-Alami); *Introduction to Zionism and Israel: From Ideology to History*; and *The Palestinian State: A Jewish Justification*.

Mary Grey

I was born in north-east England, the eldest of seven children to parents – both teachers – who were deeply religious (Roman Catholic). Their ambition was that their daughters would be nuns and their sons – priests. Well, one of my brothers is a priest, and two of us did make unsuccessful attempts to be nuns! We grew up with the stories of local Celtic and Saxon saints and loved the countryside of Northumberland associated with them. It was an upbringing rich in many ways, but narrow in others. For example, we were not encouraged to mix with Christians from other denominations, let alone with those from other faiths. Yet our parents inspired in us a deep commitment to social justice.

All this changed with the Second Vatican Council – which coincided with my time at Oxford – studying Classics and Philosophy. This opened up windows to ecumenism and to interfaith dialogue. So when I studied Theology at the University of Louvain, Belgium (by this time I was married with four children!) Christian Theology was coming to terms both with its own endemic anti-Judaism and the Church's actions – or inaction – during the Holocaust.

The second great influence that I encountered in Louvain was the rise of Christian Feminism – so I wrote my PhD thesis in this area – on Redemption in Feminist Theology which eventually became *Redeeming the Dream* (SPCK 1989). This led directly into Liberation Theology which has been my great enthusiasm since the seventies and the subject of much of my writing. Our family returned to the UK in 1979, and since them I've been lecturing in different places – with a return to the Netherlands in 1988, for a

Chair in Feminism and Christianity in Nijmegen. Increasingly, the direction of my writing is moving from liberation to reconciliation – this was the case with *To Rwanda and Back* (2007) and the writing on Israel/Palestine. It has also been a strand in my involvement in India: Nicholas – my husband – and I co-founded an NGO called *Wells for India* in 1987 and have been travelling frequently to Rajasthan for our water projects. The people of the villages will remain close to our concerns. But the struggle for justice for the Dalit (former Untouchables) peoples profoundly affected me and became another focus of my writing.

It seems that the search for freedom and liberation is an unfinished symphony – certainly more than enough for one lifetime!

Preface

Dan Cohn-Sherbok

Before we begin our discussion and debate, I want to say something about the nature of the Jewish community worldwide. It has now been over 60 years since the terrible events of the Holocaust took place. Over 5 million Jews were killed in the most terrifying fashion. The Nazis were determined to exterminate Jews wherever they lived. Gassing and cremation became stages in an efficient series of murderous acts. These terrifying events have cast a long shadow over the contemporary Jewish community. And, most significantly, in the minds of most Jews they have confirmed the vision of the early Zionists.

At the end of the nineteenth century, such figures as Theodor Herzl (the father of modern Israel) warned that Jews would always be insecure in the societies in which they lived. In *The Jewish State*, he argued that old prejudices against the Jewish nation are ingrained in Western society – assimilation, he believed, would not provide a cure of the ills that beset the Jewish population. In his view, there is only one remedy for the sickness of anti-Semitism: the creation of a Jewish state. At the first Zionist Congress in 1897, Max Nordau, one of the leading Zionist figures, spoke about the contemporary conditions of Jewry. Wherever they lived in large numbers, he stated, they were subject to misery. Proponents of Jewish emancipation have argued that if legal restrictions against Jews were lifted, this would result in the amelioration of Jewish deprivation. But this is a chimera: anti-Semitism is inevitable. Thus the Jewish people need a place of refuge.

The horrors of the Holocaust have for most Jews confirmed these fears about the fate of the Jewish people. Today Jews wherever they live are determined to ensure the survival of the Jewish nation and the continuation of the Jewish religion. In this quest, the state of Israel is central: it is regarded as a safe haven for the oppressed and persecuted. The Jewish theologian, Emil Fackenheim, has given voice to such determination and commitment. In his view, out of the ashes of Auschwitz, God issued the 614th commandment:

> Jews are forbidden to hand Hitler posthumous victories. They are commanded to survive as Jews, lest the Jewish people perish. They are commanded to remember the victims of Auschwitz lest their memory perish. They are forbidden to despair of man and his world, and to escape into either cynicism or other worldliness, lest they co-operate in delivering the world over to the forces of Auschwitz. Finally, they are forbidden to despair of the God of Israel, lest Judaism perish ... A Jew may not respond to Hitler's attempt to destroy Judaism by himself co-operating in its destruction.
> (Emil Fackenheim in Michael Morgan, p. 176)

In this theological formulation Fackenheim has expressed a universal sentiment shared by contemporary Jewry: Never Again! In a post-Holocaust world, the quest for Jewish survival has eclipsed all other matters, and has reinforced the Jewish commitment to the survival of the state of Israel. Across the religious spectrum – from strict Orthodoxy on the right to the most liberal forms of non-Orthodox Judaism – Jews are fiercely loyal to the state of Israel even if they disagree with the political direction taken by its leaders. Even those Jews who are troubled about Palestinian suffering in the Occupied Territories are determined that the Jewish state should survive and flourish.

As a liberal rabbi, I – like the vast majority of my coreligionists – am deeply concerned about the continued survival of the Jewish nation. It would be an overwhelming tragedy if Israel were destroyed by its Arab neighbours. As you know, only until recently have Palestinians embraced the notion of a two-state solution: previously they sought to drive Israelis into the sea. Indeed, such an aspiration is a central feature of Hamas policy. Since its foundation it has been committed to Islamic rule for all of Palestine. As a Catholic theologian, you may find it difficult to perceive the depth of Jewish sensitivity to this most recent threat to Jewish survival. For thousands of years, we Jews have been persecuted, hated and murdered. The most recent manifestation of such Jew-hatred – the Nazi onslaught – has profoundly affected Jewish consciousness. On the threshold of the twenty-first century we continue to feel under threat. Now it is not the Nazis who pose the greatest challenge, but the Arab world which detests us and seeks to overwhelm the small nation-state that we have built in our ancient homeland.

Mary Grey

Growing up in a tightly-knit Roman Catholic family, with its Irish background, I was not aware of the long history of anti-Semitism and suffering of the Jewish people in history, and culminating in the Holocaust until I began to study theology at the University of Louvain in the seventies. At that time Christian theology and the Christian Church was reacting with horror to the stories of the Holocaust and to its own involvement. I read everything I could find on the subject – including your own early work on the Holocaust and was deeply shocked and affected. It was made easier to understand while living in the Netherlands, visiting the Anne Frank House, in Amsterdam and hearing the stories of Christian families who had tried to help Jews by hiding them or helping them escape. At this point Rosemary Radford Ruether's book *Faith and Fratricide* was groundbreaking in its analysis of *Christian anti-Judaism* (Ruether 1974) and in my own area Katharina von Kellenbach's *Anti-Judaism in Feminist Religious Writing* (Von Kellenbach 1994). I recalled with shame the prayers that were said every year at Good Friday's liturgy praying for the conversion of the "perfidious Jews": these are words now eliminated by the reforms of the Second Vatican Council. I think that at this stage Christian theologians were genuinely delighted at the birth of the state of Israel. I remember the excitement of the 1967 war – when it was thought to be an amazing achievement that this fledgling State could defeat the combined Arab armies in the Six-Day War.

My reaction to all this was to become involved in Jewish Christian dialogue, first, joining in seminars with the Women's Group of International Commission of Christians and Jews (ICCJ) in Lille, Rome and Kiev, and then serving on their Theology Group. In Kiev with Rabbi David Rosen we visited the site of Babi-Yar, which was deeply moving – though I was not able to go to Auschwitz until 2011.

Only slowly did I become aware of the long-standing conflict in Israel–Palestine and that there was another side to the story – the suffering of the Arab people, both Christian and Muslim. The story of the Nakba – the Catastrophe, according to the Palestinians, when the inhabitants of 533 villages were driven out of their homes and forced to become refugees – is much less known in Europe and America than is the story of the Holocaust/Shoah. In England we have a Holocaust Memorial Day – but no Nakba day.

So I joined Sabeel – or Friends of Sabeel UK – soon after its founding in 1987: Sabeel (Arabic for 'The Way' or 'The Wellspring') was founded by Canon Naim Ateek, an Anglican priest and theologian, who had personally experienced the Nakba on being driven from his home, Beit Shean, as a child. Its aim is the liberation of Palestinian Christians – but Sabeel also works with Muslims both in Israel and the West Bank. I tried to struggle with the two conflicting narratives. Things came to a head at the ICCJ Conference in Kiev in 1997, where I was given the task – with the Jewish Rabbi Tikva Frymer-Kensky – of writing a Justice Policy document for ICCJ. When I asked what to do about the conflict in Palestine/Israel, I was told, 'Just leave it out!' I could not in conscience do this, so, very sadly, I resigned. I still miss the people and the theological discussions.

I think it is through my cooperation with you that I continue to wrestle with the two narratives and the urgency of doing justice to both. This is not made easier by the way it is considered as 'anti-Semitic' in some quarters to criticise the policies of the Israeli government and the Occupation of the West Bank and Gaza. I hope that in this book that our commitment to peace and reconciliation through telling the truth will go some way to winning trust on both sides of the divide.

PREFACE

Our first book *Pursuing the Dream* (2005) struggled with our respective theologies, but this one will tackle the serious issues of the conflict in some detail. I think the process will be painful – but nothing compared with the pain and suffering of all those communities caught up in what seems like an interminable conflict.

Foreword

In the Israeli-Palestinian conflict there have been two mutually exclusive discourses. The Israelis tell the story of their sufferings under anti-Semitism through the ages, culminating in the Nazi Holocaust, their need for a Jewish state to protect them from new attacks by anti-Semites today and in the future and the democratic nature and excellent accomplishments of the state of Israel. The Palestinians tell the story of their historical roots in the land of Palestine, their unjust colonisation by Britain and the Zionists, the expulsion of many of their people from Palestine, the oppression of others by Israel, and their call for justice. These two discourses tend to be mutually exclusive. They are published for and read by different audiences.

In this book by Catholic feminist theologian Mary Grey and Jewish theologian Rabbi Cohn-Sherbok, there is a courageous attempt to bring these two discourses together in one conversation. In twenty chapters Grey and Cohn-Sherbok write letters back and forth in an intense discussion of the history of this conflict between Israel and the Palestinians from its foundations in the nineteenth century Zionism, and the British proposal of a "national home for the Jewish people" that would not prejudice the rights of the "non-Jewish people of Palestine," through the twists and turns of the 20th century to the conflicts and peace movements in Palestine today. The hope is to find ways of agreeing with each other on what needs to be done between the two communities to create justice and peace between them.

FOREWORD

The book ends in a heartwarming agreement. Cohn-Sherbok is committed to a two-state solution in which there can be equal justice for the Palestinians, side by side with the state of Israel, a vision shared by Mary Grey. Whether the terms of this envisioned solution can create a Palestinian state adequate to encompass the needs of Palestinians scattered in Israel and abroad would be another discussion.

Rosemary Radford Ruether

The Palestine–Israeli Conflict (Timeline)

1862	Publication of *Rome and Jerusalem* by Moses Hess.
1881	Assassination of Tsar Alexander II followed by persecution of Russian Jews.
1882	Publication of *Autoemancipation* by Leo Pinsker.
1882–1903	Alfred Dreyfus falsely charged with espionage.
1896	Publication of the *Jewish State* by Theodor Herzl
1897	First International Congress of Zionists
1903	Persecution of Jews in Kishinev.
1905	Seventh Zionist Congress rejects alternative to Palestine as aim of Zionism.
1908–1909	Arab opposition to Zionist settlement intensifies.
1914–1918	First World War.
1915	McMahon correspondence with Sharif Hussein
1915–1916	Sykes-Picot agreement.
1917	Balfour Declaration. Arab Revolt: Lawrence takes Aqaba, Allenby enters Jerusalem.
1919	Chaim Weizmann leads Zionist delegation at Paris Peace Conference.
1919–1923	Third Aliyah
1920–1921	Arab anti-Jewish riots in Palestine.
1924–1932	Fourth Aliyah
1929	Arab riots in Jerusalem, Hebron and Safed.
1930	Passfield White paper seeks British disengagement from the Jewish National Home aspects of the Balfour Declaration and the Palestine Mandate.
1931	Irgun Tzevai Leumi established.
1933–1935	Fifth Aliyah
1937	Peel Commission recommends partition of Palestine.
1938	Evian Conference.

1939	Conference at St James Palace White Paper repudiates partition and favours an independent Palestinian state.
1939–1942	Co-operation between British forces and Jews in Palestine.
1942	Loss of Struma. Baltimore Congress.
1943	Anglo-American Conference at Bermuda on refugees.
1944	Assassination of Lord Moyne in Cairo.
1945	President Truman supports the demand for a large number of immigrants to Palestine.
1946	Truman supports demand for admission of 100,000 refugees to Palestine. This is refused by the British. Jewish sabotage operations throughout Palestine. Irgun blows up King David Hotel in Jerusalem. Truman endorses partition of Palestine and creation of a Jewish state.
1947	British Foreign Secretary, Ernest Bevin, declares intention to refer the Palestine Mandate back to the United Nations. General Assembly votes for partition of Palestine into a Palestinian and Jewish state. The British government expresses its intention to terminate its responsibility under the Mandate.
1948	Irgun, led by Menachem Begin, massacre villagers at Deir Yassin. Palestinian refugees flee en masse fearing a similar fate. Ben-Gurion declares the State of Israel. Termination of the British Mandate. Arab armies enter areas assigned to the Palestinian state under the partition plan to support Palestinian resistance. UN appoints as mediator Count Folke Bernadotte. Truce between Israel and the Arab states. Bernadotte assassinated. Fighting between Israel and Egypt. Moshe Dayan drives all Palestinian citizens from Lydda and Ramleh by force. UN Resolution 194 states that all Palestinian refugees wishing to

	return to their homes should be permitted to do so and that compensation for loss or damage to property should be paid.
1949	Israel concludes armistice agreements with Egypt, Lebanon and Syria. UN votes in favour of internationalizing Jerusalem. Ben-Gurion declares Jerusalem the capital of Israel.
1950	Beginning of Jews immigration to Israel from Arab countries. King Abdullah of Jordan formally annexes the West Bank. The Law of Return gives the right to settle in Israel to every Jew world-wide.
1951	King Abdullah assassinated in Jerusalem at Friday night prayers.
1952	Coup in Egypt by 'Free Officers'; rise to power of Nasser.
1953	Ben-Gurion retires. Moshe Sharrett becomes Prime-Minister of Israel.
1954	Increased fedayeen attacks on Israel. Israeli army attacks Nahalin in the West Bank.
1955	Israel launches a major raid against Egyptians. Military pact between Egypt and Syria. Ben-Gurion becomes Prime Minister.
1956	Israel attacks in Sinai. Israeli border guards massacre villagers at Kufr Kassem. UN Security Council Resolution calling for Israeli withdrawal from Sinai vetoed by Britain and France. British and French attack in the Canal Zone.
1957	Israel announces intention conditionally to withdraw from Sinai. Palestinian Liberation Party (Fatah) founded.
1958	Relations between Israel and the United States strengthened.
1963	Levi Eshkol becomes Prime Minister.
1964	Palestine Liberation Organisation (PLO) founded.

1966	Fedayeen activity against Israel increased.
1967	Nasser sends troops into Sinai.
1967	Nasser closes Strait of Tiran to Israeli shipping Summit at Khartoum. United Nations Security Council Resolution 242 issued.
1968	Golda Meir becomes Prime Minister. Yasser Arafat is elected as the Chairman of the Executive Committee of the PLO.
1970	Black September. Jordanian army acts against PLO guerrillas in Jordan.
1971	PLO guerrillas leave Jordan for Syria and south Lebanon.
1972	Black September Organisation seizes Israeli athletes at Munich Olympics Nine Israelis die in airport shootout.
1973	Egypt and Syria launch full-scale war against Israeli forces occupying the Sinai Peninsula and Golan Heights.
1974	Summit meeting of Arab leaders in Rabat declares the PLO the only legitimate representative of the Palestinian people.
1975	Civil war breaks out in Lebanon. Palestinian guerrillas fight alongside Lebanese leftists and Muslims against Maronite Christians.
1976	Following Syrian intervention in the Lebanese civil war, Arab leaders agree to a cease-fire.
1977	Sadat goes to Jerusalem for peace offer.
1978	Israel invades south Lebanon and attacks Palestinian guerrilla bases. Camp David Accords signed by Egypt, Israel and the USA.
1979	Egypt and Israel sign peace treaty.
1981	Katysha war between the PLO and Israel in Lebanon.

THE PALESTINE–ISRAELI CONFLICT

1982	Israel invades Lebanon again in an all-out offensive against the PLO. Israeli forces reach outskirts of Beirut. Following the siege, the PLO leaves Lebanon, establishes headquarters in Tunis and scatters its fighters throughout the Arab countries. Massacre of Palestinian refugees in Sabra and Shatila camps in Lebanon. Israeli Defense Minister Sharon forced from office. Lebanon-Israel truce.
1985	Israeli Air Force attack on PLO headquarters in Tunis. Palestinian Liberation Front hijacks Achile Lauro in the Mediterranean. Palestinian Intifada begins in the Israeli-occupied Gaza Strip and the West Bank. Khalil al-Wazir (Abu Jihad) assassinated by Israeli commandos in Tunis. Jordanian disengagement from the West Bank. Palestinian National Council declares an independent Palestinian state. Arafat recognizes Israel and renounces terrorism before the UN at Geneva. USA agrees to open dialogue.
1990	Iraq invades Kuwait.
1991	Gulf War: Allied bombing campaign against Iraq. Middle East Peace Conference in Madrid.
1992	Labour Party under Rabin wins Israeli election and engages the PLO in dialogue.
1993	PLO declaration of principles on interim self-government.
1994	Jewish settler Baruch Goldstein murders Palestinian Muslims worshipping at Hebron Mosque. Cairo Agreement between Israel and PLO. Israel-Jordan Peace Treaty; Whitehouse lawn handshake between Rabin, Peres and Arafat, who are jointly awarded the Nobel Peace Prize. Israel forces commence withdrawal from Jericho and the Gaza Strip.
1995	Rabin assassinated by Jewish extremist at a peace rally in Tel Aviv.
1996	Benjamin Netanyahu becomes Prime Minister.

1998	Wye River agreement between Netanyahu and Arafat.
1999	Netanyahu loses Israeli election to Ehud Barak. King Hussein of Jordan dies and is succeeded by his eldest son, Abdullah.
2000	Israel withdraws from Lebanon. Death of President Hafez al-Asad of Syria. Palestinian uprising. Final collapse of Wye Accords as Palestinians reject Israeli plan that would keep large areas of the West Bank under Israeli control. Visit by Ariel Sharon to al-Haram al-Sharif/Temple Mount triggers Al-Aqsa Intifada.
2001	Ariel Sharon elected Prime Minister of Israel. 'Dolphinarium' discotheque in Tel Aviv hit by suicide bombs. 'Sbarro' pizzeria suicide bombing in Jerusalem by Islamic Jihad. Israel assassinates Abu Ali Mustafa. Terror attacks on the World Trade Centre. PFLP assassinates Israeli tourism minister Rehav'am Ze'evi.
2002	Saudi Prince Abdullah announces a Peace plan. Israel mounts operation 'Defensive Wall' in retaliation for suicide bombings. Invasion of Jenin refugee camp and West Bank towns. Chairman Arafat imprisoned in the 'Mukata' compound in Ramallah. End of sieges in Mukata and Church of Nativity. Chairman Arafat signs the 2002: PNA Basic Law. Israel commences building of the 'Separation Fence'. President Bush calls for Israeli withdrawal and a Palestinian state, but insists that PNA be reformed and current leaders replaced. Israel assassinates Saleh Shehadeh. Israel's government unstable due to resignations in the Labour Party.
2003	Cairo conference of Palestinian groups. Ariel Sharon re-elected Prime Minister. United States and Britain invade Iraq overthrowing the regime of Saddam Hussein. Mahmoud Abbas appointed

	Prime Minister. Arafat under siege in Ramallah headquarters.
2004	Operation Rainbow. Operation Days of Penitence. Ramallah siege continues Arafat delegates powers to Mahmoud Abbas. Death of Arafat.
2005	Mahmoud Abbas elected President. Ariel Sharon resigns as leader of Likud party and sets up Kadima. Israeli disengagement from the Gaza Strip.
2006	Ariel Sharon suffers stroke. Ehud Olmert elected Prime Minister of Israel. Hamas wins a majority of seats in the Palestinian legislature. Israel-Lebanon War Hamas and Fatah agree to a cease fire.
2007	Fighting continues between Hamas and Fatah. The armed wing of Hamas announces that the truce with Israel has ended.
2008	Bush tours Middle East. Popular breakout from Gaza into Egypt to buy essential supplies.
2009	Barack Obama elected President of the USA. US Secretary of State Hilary Clinton goes to Israel. White House announces negotiations to take place between Israel and the Palestinians. Israel imposes construction freeze on settlements in the West Bank.
2010	Israel carries out Gaza flotilla raid. Negotiations take place between Israel and the Palestinians.
2011	Fatah and Hamas sign a unity agreement Mahmoud Abbas appeals to the UN General Assembly to recognize Palestine as a nation state.
2012	Israel begins Operation Pillar of Defense in the Gaza Strip. The Palestinian Authority applies to the UN for admission as a Non-member state.
2013–2014	Israeli and Palestinian Negotiators engage in direct negotiations.

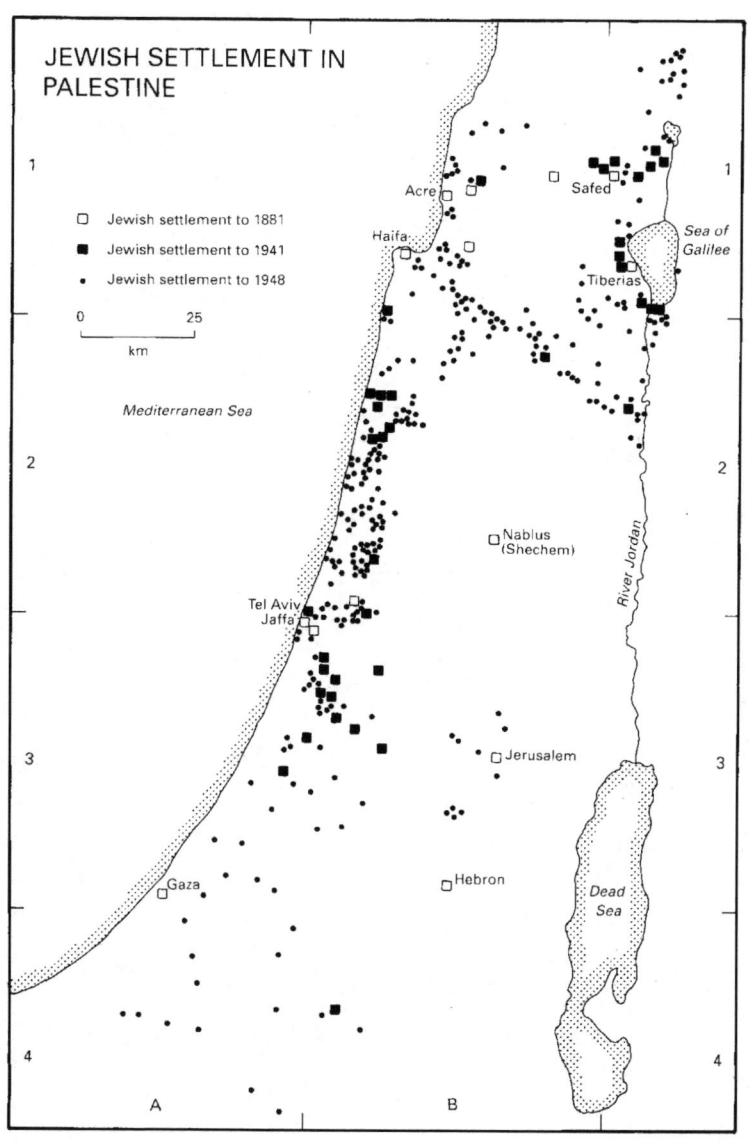

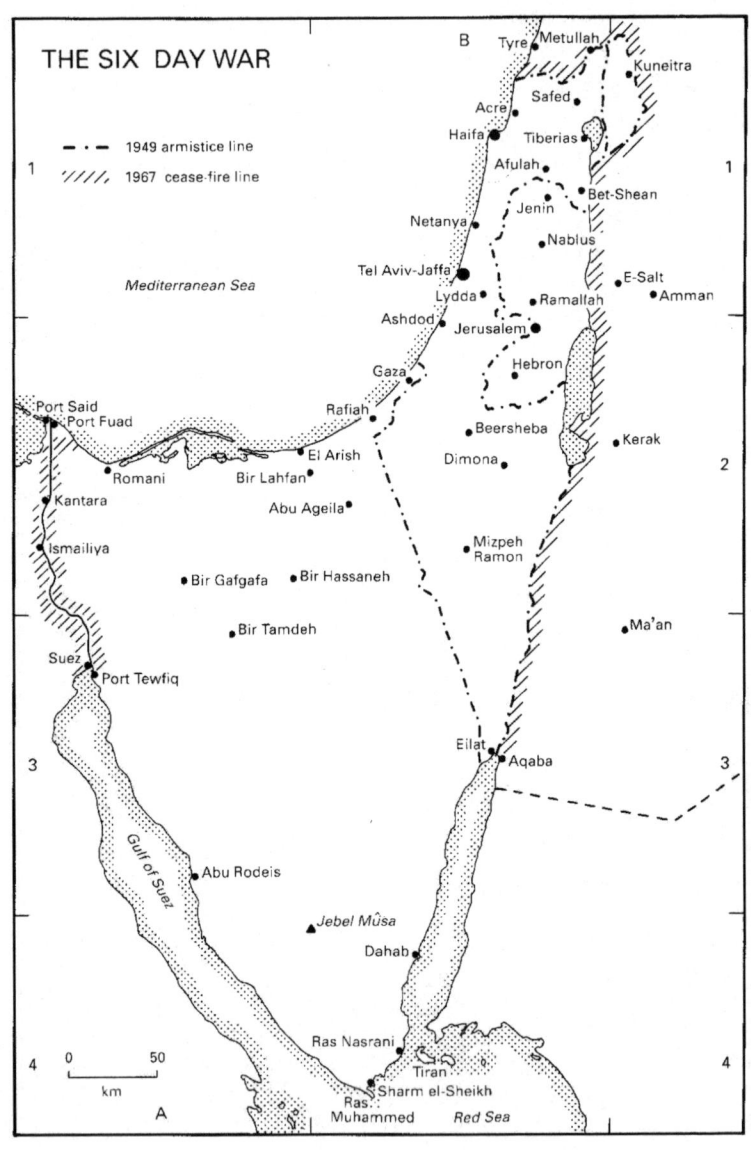

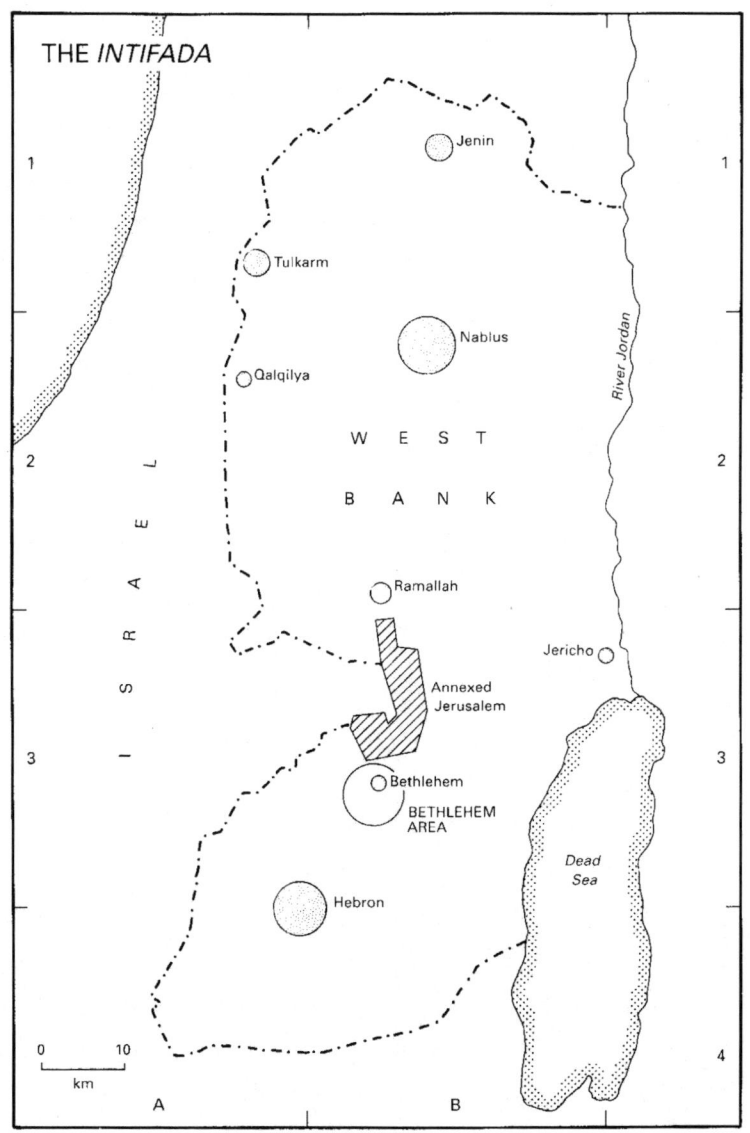

Chapter 1
Nineteenth-Century Anti-Semitism

The Problem of Anti-Semitism
Dan Cohn-Sherbok

You may not have realized that at the end of the nineteenth century most Jews were not in favour of the creation of a Jewish state. It was only after the Holocaust that Jewry united in supporting the establishment of Israel. Prior to that time, the vast majority of Orthodox Jews were anti-Zionists for religious reasons. Although the Torah maintains that it is the duty of the pious to return to Zion, these Orthodox Jews pointed out that such an ingathering must be preceded by messianic redemption. These critics maintained that Zionism is a heretical attempt to usurp the privilege of the Messiah to establish a Jewish kingdom in the holy land. For these reasons Agudat Israel, the mainstream Orthodox European movement, denounced the policies of modern Zionists as well as religious Zionist parties such as Mizrahi. In Palestine itself its leaders protested to the British government and the League of Nations about the Zionist quest to make a national home in the Holy Land. At times it even joined forces with Arab leaders.

Paralleling the Orthodox critique, liberal Jews attacked Zionism for its utopian character. According to these critics, it is simply impossible to bring about the emigration of millions of Jews to a country which was already populated. In the view of Reform Jewish leaders and others, assimilation provided the solution to the problem of Jew-hatred. Some of these liberals were determined to refute the principles of Zionism. Felix Goldman, a German and anti-Zionist rabbi, for example, contended that Jewish nationalism is a product of the general chauvinistic movement which had poisoned contemporary history, but would be swept away by universalism. Jewish socialists, too, voiced their criticism. In their view, it was an error to emigrate from the countries where they resided. Assimilation and integration into a socialist society was the key to Jewish survival.

These currents of anti-Zionism were met by fierce opposition on the part of secular Zionists. As early as 1862 Moses Hess, the Jewish socialist and colleague of Karl Marx, published *Rome and Jerusalem* in which he argued that the only remedy for anti-Semitism was Jewish nationalism. Anti-Jewish sentiment, he argued, is unavoidable. Progressive Jews think they can escape from Judeophobia by recoiling from any form of Jewish national expression. Yet the hatred of Jews is inescapable. No reform of the religion, he wrote, is radical enough to avoid such sentiments, and even conversion to Christianity cannot relieve the Jew of this disability. For Hess, Jews will always remain strangers among the nations: nothing can alter this state of affairs. The only solution to the problem of Jew-hatred is for the Jewish people to come to terms with their national identity.

Another early Zionist, Leo Pinsker, was deeply affected by the Russian pogroms of 1881. Previously he had been an advocate of Jewish emancipation in Russia. However, after witnessing the fury unleashed against the Jews, he embraced Zionist ideology. In *Autoemancipation*, published in 1882, he wrote: 'The Jewish people has no fatherland of its own, though many motherlands; it has no rallying point, no centre of gravity, no government of its own, no accredited representatives. It is everywhere a guest, and nowhere at home' (Pinsker 1932, p. 6). Thus, among the nations of the world, the Jews are like a nation long dead; the dead walking among the living. Having no home, the Jew can never be anything other than an alien. He is not simply a guest in a foreign country rather he is more like a beggar and a refugee. The only way to escape discrimination, persecution and murder, is for Jewry to have a country of their own.

Echoing such views, Theodor Herzl, a Viennese journalist was deeply disturbed by the Dreyfus case in France. Falsely accused of treason, Captain Alfred Dreyfus was subject to intense anti-Jewish sentiment. Confronted by such antagonism, Herzl came to the conclusion that Jews will never be free of anti-Semitism unless they possess a country of their own. In *The Jewish State*, published in 1896, he argued that old prejudices against Jewry are ingrained in Western society – assimilation will not act as a cure for the ills that beset the Jewish people. There is only one remedy for the malady of anti-Semitism: the creation of a Jewish commonwealth. Considering where such a Jewish homeland should be located, Herzl stressed that Palestine was the Jews' historic homeland.

I wonder what you make of such Jewish aspirations. Obviously you do not subscribe to the views of Orthodox critics of Zionism. In their opinion, Jewish settlement in Palestine must be preceded by the arrival of the long-awaited Messiah. But what about the assimilationist critics? Do you think they were right that Jews can fully integrate into the societies in which they live and thereby escape anti-Jewish attitudes? In a post-Holocaust world, is such a stance viable? Or do you agree with the secular Zionists that a Jewish state is vital for Jewish survival? If you are persuaded by thinkers like Hess, Pinsker and Herzl, then where should such a state be located? Would you have been opposed to the creation of a Jewish homeland in Palestine? In essence, what do you make of the problem of anti-Semitism, and what solution is there to this ancient hatred?

Anti-Semitism – A Christian Counter-Current

Mary Grey

You end with the most challenging question of all:

> *What do you make of the problem of anti-Semitism, and what solution is there to this ancient hatred?*

You are well aware that there is no easy answer: but the first imperative is to tell the truth. So I fully admit the evil of anti-Semitism through history and the responsibility of Christians – for keeping this alive, and for causing untold suffering on the Jewish people. Our own age struggles to make amends and to make it clear that anti-Semitism, like racism, is *sin*. Jewish-Christian conversations are very clear on this. But this has not prevented new outbreaks of anti-Semitism in different parts of the world, such as the desecration of Jewish graves.

You describe Jewish Zionist efforts – which the assimilationists opposed – to awaken interest and commitment to a Jewish homeland in Palestine.

But I'm sure you are aware that from the sixteenth century there was also a deep Christian (Protestant) interest in the same ideal (Sizer 2005, 2007).

Of all the protagonists in this cause, none was more influential than Lord Shaftesbury, Anthony Ashley-Cooper. Shaftesbury, a puritanical Protestant, was a proponent of the restoration of the Jews and became President of the London Jews' Society from 1848 until his death in 1885. He loved the biblical Book of Chronicles because it was 'full of hope for the Restoration of Israel'. Much of the influence he had was through Lord Palmerston, whose daughter he married.

Shaftesbury helped persuade Palmerston to send a British consul to Jerusalem in 1838. He argued for a Jewish return to Palestine both because of what he saw as the political and economic advantages to England and because he believed that it was God's will. He saw the conversion of the Jews as a means of bringing the whole world to faith before Christ returned – not an argument which endears him to Jews!

In January 1839 Shaftesbury published an article in the Quarterly Review, which provided the first proposal by a major politician to resettle Jews in Palestine:

> The soil and climate of Palestine are singularly adapted to the growth of produce required for the exigencies of Great Britain; the finest cotton may be obtained in almost unlimited abundance. . . . Capital and skill are alone required: the presence

of a British officer, and the increased security of property which his presence will confer, may invite them from these islands to the cultivation of Palestine; and the Jews, who will betake themselves to agriculture in no other land . . . , will probably return in yet greater numbers, and become once more the husbandmen of Judaea and Galilee.

(Shaftesbury in *Quarterly Review* 1838, Vol 64, pp. 104–108)

On the 4 November 1840 he placed an advert in *The Times* to make his purpose clear and then succeeded in the appointment of a vice-consul, William Young, and then a bishopric in Jerusalem – in 1841. Shaftesbury's next step was to map Palestine and he became the founding President of the Palestine Restoration Fund (PEF) in 1865. He made it clear that the purpose was to prepare the land for the return of its ancient possessors.

The lead-up to the Crimean War (1854) signalled an opening for realignments in the Near East. In July 1853 Shaftesbury wrote *these vast and fertile regions will soon be without a ruler, without a known and acknowledged power to claim dominion. The territory must be assigned to someone or other . . . There is a country without a nation; and God now in his wisdom and mercy, directs us to a nation without a country.* This is commonly cited as an early use of the phrase, 'A land without a people for a people without a land' which had inspired Israel Zangwill and Theodor Herzl to coin the phrase 'A land of no people for a people with no land.'

Shaftesbury's support for the Jewish restoration was not only a question of public campaigning but reflected in personal meditations and a deep reverence for Jewish people. His efforts for their restoration never declined. In the end, although he did not live to see his 'promised land' through his lobbying, writings and public speaking, he did more than any other British politician to inspire a generation of Joshuas to translate his religious vision into a political reality (Sizer 2005, p. 67).

Yet, evaluating his contribution, we need to admit that he overestimated what he considered the universal desire of European Jews to return to Palestine as well as the number of Jews in Palestine.

He had never been to Palestine and can be criticized for never giving the situation of the Arab people any consideration. Although his personal respect for the Jewish people is beyond question, *it is doubtful if Lord Shaftesbury ever thought of them as a people with their own language and traditions, their own Torah and law and spiritual guides honoured through a hundred generations* (Tuchman 1956, p. 115).

So, even if Shaftesbury's enthusiasm for restoration was permeated by Christian and political motives, he does represent a countercurrent to anti-Semitism. My question to you is, why did he and subsequent leaders – both Jewish and Christian – ignore the Arabs already living in the land for centuries? Didn't they all sow the seeds of future tragedy by doing this?

A Jewish State?

Dan Cohn-Sherbok

I am certainly aware of Lord Shaftesbury's support for the creation of a Jewish homeland in Palestine. He, like many other early Christian Zionists, was convinced that the restoration of the Jewish homeland in Eretz Israel would serve as a prelude to Christ's Second Coming. Their convictions were grounded in fervent religious belief about Jesus' eventually reign on earth. Another early Christian supporter who had a profound influence on the course of Zionism was William Hechler, a British clergyman of German origin. Born in South Africa, he studied theology and became a Protestant pastor; eventually he became private tutor to Prince Ludwig, son of Frederick, the Grand Duke of Baden. In 1883 he wrote *The Restoration of the Jews to Palestine*. In his work he argued on the basis of biblical prophecy that the Jews would be restored to the Land between 1897 and 1898. Two years later Herzl published *The Jewish State*, and in March 1896 Herzl and Hechler met. In his diary Herzl recorded his impressions:

> The Reverend William Hechler, Chaplain to the English Embassy here, came to see me. A sympathetic, gentle fellow, with the long grey beard of a prophet. He is enthusiastic about

my movement, a 'prophetic turning point'—which had foretold two years before.

(Herzl, in *Sizer*, p. 63)

What is crucial to note about such early Christian proponents of Zionism was their religious commitment to a view which has no resonance in Jewish thought: Jesus will come again to redeem humankind once the Jewish nation reclaims its homeland. In modern times, Christian Zionists have similarly been vociferous supporters of a Jewish state. Such figures as the Christian novelist Hal Lindsay describes the end of the world in *The Late, Great Planet Earth*: in this work he argues that the settlement and integration of the Occupied Territories in Israel is essential to maintain the promises made to Abraham. In his view, the occupation of Jerusalem is of fundamental significance – it signifies the return of Jesus. Eventually Jerusalem will become the spiritual centre of the entire world. All peoples will come there to worship Jesus who will rule from Jerusalem. While Zionist Jews are deeply grateful for Christian Zionist support, they utterly repudiate such Christological interpretations of history, as I'm sure you do.

You are right that in their quest to settle Palestine these Christian writers and others including many Zionists have been insensitive to the needs of the hundreds of thousands of Arabs living in the Holy Land. But the question I asked you about anti-Semitism remains. Given the thousands of years of suffering endured by the Jewish people, do you agree with the Zionists that the problem of Jew-hatred can only be solved by the creation of a Jewish state? Do you think Hess, Pinsker and Herzl were right in their analysis of the Jewish problem? Let me put the matter this way: if you had been in attendance at the Zionist Conference in Basle in 1897 would you have agreed with the delegates that the Jews must have a state of their own if they are to escape from persecution and suffering? Would your sympathies with the downtrodden and the homeless have led to the same conclusion as that reached by these early Zionists? Or alternatively, would you have been on the side of the assimilationists? Would you instead have joined ranks with liberal Jews who regarded Herzl's dream of a Jewish state as an unrealistic delusion?

This question is central and prior to any consideration of where the Jewish state should be located. You will remember that at one stage the Zionist Congress agreed to the British proposal for a Jewish settlement in East Africa. Attacks on Jewry in Eastern Europe exacerbated the quest for a place of refuge. At the Congress in 1903 Herzl stressed that the plight of Jewry was becoming increasingly worse. There had been a pogrom in Kisinev and there was the danger of further massacre in Russia and elsewhere. Let us save those who can be saved, he proclaimed. If you had heard this impassioned speech, what would have been your reaction? In answering this fundamental question, you should also consider the tragedy of the Nazi era. Do the terrible events of the Holocaust confirm Zionist predictions about the plight of Jewry? And, if you come to the conclusion that the Jewish people do need a home of their own, where should it be? In Africa, or Australia, or America? Where?

A Separate Homeland Is Not the Only Solution

Mary Grey

You are right, that I utterly repudiate the suggestions of the Christian Zionists – then and now – that Jews should return to the Holy Land in order to prepare for the Second Coming of Jesus. The suggestion is based on false theological premises and is insulting to Jews – who would need to convert to Christianity or be damned. I've never quite understood this uneasy alliance but agree that it continues to be popular among Christians.

Going back to your argument: you ask the same question, but with greater intensity. What would I have done if I'd been there, in the first Zionist Congress, convoked by Herzl? Would I have gone along with the tide of passion calling for a homeland for the Jews? In response, I argue first, this is a question impossible to answer for historical reasons. This is the twenty-first century not the nineteenth. One hundred and sixteen years have passed since those momentous days: I got a strong impression as to how momentous when I visited the Jewish Museum in Vienna which has an impressive account of Herzl's achievement. But, I know from my Palestinian friends that in those days, there were few Jews in Palestine. And Jews and Arabs were able to coexist peaceably – in fact, when the first waves of immigration began, Jews were welcomed by Palestinians, who simply assumed that this peaceable existence would continue.

But to give an honest personal answer, if I was as keen then on social justice as I am now, if I had been as conscious of the suffering and oppression of Jews throughout history, then I think I would have been strongly in favour of a Jewish homeland. I would probably have taken the stance of the novelist, George Eliot (Mary Ann Evans), who, in her last novel, *Daniel Deronda* (Eliot 1876, 1995) creates a hero who recognizes his Jewish identity, and feels his vocation is to sail to Israel with his newly wedded bride, Mirah:

> 'I am going to the East to become better acquainted with the condition of my race in various countries there' said Deronda.... The idea that I am possessed with is that of restoring a political existence to my people, making them a nation again, giving them a national centre, such as the English have, though they too are scattered over the face of the globe. That is a task that presents itself as a duty ...
> (Eliot 1876, 1995, p. 803)

But, it is important to remember that Eliot, like many of the characters we have been discussing, was part of that somewhat idealized nineteenth-century Restoration movement. I think I would have shared this then – but I would have been wrong. The question as to the reactions of the indigenous peoples were simply not on the radar screen of the principal protagonists – remember this is the height of the British Empire – and we'll need to come back to that issue as the story develops. It is almost impossible for us to take on board now that politicians could discuss giving away the land of other peoples so freely – as indeed was discovered when the options of Cyprus or Uganda were considered as homeland and then rejected.

It is still a burning issue: is the solution to anti-Semitism to remove the victimized population to another country? This was not the preferred option in South Africa or in the United States, even at the height of the race riots. In both cases, harmonious relationships in the land itself were sought. A closer analogy could be Gandhi's fight against the partition of India: he fought – non-violently – for a united India but lost, and was assassinated. And this divided country has never been healed from the wounds of separation. And surely, the fact that Jews have moved to great prosperity in the United States, and are prominent in public and professional life, shows that anti-Semitism can be overcome by other means than creating a separate homeland? As you know the assimilationist argument was also powerful and would remain so up till the decision to create a home land for the Jewish people. The move to Israel was really achieved by other arguments, namely, that the land actually belongs to the Jews who, it was argued, have strong historical claims: this would be the argument that finally forged the decision: not simply the need to find a solution, the solution to anti-Semitism.

The Question of a Jewish Homeland
Dan Cohn-Sherbok

Yes, I can imagine you sitting at the first Zionist Congress in Basle, dressed in a flowing gown amongst the male delegates all wearing formal dress. There you would be, intently listening to the impassioned pleas of Herzl and others to save the Jewish people from suffering and despair. Like George Eliot, you would no doubt have been moved to find a meaningful solution to the problem of the victimisation and persecution of the Jewish people. Yet at the same time, I am sure you would have been aware that there were hundreds of thousands of Arabs living in the Holy Land whose lives could be threatened by a massive influx of Jewish immigrants.

You may not know that a number of early Zionists who heard such fervent speeches in favour of Jewish nationhood were acutely conscious of the needs of the Arab population in Palestine. Ahad Ha-Am, for example, warned about the dangers of ignoring the Arab presence and trampling on their rights:

> One thing we certainly should have learned from our past and present history, and that is not to create anger among the local

population against us. . . . We have to treat the local population with love and respect, justly and rightly. And what do our brethren in the land of Israel do? Exactly the opposite. Slaves they were in their country of exile, and suddenly they find themselves in a boundless and anarchic freedom, as is always the case with a slave that has become king; and they behave toward the Arabs with hostility and cruelty, infringe upon their boundaries, hit them shamefully without reason and even brag about it.

(Ha-Am, in *Avineri*, p. 123)

So, like Ha-Am, you would have been right to be troubled about Zionist aspirations to create a Jewish state in the Holy Land. Herzl, Zangwill and others were misguided to think that Palestine was 'a land of no people, for a people of no land'. This was never the case. But, you must face up to the central question that I have been asking you: 'Do you think that Jews will inevitably be subject to persecution, suffering and murder if they have no land of their own?' This is the key issue that Jews struggled with at the end of the nineteenth century. Orthodox Jews were virulent critics of the Zionists, not because they disagreed with their analysis of the Jewish problem. Rather, as I noted previously, their opposition was based on their interpretation of God's providential plan for his chosen people. In their view, the arrival of the Messiah must occur before the Jewish people return en mass to Zion. Secular anti-Zionists, on the other hand, had no such religious misgivings. Their critique of Zionism was grounded in an optimistic assessment of the advantages of Jewish emancipation and assimilation. The socialist anti-Zionist, Karl Kautsky, for example, maintained that in the past Jews had been an exclusive hereditary caste of merchants, financiers, intellectuals and artisans. Yet with the rise of industrial capitalism, Jews had obtained equal rights and been assimilated into their adopted countries. Anti-Semitism had re-emerged, he believed, by the reaction of the petty bourgeoisie against liberalism. Eastern European Jews had responded to this threat by calling for national solidarity. But, in his opinion, Zionism has no future. Where, he asked, could space be found for a Jewish state? How could Jews be persuaded to engage in agricultural labour or build a massive industry in

Palestine? These were insurmountable obstacles to the realization of Zionist aspirations.

The Zionists disagreed with such an analysis. The lessons of Jewish history, they argued, must guide current Jewish thought and action. Judeophobia is an inherent aspect of modern society, and those who champion liberal ideologies such as socialism would inevitably be disappointed. In the words of Max Nordau, 'Socialism will bring the same disappointments as did the Reformation, the Enlightenment, the movement for political freedom. If we should live to see Socialist theory become practice, you'll be surprised to meet again in the new order that old acquaintance, anti-Semitism.' (Nordau in *Laqueur*, p. 388).

So, Mary, again I ask you the same question: Do you think the Zionists were misguided in their analysis of the problem of Jew-hatred? Or are you on the side of the assimilationists? You say at the beginning of your last response that this is a question impossible to answer for historical reasons. But I don't agree. This is a central problem that transcends specific historical circumstances. This chapter is entitled 'Nineteenth-Century Anti-Semitism'. At its heart is this fundamental issue which split Jewry at the turn of the twentieth century: How are Jews to escape Judeophobia? Is a Jewish state the only answer? Or is assimilation the way forward? We are not speaking here about Palestine. That is only one half of the equation. The other half is the solution to over 3,000 years of Jewish suffering.

Assimilation Can Never Be the Answer!

Mary Grey

You keep returning to the burning question at the heart of this chapter, namely, 'the fundamental issue which split Jewry at the turn of the twentieth century: How are Jews to escape Judeophobia? Is a Jewish state the only answer? Or is assimilation the way forward?' Do the terrible events of the Holocaust confirm Zionist predictions about the plight of Jewry? We seem to be no nearer agreement than when we started off, mostly because of differing views as to whether the particularities of historical context alter the framework of the debate!

I agreed with you, that in the nineteenth century I would have concurred with the views of George Eliot – and thanks for the image of me at the Zionist conference! – but choices are not offered in the same way in every historical period. As we have begun to discuss, the question of a homeland for the Jewish people would not have arisen without the long build-up of the Restorationist movement since the times of Oliver Cromwell.

But it could be argued that the very fact of possessing a homeland – in this case Israel – has in itself not solved the entire problem. There are still outbursts of anti-Semitism in different parts of the world – and the actions of the Israeli government against the Arab population has itself exacerbated anti-Jewish sentiment. I'm glad you cite an example of the wish to respect the indigenous Arab population by some Jews – that is heartening. My own deep respect is for Martin Buber and some of his colleagues, who went some way in urging the formation of a bi-national state before the creation of the state of Israel.

Where I fundamentally disagree with you is that assimilation is the only alternative to a Jewish homeland. (And we'll need to return to this when we discuss the Balfour Declaration.) The problem is that assimilation appears to demand that the minority group suppress its own (unique) identity to 'fit in' with the so-called dominant culture. It is possible to make the analogy with the struggle for acceptance of the black communities: it is still the case that – in following the struggle for assimilation into a white culture – that *blackness* can be suppressed in favour of attaining a white-as-possible skin. Hence, in providing an alternative to this, the movements celebrating black culture/music/literature and so on. But the opposite is happening with Jewish communities here and in the US: Jewish culture and faith are not suppressed or denied but celebrated. Jews form a large part of professional life here – our would-be Prime Minister is Jewish, to cite one example.[1] The Chief Rabbi broadcasts on Radio 4 whenever there is a Jewish feast: so there is an assumption that the wider community will be interested and show respect.

So, my reply to you is twofold. In the nineteenth century there was an unstoppable movement for the creation of a Jewish

---

[1] I realize that this example is restricted to Britain.

homeland. And, yes, I agree with you that at that point in history, anti-Semitism was vicious, violent and at that time appeared incurable. So the process of setting in motion and furthering the plan for a Jewish homeland made a lot of sense – even if some of the methods for attaining it were questionable. And now that the State of Israel exists, to deny its right to exist is to embark once more on the trajectory of anti-Semitism. But there could so easily have been a different course.

It took the tragedy of the Holocaust (Shoah) of the Second World War to make this fundamental shift of attitude and policy. The impact of the indescribable horror and suffering of the Jewish people created shock waves still reverberating. Christian theologians and Churches began to ask themselves what had been their own responsibility during this period: and a process of repentance was set in motion that involved dialogue, shared prayer and a diverse programme of interactions where Christians embarked on concrete actions of solidarity. But we also realized that our own theology was at fault: tracing anti-Judaism right back to the death of Christ and the act of blaming the Jews for this was seen as the origin of a deep-seated historical process leading to outbreaks of anti-Semitism throughout history.

That this was never tackled until the last century has led to the impasse you have alluded to throughout this chapter. Was the creation of a homeland of the Jews the only solution to anti-Semitism? I have argued that there was another alternative: face the underlying roots of this. But before we go further, the sheer power and character of Zionism needs to be faced head-on.

Chapter 2
Zionism

The Many Faces of Zionism

Mary Grey

We have already opened up the discussion on Zionism with reference to Theodor Herzl and the nineteenth-century movement for a Jewish homeland. But to speak about Zionism is to cut to the heart of the Jewish–Palestinian conflict today. How can we address the subject without intensifying divisiveness?

It is well known that Zionism in its present form emerged in the late *nineteenth century* in central and Eastern Europe as a nationalist revival movement when Jewish hopes were at a low ebb, and Jewish communities particularly in Russia were experiencing persecution (Christian Zionism, as I have related, had earlier roots).[1] So the historical context was one of both nationalism and imperialism. The focus of the movement soon concentrated on creating the longed-for Jewish homeland: this desire became centred on *Palestine*, then, of course, a part of the *Ottoman Empire.*

But Zionism has taken many forms in the last 150 years – and is still not a unified movement. Although the symbol of Mount Zion

---

[1] See section 'Anti-Semitism – A Christian Counter-Current' in Chapter 1.

must be central in Jewish sentiment, the term may also refer to non-political *cultural Zionism*, represented most prominently by *Ahad Ha'am*; it can refer to political support for the *State of Israel* by non-Jews, as in *Christian Zionism*. It can also mean *Labour* or *Socialist* Zionism, which originated in Eastern Europe. Socialist Zionists believed that centuries of oppression in anti-Semitic societies had reduced Jews to a weak, hopeless existence that itself was vulnerable to further anti-Semitism; they argued that a revolution of the Jewish soul and society was necessary and achievable in part by Jews moving to Israel and becoming farmers, workers and soldiers in a country of their own. Most socialist Zionists rejected the observance of traditional religious Judaism as perpetuating a 'Diaspora mentality' among the Jewish people, and established rural communes in Israel called '*kibbutzim*'. (I used to have huge admiration for the kibbutz movement until the truth dawned on me – that the land cultivated by these idealistic people had been taken from its Arab owners.) It's not hard to understand that this progressive Socialist Zionist would have an uneasy relationship with *Orthodox Judaism*.

We need also to mention *liberal* Zionism – initially the dominant trend within the movement from the *First Zionist Congress* in 1897 until after the First World War – these Zionists identified with the liberal European middle class. There is also *National or Revisionist* Zionism led by the Russian, *Jabotinsky*, founder of the Jewish self-defense organisation.[2]

But I want to focus more on Religious Zionism – because I believe that this has been extraordinarily influential in changing perceptions. This movement derives from Rabbi *Abraham Isaac Kook* (the first *Chief Rabbi of Palestine*) and his son Rabbi Zevi Judah Kook, active in the 1920s and 1930s. Before them Zionism had been largely a secular movement. The Rabbis Kook now transformed it into a religious one, teaching that Orthodox (Torah) Judaism nurtures Zionism's positive ideals, such as the ingathering of exiles to Jerusalem, and justifies political activity to create and maintain a Jewish political entity in the Land of Israel. Religious

---

[2]Revisionists left the World Zionist Organization in 1935 because it refused to state that the creation of a Jewish state was an objective of Zionism.

Zionists have been at the forefront of the (illegal) Jewish settlements in the West Bank and efforts to assert Jewish control over the *Old City* of Jerusalem. They have been able to overcome the initial Orthodox resistance to Zionism – which believed that only when the Messiah came would Jews once again inhabit the Holy Land. This approach has also paved the way for the use of the Bible to justify possession of this 'Promised Land'.

All of this is familiar territory for you. You will also be familiar with the many critiques of Zionism – which are not hard to find. For example, it is a racist ideology; it is based on illegal, ruthless land confiscation and on expulsions of thousands of Palestinians, which involves the countless daily humiliations consequent on Israel's occupation of the West Bank and Gaza.

As you know from our previous discussion, I would have had much sympathy with the nineteenth-century movement for a Jewish homeland. Now I know it was based on false premises – 'a land without a people', for example, largely ignoring the existence of the Arabs. The difficulty, and this is my question to you, is that criticism of, and opposition to Zionism can be hard to distinguish from anti-Semitism. How is it possible to criticize the unjust and illegal actions of the Zionist government today, without incurring the label of being anti-Semitic?

The Zionist Quest

Dan Cohn-Sherbok

You say that you would have been sympathetic to Zionism in the early nineteenth century. However, you now think that would have been mistaken since it was based on false premises. In this context you refer to various critiques of the movement: it is a racist ideology; it is based on illegal, ruthless land confiscation and on the expulsion of thousands of Palestinians; and it involves countless daily humiliations of Arabs. Such a characterisation, however, is not at all consonant with the earliest stages of Zionism. You stress that we must pursue the truth: thus, I want to take you back to the origins of Zionism and ask you again what your attitudes would have been then to the Zionist desire to have a Jewish homeland.

The first Zionist Congress took place on 29 August 1897 in the concert hall of the Basle Municipal Casino. Herzl gave instructions that the delegates should attend the opening session in formal dress, tails and white tie. Around 200–250 men and women from 24 states and territories were in attendance. This gathering also included a number of non-Jewish guests like William Hechler. At the Congress, Herzl declared:

> Let our Congress be serious and lofty, a blessing for the unfortunate, a threat to nobody, a source of honour to all Jews and worthy of the past.
> (Herzl 1911, *Protokoll des I. Zionistenkongresses*, pp. 15–20)

At the Congress, Max Nordau spoke about the contemporary condition of Jewry. Wherever they lived in large numbers, he stated, they were subject to misery. In such a situation, he stressed, the Jew had become a cripple. The Congress lasted three days during which delegates heard reports on the conditions of Jews in various countries. At the end of the Congress, delegates agreed that the movement should (1) seek the advancement of the settlement of Palestine with Jewish farmers, artisans and tradesmen; (2) strengthen Jewish national feeling and consciousness; and (3) make preparatory moves towards obtaining such governmental consent as will be necessary to the achievements and aims of Zionism (Vital 1982, *Zionism: The Formative Years*, p. 4).

After the Congress, Herzl pressed forward with the plan to obtain such consent. After much effort, he eventually had an interview with the Sultan of the Ottoman Empire on 11 May 1901. The aim of this meeting was to obtain permission to establish a Jewish settlement in Palestine. The interview was cordial and lasted two hours. Herzl did not discuss the Zionist movement nor a charter. Instead he explained how Jews could offer services to the Ottoman state. If it were accepted, then such support should involve a reciprocal gesture from the Turkish sovereign. In the end, a general agreement was reached: although unspecified, the principle was accepted that Jewish financial support would be provided in exchange for political concessions. However, after fourteen months passed involving various exchanges in writing and visits to Constantinople, nothing was achieved.

Herzl's unsuccessful efforts with the Sultan were followed by an attempt to persuade Britain of the need for the creation of a Jewish homeland. On 22 and 23 October 1902, Herzl met with Joseph Chamberlain, the Colonial Secretary. During their meeting Chamberlain accepted Herzl's analysis of the Jewish question and agreed with his solution. In response to Herzl's reference to the three British controlled territories where Jews could be settled, Chamberlain suggested that El Arish might be a possibility. The land was largely uninhabited, and it could serve as a rallying point for the Jewish people. Following a subsequent meeting with Herzl, Lord Lansdowne wrote to Lord Cromer, the British governor of Egypt, explaining that Herzl had wished to get hold of a tract near El Arish and establish a colony of Jewish people there. Eventually, however, a Royal Commission that was sent to explore this possibility ruled that the land was unsuitable for settlers, and the plan was dropped.

Your characterisation of early Zionism as a racist policy intent on displacing Arab inhabitants of Palestine thus has no basis in fact. Herzl and others were pragmatists who simply sought a place of refuge for Jews who were persecuted in Europe and elsewhere. The Zionist quest was not an expansionist policy intent on ignoring the hundreds of thousands of Arabs living in Palestine. Instead, the early Zionists were preoccupied with the plight of their co-religionists – their aim was to obtain legal permission from governments in control of the area so that a tract of land either in Palestine itself or Egypt could serve as a home for those fleeing from persecution. Would you really not have been a supporter of Herzl's efforts?

The Bible Is Our Mandate!

Mary Grey

I think you've missed the point about my titling my last letter to you as 'The Many Faces of Zionism'. Yes, I agreed that as a Christian in the nineteenth century, I might have been very influenced by Lord Shaftesbury's movement of Restoration and a homeland for the Jews. I told you how moved I was by George Eliot's novel, *Daniel Deronda* – and I know Herzl himself was stirred by it. I remained supportive of all those early efforts, until I discovered what the consequences had been for Palestine's indigenous peoples. Zionism's idealistic and hopeful beginnings, its dreams of a different future for the Jewish people, all this has been soured by the contemporary realities of Zionism in Palestine. And the face that became one of the most influential was the way Zionism has used the Bible to justify Jewish claims to the land and therefore to seizing land from the Palestinians.

This was expressed powerfully by Israel's first Prime minster, David Ben-Gurion (1886–1973). In fact, Ben-Gurion had renounced religion when a boy, becoming known as a 'religious non-theist'. So, as you are aware, he accepted the Biblical revelation of a Chosen People and Promised Land. In fact when addressing the Peel Commission in Jerusalem – sent in 1936 by the British Government – he dramatically exclaimed this historic phrase, 'The Bible is our Mandate!'

His passion for Zionism, which began early in life, already led him to become a major Zionist leader and Executive Head of the World Zionist Organization in 1946. As the head of the Jewish Agency for Palestine, he became the *de facto* leader of the Jewish community in Palestine, and largely led its struggle for an independent Jewish state. It was a great surprise to me to discover that Ben-Gurion has written extensively on the Bible as inspiration for occupying Palestine and gathered a number of scholars around him in 'The Prime Minister's Bible Circle' (Ben-Gurion 1969).[3]

He saw the Jewish people of the new state in direct continuity with the Biblical Jews – who had held the same racist views with regard to the neighbouring tribes:

> Israel was not alone in feeling and fighting the impact of ancient Egypt and Babylon. Its neighbours – Edom, Moab, Ammon, Philistia, Tyre, Sidon, and Aram – were in a similar position. The names are common enough to any student of the Bible, but what vestige of their owners is in existence today,

---

[3] The following quotations are from these texts or paraphrases thereof.

beyond archaeological findings? It is difficult to conceive how all these people were physically obliterated. Of their tongues, their cultures, their creeds, nothing lives.

(Ben-Gurion 1969)

He argued further that the Jewish people in the Land of Israel were the only people in the whole of the Middle East who still spoke the language of their ancestors, who still held to a religion that sprang from the Patriarch Abraham and Moses. *Yet never once did they sever their links with the land* (my italics).

This is a highly contentious view. Even if you could prove half of this, what of the Arab attachment to their land, given scant attention by colonizing powers? Ben-Gurion did recognize the strong attachment of *Palestinian Arabs* to the land but hoped that this would be overcome in time. In an address to the United Nations and the British Mandate, he also doubted the likelihood of peace with the future Arab nations and wrote many times of the obliteration of the Canaanite people, but in contrast, the continuity of the present day Jews with the ancient nation:

> The line of development of the ancient nations was completely severed: their language, their religion, their culture, their tradition, and their name – all vanished from off the face of the earth; and the Jewish people – though it was physically uprooted from its birthplace more than 2,000 years ago – is the only nation which continues its ancient tradition, its own language and culture, as if there had been no break in its historical continuity.
>
> (Ben-Gurion 1969)

He makes his vision very clear that the Jewish people, after a long adventure on the stage of world history for 4,000 years in all countries of the world, have returned to the point of origin and founded the third government of Israel – and will not divest of the vast and rich international experience accumulated. What is the historical veracity of these biblically based claims when Biblical scholarship and archaeology – of both Jews and Christians – raise serious challenges to them? How far do contemporary Zionist claims depend on the literal truth of Biblical stories?

An Historic Mandate

Dan Cohn-Sherbok

I want first to address the point you make at the beginning of your last exchange. You maintain that you were supportive of the efforts of the early Zionists until you discovered what the consequences had been for Palestine's indigenous peoples. In particular you say that Zionism's early dreams have been soured by the contemporary realities of Zionism in the Holy Land. I think you are making a mistake here. The question is not whether the dreams of Herzl and others have been clouded by recent events. Rather, the issue is whether Zionism at the turn of the century was a valid way forward for the Jewish people? The events then should be judged in context. Surely you would not want to evaluate Jesus' teaching about God's Kingdom on earth on the basis of the Inquisition or the Church's acquiesce to the Nazis during the Third Reich. The point of my last letter was to illustrate that the quest of Zionists at the end of the nineteenth century and the beginning of the twentieth century was to obtain a strip of land in the Middle East as a refuge for Jews suffering discrimination and persecution in Eastern and Western Europe. Herzl's hope was that governments controlling this area would accede to his plea. The Zionists did not seek to divest the native population of the land they owned or cause them suffering and humiliation.

You then go on to focus on the way the Bible has been used by Zionists, citing the writings of Israel's first Prime Minister, David Ben-Gurion. You acknowledge that you are skipping ahead at least thirty years in focusing on Ben-Gurion's views. I appreciate that Ben-Gurion's attitudes are of critical importance in assessing the growth and development of the Jewish state. But I think we must keep to our time frame; otherwise we will lose track of the historical events under consideration. Hence I think we should examine what Zionists at the beginning of the century had to say about the Jewish connection with Eretz Israel.

Despite Herzl's initial attempts to interest the Sultan and the British government in a solution to the Jewish problem, the Zionists were frustrated in their efforts. However, on 23 April 1903 Herzl met again with Joseph Chamberlain, the Colonial Secretary who proposed a tract of land in East Africa for Jewish settlement. At the Sixth Zionist Congress, the delegates reluctantly agreed to accept this proposal; it was seen as a stepping stone to Palestine and a means of gaining international status for Zionism. The Russian delegation, however, was incensed and walked out the Congress hall. In their view, such a suggestion was a travesty of Zionist aspirations. The delegates from Kishinev in particular were determined to thwart this scheme. In November 1903 they met at Kharkov and an ultimatum was sent to Herzl; he was to withdraw the East Africa project, or a new independent organisation would be formed. Throughout all these negotiations, Zionists were determined that if a Jewish state were to be established it should be located in the Jewish people's ancient homeland. For Herzl, the immediate goal was to find a place of refuge for Jews who were currently suffering persecution, but he never lost sight of the ultimate aim of a Jewish settlement in Palestine.

You are right to point out that the Bible was of fundamental importance for the early Zionists. For over a thousand years, Jews had lived in Eretz Israel, and the Bible is a record of their history. The early secular Jewish pioneers were not religiously motivated to settle the land; rather they simply wished to reclaim the soil of their ancestors. These settlers had no desire to drive the indigenous Arab population into the sea and confiscate their lands. It was their wish simply to find a place of refuge for Jews who wished to flee from oppressive regimes. It is simply a fact that Jews were uprooted from Judaea by the Romans in the first century, and for nearly 2,000 years lived in other countries. I am reluctant to skip ahead to consider Ben-Gurion's attitudes and actions, but since you refer to him I will conclude with a passage from Israel's Declaration of Independence which was read out by David Ben-Gurion on 18 May 1948 which, I believe, correctly encapsulates the Jewish perception of the nation's connection to the land:

> The Land of Israel was the birthplace of the Jewish people. Here their spiritual, religious and national identity was formed.

Here they achieved independence and created a culture of national and universal significance. Here they wrote and gave their Bible to the world. Exiled from Palestine, the Jewish people remained faithful to it in all the countries of their dispersion, never ceasing to pray and hope for their return and the restoration of their national freedom.

(Cohn-Sherbok 2003, Judaism: History, Belief and Practice, p. 319)

The *Eretz Israel* Has a History for Palestinians Too!

Mary Grey

If you want to insist that we stick to the question as stated in the twentieth century, so be it. But you cannot avoid the truth that people form attitudes not only on the basis of the past, but how the issue now presents itself. We do not judge Russia today on the track record of Ivan the Terrible but on present day ambition. Similarly, you are right that I wouldn't dismiss Jesus' teaching on the Kingdom of peace and justice on the basis of Church events like the Inquisition: but that is a false contrast. I would not dismiss Isaiah's ideas on the Messianic Kingdom on the basis of today's reality of Zionist ambition.

As I argued with reference to Ben-Gurion, the Biblical narratives would form a large part of Zionist claims to the land of Israel. You yourself admit that Biblical history was of fundamental importance for the early Zionists, even though they were secular and not religiously motivated. You use phrases like 'the Bible is a record of their history' and that they wished to reclaim the 'soil of their ancestors'.

Given that, I want to make three points. The first is that you must know that the Bible is not straightforward history. It is history, myth, poetry, prophecy and wisdom literature – all of this. It is now highly disputed as to how much of the earlier narratives are historical. Secondly, you will also know the work of Shlomo Sand who casts doubt on the claim that all the Jewish people are descended from those who left in 70 CE at the conquest of the Romans. In reaction to his book *The Invention of the Jewish People* (Sand 2009), critics argue that the book is an attempt to prove that the Jewish people never existed as a 'nation-race' with a common origin, but rather is a colorful mix of groups that at various stages in history adopted the Jewish religion. He also argues that for a number of Zionist theorists, the mythical perception of the Jews as an ancient people led to truly racist thinking. He has suggested that much of the present day world Jewish population are individuals and groups, who converted to Judaism at later periods. Additionally, he suggests that the story of the exile was a myth promoted by early Christians to recruit Jews to the new faith. Sand argues that most of the Jews were not exiled by the Romans, and were permitted to remain in the country, putting the number of those exiled at tens of thousands at most. He further argues that many of the Jews converted to Islam following the Arab conquest, and were assimilated among the conquerors. In addition, the birth of the myth of a Jewish people as a group with a common, ethnic origin was a retrospective German invention.

I do not for a moment think you will accept this thesis – and I myself think it is far fetched. But what I do want to argue seriously, is for you yourself to take the context in more depth: not only of the growing enthusiasm of Zionism and Herzl's efforts to secure a piece of the land; but that this was a context of both nationalism and imperialism – and of Arab nationalism too. At this time, when Palestine was under the control of the Ottomans, the population was about 600,000, of which 10 per cent were Christian, 4 per cent Jews and the majority were Sunni Muslims. The middle nineteenth century saw the opening up of Jerusalem to every sort of Christian denomination (following Shaftesbury's efforts) – and it was these Christian communities that first expressed alarm at increasing Jewish immigration. (The first unrest between peasants and settlers was in 1898.)

So, although I expressed sympathy with the Zionist longing for a homeland as new beginning after two centuries of suffering, I also have sympathy with the Arab people living under Turkish domination. And I also know from friends in Palestine that at first the people welcomed the Jewish settlers. They presumed that they could live side by side as neighbours. Later, in 1948, survivors of the tragedy related that they could not believe that the people they had welcomed would be expelling them from the land. *Zionism cannot make room for two peoples who have a claim to the same piece of land.*

The Bible and History

Dan Cohn-Sherbok

You are of course right that the Hebrew Bible is a mixture of history, myth, poetry, prophecy and wisdom literature. Further, archaeologists have demonstrated that a number of the stories in Scripture have no basis in fact, or are simply incorrect. For example, the various accounts of the conquests of Canaan do not conform to the findings of archaeologists. In addition, it appears that the history of the first kings of Israel – Solomon, Saul and David – have little foundation. Nonetheless, there is no question that the ancient Israelites did settle in the Holy Land and that there was a Jewish presence there for over a thousand years.

Let me give you several examples which demonstrate that this is so. Archaeologists have uncovered the remains of the ancient Temple in Jerusalem; as you know, pious Jews today pray at the Western Wall which was part of the Temple complex. Hence, we have concrete evidence that Jews did in fact build a Temple on this site and worshipped there in ancient times. You might have seen the Black Obelisk which is in the British Museum in London: this sculpture from the city of Nimrud during the reign of King Shalmaneser III shows a scene of Jehu, the king of Israel in the ninth-century BCE, bringing tribute to the Assyrian king. On the obelisk is this passage: 'The tribute of Jehu, son of Omri. Silver, gold and golden bowl, a golden vase, golden cups, golden buckets, tin, a staff for the royal hand, puruhati-fruits' (The Black Obelisk in DOTT, p. 48). In the British Museum you will also find bas-reliefs of the conquest of the Israelite city of Lachish by the Babylonians in the eighth-century BCE, an event recorded in the Bible. It is thus indisputable that the ancient Israelites did live in what is now Israel in the first millennium BCE. The Bible was not meant to be an accurate historical record of the history of the Jewish nation: it is a blend of various elements. But it is in part history. And it is this history which serves as the basis for the Zionist claims which I mentioned in my last exchange.

Let me turn now to the argument put forward by Schlomo Sand. As you note, he has questioned the claim that Jews today are descended from those who left Judaea in the first century following the Roman conquest. It is his contention that the Jewish people are a mix of groups that at various stages adopted the Jewish religion. Much of the present day world Jewish population, he contends, are individuals and groups who converted to Judaism through the centuries. The implication of this observation is that, because of such mixed ancestry Jews today have no historical claim to the Holy Land. There are, I think, fundamental flaws with this theory. First, there could be no way to demonstrate that modern Jews are the descendants of the ancient Israelites: no DNA test exists which could prove that this was so. And the same would be true of citizens of any country who sought to prove a genetic connection with its original inhabitants. But more importantly, such a lack of proof does not in any way mean that the current inhabitants of a particular country do not feel linked to their nation's history. Let me put the point this way: I am an American citizen. But my great grandparents were Hungarians who settled in the United States at the beginning of the twentieth century. Genetically, therefore, I have no connection with the early Americans who settled in the colonies in the sixteenth century. Yet, American history is MY history; the Declaration of Independence has meaning for me even though those who signed this document are in no way my relatives. The American Civil War is an indelible part of my history even though when it took place my ancestors were living in Jewish villages in Eastern Europe at the time it took place. I grew up in Colorado; my grandparents moved there in 1915 because my grandmother was threatened with tuberculosis and needed a warm climate. The family had nothing to do with cowboys and Indians. Yet the story of the opening up of the West is MY history. Similarly, the history of the Jewish people in ancient Israel is my history because I am a Jew: it makes no difference whether I can prove a genetic connection with the first Jewish inhabitants of the Holy Land.

So, I return to my original contention: the Zionists were correct in asserting an historical link to Palestine. Although Jews have lived in numerous lands for nearly 2,000 years after the Roman conquest in 70 AD, they have always regarded Israel as sacred and prayed for their eventual return. It is entirely understandable why Herzl and other Zionists were intent on obtaining a tract there for Jewish settlement. As you note, there were already a small number of Jews living in Palestine during the nineteenth century. It was the Jewish hope that as their numbers increased, they could live peacefully with their Arab neighbours. The Zionist aim was not to drive out the indigenous population, and confiscate their lands. In your presentation you are anxious to portray Zionists as colonial usurpers, insensitive to Arab rights. But it is a mistake to judge this early period of Zionist history on the basis of events that took place decades later.

Chapter 3
The Balfour Declaration

The Road to Balfour

Dan Cohn-Sherbok

The last power to control Palestine before modern times was the Ottoman Turks. In 1516 they swallowed up Palestine, and for the next 400 years Palestine remained under Ottoman rule. During this period the majority of the population were Arab-speaking Muslims, but there were also a few thousand Jews living in the region. During the early years of the nineteenth century, a relatively small number of Jewish settlers entered the country. Two waves of immigration (known as the First and the Second Aliyah) took place from 1882 to 1903, and 1904 to 1913. This was in no sense an invasion or conquest; on the contrary, these settlers purchased land with the help of rich Jews like Baron Edmund de Rothschild and later the Jewish National Fund and the Palestine Land Development Fund.

Although some Arabs expressed alarm about this influx of Jewish immigrants, confrontation between Jews and Arabs was not inevitable. Herzl had expressed a wish that Jews and Arabs would be able to live together in harmony. With the outbreak of the First World War, Turkey sided with Germany and Austria-Hungary against Britain, France and Russia. Caught in the midst of this conflict, Jews in Palestine suffered from war conditions and were regarded with increasing suspicion by Turkish military officials. On 17 December 1914 the Turkish governor of Jaffa ordered the expulsion of 6,000 Russian Jews living in the city. Within the month 7,000 Jews fled Palestine; the remainder who were unable to leave so quickly feared for their lives.

As this conflict intensified, Vladimir Jabotinsky (a charismatic Zionist leader) attempted to create a Jewish legion for battle against the Turks in Palestine. In March–April 1915 about 500 Jews were accepted for enlistment in a special transportation unit, the Zion Mule Corps which disembarked on the beaches of Gallipoli. In the midst of this conflict, leading Zionists such as Chaim Weizmann sought to persuade the British of the need for a Jewish homeland in Palestine. With the election of Lloyd George as the Prime Minister with Lord Balfour as a foreign secretary in the last weeks of 1916, a partnership with the Zionists became a strong possibility. Pressing his case, Weizmann drew upon the religious sympathies of those whom he sought to persuade. In the minds of Welsh and Scottish Protestants, the Holy Land was sacred. Lord Balfour, for example, expressed a life-long interest in biblical Israel. Such figures and others fervently believed that Christianity had an obligation to the Jewish nation.

Determined that Britain should offer the Jewish people a safe haven, the Zionists formulated a proposal. On 4 October 1917 the declaration was put before the British cabinet. Although it was opposed by Edwin Montagu, the Secretary of State for India and the only Jew in the cabinet, Lloyd George and other Zionist sympathizers persisted. With the support of the President of the United States, Woodrow Wilson, the War Cabinet voted for the declaration on 31 October. The declaration took the form of a letter sent by Balfour on 2 November 1917 to Lord Rothschild, the president of the British Zionist Federation:

> Dear Lord Rothschild, I have much pleasure in conveying to you, on behalf of His Majesty's Government, the following declaration of sympathy of Jewish Zionist aspirations which has been submitted to, and approved by, the Cabinet: 'His Majesty's Government view with favour the establishment in

Palestine of a national home for the Jewish people, and will use their best endeavours to facilitate the achievement of this object, it being clearly understood that nothing shall be done which may prejudice the civil and religious rights of existing non-Jewish communities in Palestine, or the rights and political status enjoyed by Jews in any other country.'

(Mendes-Flohr (eds) 1995, *The Jew in the Modern World*, p. 582)

Now, I am sure you will say that the British had no right to give such an assurance to the Zionists. I imagine you will regard such a step as a manifestation of colonial arrogance and insensitivity. Yet, given the plight of Jews in Eastern Europe and elsewhere, was it unreasonable to enable Jewry to escape from persecution, suffering and murder by providing them with a safe haven in their ancient homeland? Certainly, it was the avowed intention of the British not to harm the interests of the indigenous population: this was the explicit intent of the final sentence of the Balfour Declaration itself. Was this not a cause for celebration?

The Road to Balfour – Contradictory Promises

Mary Grey

You are grossly over-simplifying a complex – and devious – story, the consequences of which are the backdrop of much suffering today in Israel/Palestine. As Tom Segev wrote:

> The Declaration was neither the product of military nor diplomatic interests but of prejudice, faith and sleight of hand. The men who sired it were Christian and Zionist and, in many cases, anti-Semitic.
>
> (Segev 1999, p. 33)

First, the context of this Agreement was British Imperialism and its ambitions in the Middle East. The conquest of Mesopotamia would offer a secure route to India, still at the time 'the Jewel in the Crown' of Empire. David Fromkin agrees:

> As of 1917, Palestine was the key missing link that could join together the parts of the British Empire so that they could form a continuous chain from the Atlantic to the middle of the Pacific.
>
> (Fromkin 1989, p. 282)

And there were various key figures in this plan. Where I agree with you is in the vital part played by Chaim Weizmann, who, as it were, took over Herzl's role after his death. Without his persistence and enthusiasm – and influence on Balfour – I don't think there would have been an agreement.

Sir Mark Sykes – 6th Baronet of Sledmere is obviously a key figure in the imperialistic plan. He was passionate about the Middle East, anti-Semitic, but capable of changing his mind – he would became Weizmann's staunchest ally and an ardent Zionist. With the French Ambassador, François Picot, a diplomat with expertise in the Middle East, he was responsible for a key Anglo-French-Russian agreement in May 1916. Jonathan Schneer writes:

> It did not take long. Sykes was a human dynamo, bubbling with enthusiasm, teeming with ideas . . . Picot was urbane and reserved. . . . The two men developed a working relationship that they preserved for the duration of the war . . . together Sykes and Picot redrew the Middle Eastern map. We may picture them in the grand conference room in the Foreign Office, crayons in hand. They coloured blue the portions on the map they agreed to allocate to France, and they coloured red the portions they would allocate to Britain. . . . Since both parties coveted Palestine, with its sites holy to Christians, Jews and Muslims alike, they compromised and coloured the region brown, agreeing that this portion of the Middle East should be administered by an international condominium.
>
> (Schneer 2010, p. 79)

As if this was not imperialistic enough, another contradictory promise had been made. In 1915 Britain promised Hussein, the Sharif of Mecca, that it would support an independent Arab kingdom under his rule in return for his mounting an Arab revolt against the Ottoman Empire, Germany's ally in the war. The promise was contained in a letter dated 24 October 1915, from Sir Henry McMahon, to the Sharif of Mecca in what became known as the McMahon–Hussein correspondence. This seemed to promise the Arabs their own state stretching from Damascus to the Arabian Peninsula in return for fighting the Ottomans. Before McMahon's letter, Lord Kitchener (Minister of war) had already promised Hussein that, if he would come out against Turkey, Britain would guarantee his retention of the title of Grand Sharif and defend him against external aggression. It hinted that if the Sharif were declared Caliph he would have Britain's support, *and it included a general promise to help the Arabs to obtain their freedom:*

> McMahon to Sharif Husayn . . . *I am authorised to give you the following pledges on behalf of the Government of Great Britain, and to reply as follows to your note: That subject to the modifications stated above, Great Britain is prepared to recognise and uphold the independence of the Arabs in all the regions lying within the frontiers proposed by the Sharif of Mecca.*
>
> (McMahon correspondence)

However, not only was the correspondence deliberately imprecise but the status and ability of the Sharif of Mecca to speak for all of the Arabs was also an issue. This is how the ambiguity appears:

> *In the Arabic version sent to King Hussein this is so translated as to make it appear that Britain is free to act without detriment to France in the whole of the limits mentioned. This passage, of course, had been our sheet anchor: it enabled us to tell the French that we had reserved their rights and the Arabs that there were regions in which they would have eventually to come to terms with the French. It is extremely awkward to have this piece of solid ground cut from under our feet.*
>
> (James Barr 2011, pp. 118–119)

So, at the same time that Britain was negotiating with the Sharif Hussein over the future of the Asian provinces of the Ottoman Empire it was discussing the same subject with France and Russia and keeping the two sets of negotiations separate! This was clearly practising deceit towards the Arabs, although the British could claim that they were involved in a deadly war. Small wonder that T.E. Lawrence became disillusioned! So, writes Avi Shlaim:

> *By a stroke of the imperial pen, the Promised land [thus] became twice promised. Even by the standards of Perfidious Albion, this was an extraordinary tale of double-dealing and betrayal, a tale that continued to haunt Britain throughout the 30 years of its rule in Palestine.*
>
> (Shlaim 2003)

Imperialism cannot be omitted from *the Road to Balfour!*

British Betrayal

Dan Cohn-Sherbok

You are of course correct: imperialistic concerns were a central feature in Britain's dealing with the Arabs. The Middle East was vital to the British because of the strategic position on the route to possessions in India and the Far East. With huge numbers of troops tied down on the Western Front, British diplomats looked for allies in their campaign against the Turks. Resentful of Turkish overlordship, the Arabs were perceived as potential allies.

As you note, in 1915–1916, Sir Henry McMahon, the British Consul in Egypt, engaged in a lengthy correspondence with Hussein, the Grand Sharif of Mecca. As head of the Hashemites, he was guardian of the Muslim holy cities of Mecca and Medina, and therefore had a good claim to speak for the Islamic Arab people. Speaking for the British government, the Consul General stated that his country would support Arab independence and help the Arabs establish an Arab Kingdom. Yet areas west of the districts of Damascus, Homs, Hama and Aleppo were excluded from the agreement since Sir Henry felt that they were not purely Arab. Regrettably this correspondence was not accompanied by maps.

The Grand Sharif accepted the terms and, led by his son Faisal and assisted by T.E. Lawrence, the Arabs rose up in the Hejaz and drove north to link up with British forces that had advanced into Palestine from Egypt. However, despite British assurances, full Arab independence did not follow British victory. As you explained, six months after Sir Henry's promise to support Arab independence, Sir Mark Sykes negotiated a secret understanding with his French counterpart Francois George-Picot. Fearing that Arab portions of the Turkish Empire might come under Russian influence, the Sykes-Picot agreement divided the Middle East into five parts. Britain and France were each to have an area they controlled directly, and another that lay within their sphere of influence. This was, as you indicate, a betrayal of promises made by the British to the Arabs. It is a dark chapter in the history of British imperialism in the region.

But the central issue we are discussing is whether the Balfour Declaration was a deceitful act. As you will know, politicians and scholars have focused on McMahon's letter to Sharif Hussein in seeking to ascertain whether Palestine was included in Sir Henry's conception of an Arab Kingdom. If this were the case – if Britain in fact had promised the Sharif that Palestine was to be accorded to the Arab people – then Lord Balfour had no right to promise Jewry a homeland in Palestine. The Arab position is that the portions of Syria lying to the west of the districts of Damascus, Homs, Hama and Aleppo which were excluded from the agreement could not have included Palestine since it lays well to the south of the named places. The British position, however, was that Palestine was intended to be included – this was a view it held consistently from 1916. In support of their view, the British stressed that the McMahon reference to areas which 'cannot be said to be purely Arab' applies to Palestine since there were Jewish and Christian minorities in the region.

In 1922 the Churchill White Paper stated:

> It is not the case, as has been represented by the Arab Delegation, that during the War His Majesty's Government gave an undertaking that an independent national government should be at once established in Palestine. This representation mainly rests upon a letter dated the 24th October, 1915, from

Sir Henry McMahon, then His Majesty's High Commissioner in Egypt, to the Sharif of Mecca, now King Hussein of the Kingdom of the Hejaz. The letter is quoted as conveying the promise to the Sherif of Mecca to recognise and support the independence of the Arabs within the territories proposed by him. But this promise was given subject to a reservation made in the same letter, which excluded from its scope, among other territories, the portions of Syria lying to the west of the District of Damascus. This reservation has always been regarded by His Majesty's Government as covering the vilayet of Beirut and the independent Sanjak of Jerusalem. The whole of Palestine west of the Jordan was thus excluded from Sir Henry McMahon's pledge.

(en.wikipedia.org/wiki/McMahon-Hussein_Correspondence)

It should be noted that in a 1922 letter to Sir John Shuckburgh of the British Colonial Office, McMahon wrote the following to clarify the position:

It was my intention to exclude Palestine from independent Arabia, and I hoped that I had so worded the letter as to make this sufficiently clear for all practical purposes.

(en.wikipedia.org/wiki/McMahon-Hussein_Correspondence)

The White Paper and Sir Henry McMahon's statement thus make it clear that the Arab claim that the British government had betrayed a promise made during the war to the Sharif of Mecca about the status of Palestine is without foundation. You are right that the British failed to keep their word to the Sharif about the establishment of an Arab Kingdom: this is reprehensible. But it would be a mistake to believe that the McMahon correspondence rules out the possibility of a Jewish settlement in Palestine. Lord Balfour was entirely justified in making such a promise to Lord Rothschild in an effort to find a place of refuge for Jews who sought to escape from humiliation and persecution in Eastern Europe and elsewhere.

Balfour – A Web of Deceit

Mary Grey

You cannot refer to the McMahon–Hussein correspondence as if it were totally clear. Jonathan Schneer writes: ' . . . the fatal McMahon-Hussein correspondence, whose conflicting interpretations have divided Jews, Arabs and Britons for over a hundred years' (Schneer 2010, p. 59). It is true that Sharif Hussein wanted to include Palestine in the Arab Kingdom he dreamed of, but McMahon was deliberately ambiguous and evasive:

> . . . on the 24th October he offered Hussein a woolly declaration that Britain would recognise his claim to most of the area he wanted, excluding two of its most fertile zones. One was the bridgehead at the head of the Persian Gulf which the British army already occupied. The other was a coastal portion of Syria coveted by the French which he only sketchily defined. The meaning of his wording has been debated ever since, which is not surprising for it was never intended to be clear.
>
> The evolution of the key sentence in this letter proves that McMahon was deliberately trying to deceive the Sharif.
>
> (Barr 2011, p. 26)

In other words, we are back in the intrigues of British imperialism, and the McMahon promise – or false promise – has to be reckoned with, when considering the real motives for the Balfour Declaration. Certainly the Sharif believed he had been promised Palestine.

But the most shameful aspect of this is the callous way the British never indeed planned to honour the clause in the Declaration which committed them to respect the rights of the 'non-Jewish population'.

As Balfour wrote to Lord Curzon in 1919: 'in Palestine we do not propose even to go through the form of consulting the wishes of the present inhabitants of the country. . . . The Four Great Powers are committed to Zionism. And Zionism, be it right or wrong, good or bad, is rooted in age-long traditions, in present needs, in future hopes, of far profounder import than the desires and prejudices of the 700,000 Arabs who now inhabit that ancient land.... In short, *so far as Palestine is concerned, the Powers have made no statement of fact which is not admittedly wrong, and no declaration of policy which, at least in the letter, they have not always intended to violate.*

(Ingrams 1972, p. 73)

We now know much more about the intentions of the Cabinet of the time. For a collection of state documents has been compiled by Doreen Ingrams, called 'Palestine Papers 1917–1922: Seeds of Conflict' (Murray 1972). Recognizing that the conflict began with the publication of the Balfour Declaration, she takes us back to hidden motives. She lays bare the cynicism with which British Ministers committed themselves to the creation of a Jewish state in Palestine, with deliberate disregard for the rights and interests of the Arabs (then 92 per cent of the population).

Like you have implied, most people have been inclined to believe in the good intentions of Balfour and his colleagues – that to the British Government the Balfour Declaration meant no more and no less than it said, when it proclaimed that Britain would help to establish a 'national home' for the Jewish people in Palestine without prejudice to the rights of the existing population. So, perhaps it was Weizmann's doing that 'a home for the Jews' became a national state, the fulfilment of the Zionist dream. Was what happened to the Arabs a result more of weakness than duplicity?

Ingrams argues on the basis of State Papers that this is an illusion. She shows how, in document after document, that Balfour and his colleagues – with the exception of Lord Curzon and Edwin Montagu – were determined to help the Zionists to fulfil their aims. But worse than this, the Government set out to deceive the Arabs in Palestine as to their real intentions, with promises and guarantees that Britain would 'never consent' to a Jewish Government being set up to rule their land.

The Cabinet minutes of that period show, that Balfour envisaged an outcome far beyond what the language of his letter to Lord Rothschild had said. He made it clear that a Jewish home would become a state 'in accordance with the ordinary laws of political evolution'. Moreover, Weizmann admitted several years later that both Balfour and David Lloyd George had no hesitation in telling the Zionist leader that in using the phrase 'national home' in the declaration, 'We meant a Jewish state.' The protests of Montagu and Curzon were ignored: the British Government never intended to allow the Arab majority any voice in shaping the future of their own country. As Balfour wrote to Lloyd George in February 1919:

> The weak point of our position is of course that in the case of Palestine we deliberately and rightly decline to accept the principle of self-determination.

Clearly if the Arabs had been consulted they would scarcely have approved the new homeland for the Jews. The most damning statement is the following, as cited above:

> In short, so far as Palestine is concerned, the Powers have made no statement of fact which is not admittedly wrong, and no declaration of policy which, at least in the letter, they have not always intended to violate.
>
> (Ingrams, in *Nutting*)

With this evidence from Cabinet Papers it is impossible to deny that the British government – from whatever motive – practiced a web of deceit.

Settlers and Incomers

Dan Cohn-Sherbok

You are right to point out that scholars have debated the intention of the McMahon–Hussein correspondence for nearly a century. What is clear is that the British bargained with Sharif Hussein over the terms under which the Arabs would revolt against the Turkish Ottoman Empire. The correspondence which began in July 1915 was conducted in evasive language on both sides. The core of the correspondence, concerns Arab demands for independence. Specifically, the British were reluctant to delineate the area of such Arab independence. All the correspondence was in Arabic, with the British translating their original English text with varying degrees of accuracy. As you know, Palestine itself was not mentioned in the correspondence. Following the War, the British Mandate subsumed the Turkish Ottoman administrative regions of Sanjaq of Jerusalem and part of the Bilayet of Beirut. In modern-day terms, this region includes all of Israel, the West Bank and Gaza. As I noted, the British argued that this territory was not included within the area of Arab independence because McMahon's letter excluded portions of Syria lying to the west of the districts of Damascus, Homs, Hama and Allepo.

I think you are right that McMahon was deliberately ambiguous. British political concerns were paramount at the time. This was manifested most clearly in the Sykes-Picot agreement. In January 1916 these emissaries determined their countries' postwar spheres of influence in the Arab world. Britain would be invested with supervision over Arab territories encompassing the largest part of Mesopotamia, most of Transjordan and southern Palestine. The French were authorized to exercise varying degrees of ascendancy over southern Turkey, Syria, northern Palestine and the Mosul area of upper Mesopotamia. Such a secret arrangement was a violation of the promises made to Sharif Hussein of an independent Arab kingdom. Like you, I believe this was a British betrayal of the Arabs.

But this is a separate matter from the situation of Palestine. It does not appear that Britain ever intended to relinquish control of Palestine to the Arabs. Certainly that has always been the British position, and McMahon himself explained that this was his view at the time he engaged in correspondence with Sharif Hussein. What surprises me in your account of the Balfour Declaration is your total lack of sympathy for Jewish suffering. You clearly do not share Balfour's genuine concern about the situation of Jews in Eastern Europe and elsewhere. It would be naive to think that the British had no political interest in the region: they did. But their compassion for Jewry was genuine. Balfour had a deep and consistent dislike of anti-Semitism. When Parliament was debating restrictions on the free immigration of aliens, he declared that the 'medieval treatment of the Jews was a permanent stain on European annals', and he agreed that if the government could do anything to wipe it out, they should do so. It was under his premiership that negotiations with the Zionists, first on El Arish, and then in East Africa, had taken place. In his discussions with Zionists, he accepted the terms of their arguments; in reality he had become a Zionist.

You have said earlier in our correspondence that had you been present at the first Zionist Congress you would have been moved by the impassioned pleas of Herzl and others to safeguard the lives of persecuted Jews. But in your discussion of the Balfour Declaration, you appear to be completely unconcerned by their plight. I fear your sympathy for the Arabs has blinded you to the predicament of early twentieth-century Eastern European Jewry. You simply do not share the attitude of Balfour and others. Indeed, I wonder whether you support the Arab acts of violence against the early Jewish settlers. Let me conclude with an analogy. As you know we live in Wales. For some time the native Welsh have felt hostile towards English incomers. The chapels refuse to use English in their services, and in the past some English homes have been burned down in protest against English settlement even though these houses were legally purchased from the Welsh themselves. Do you approve such attitudes? Palestine at the beginning of the twentieth century was in many respects a similar case: during the First and Second Aliyah (1882–1913), Jews bought property from Arabs. They did not steal the land. Such acquisition was resented by the native Arabs (even though the vendors themselves were Arabs and sold their land willingly). Violent attacks against these settlers became a frequent occurrence. Do you justify such hostility in both these cases?

There Were Other Ways!

Mary Grey

I am blind neither to Jewish nor Arab suffering: the fact that I am sensitive to both is the catalyst for our correspondence. My intuitions concerning the road to peace in Palestine/Israel call for an ability to enter the truth of both Jewish and Arab stories. My explorations around the history of the Balfour Agreement struggle towards this: what were the true motivations of all parties? I do not think we have yet come to the heart of it: we have not sufficiently factored in the Great War and the desire to get America into it, the involvement of American Jews and the deep concern for Russian

Jews. One last issue is the attitude of Edwin Montagu – mentioned earlier – as an influential politician favouring assimilation.

But his arguments are strong and he even accused the British government of Anti-Semitism! In a memorandum to the Government in August 1917, Montagu wrote:

> I have chosen the above title for this memorandum, not in any hostile sense, not by any means as quarrelling with an anti-Semitic view which may be held by my colleagues, not with a desire to deny that anti-Semitism can be held by rational men, not even with a view to suggesting that the Government is deliberately anti-Semitic; but I wish to place on record my view *that the policy of His Majesty's Government is anti-Semitic in result will prove a rallying ground for Anti-Semites in every country in the world.* (my italics)[1]

Recognising that the decision to create new homeland for the Jews is being made in a war context, where national security has become a priority, Montagu wrote:

> Zionism has always seemed to me to be a mischievous political creed, untenable by any patriotic citizen of the United Kingdom. If a Jewish Englishman sets his eyes on the Mount of Olives and longs for the day when he will shake British soil from his shoes and go back to agricultural pursuits in Palestine, he has always seemed to me to have acknowledged aims inconsistent with British citizenship and to have admitted that he is unfit for a share in public life in Great Britain, or to be treated as an Englishman. I have always understood that those who indulged in this creed were largely animated by the restrictions upon and refusal of liberty to Jews in Russia. But at the very

---

[1] *Source:* Great Britain, Public Record Office, Cab. 24/24, August 23, 1917. Lord Edwin Samuel Montagu (1879–1924), Anglo-Jewish statesman, was British Minister of Munitions, 1916, and Secretary of State for India, 1917–1922. *The Anti-Semitism of the Present Government*, August 23, 1917, NA, Cab24/24. Cited in Jonathan Schneer, *The Balfour Declaration*, London: Bloomsbury, 2010, p. 337. Extracts are from the Cabinet papers.

time when these Jews have been acknowledged as Jewish Russians and given all liberties, it seems to be inconceivable that Zionism should be officially recognised by the British Government, and that Mr Balfour should be authorized to say that Palestine was to be reconstituted as the 'national home of the Jewish people'. I do not know what this involves, but I assume that it means that Mahommedans and Christians are to make way for the Jews and that the Jews should be put in all positions of preference and should be peculiarly associated with Palestine in the same way that England is with the English or France with the French, that Turks and other Mahommedans in Palestine will be regarded as foreigners, just in the same way as Jews will hereafter be treated as foreigners in every country but Palestine.

In addition, he laid down four principles: the first was that there is no Jewish nation. Secondly, he thought that when the Jews are told that Palestine is their national home, every country would immediately desire to get rid of its Jewish citizens, and

you will find a population in Palestine driving out its present inhabitants, taking all the best in the country, drawn from every all quarters of the globe, speaking every language on the face of the earth, and incapable of communicating with one another except by means of an interpreter.

He argues passionately that the lives and contributions that Jews have made in Britain means that they should be regarded not as British Jews, but Jewish Britons. Montagu does not even agree that the Jews have a special claim on Palestine:

I deny that Palestine is to-day associated with the Jews or properly to be regarded as a fit place for them to live in. The Ten Commandments were delivered to the Jews on Sinai. It is quite true that Palestine plays a large part in Jewish history, but so it does in modern Mahommendan history, and, after the time of the Jews, surely it plays a larger part than any other country in Christian history. The Temple may have been in Palestine, but so was the Sermon on the Mount and the Crucifixion.

Montagu ended his dramatic memorandum this way:

> I would say to Lord Rothschild that the Government will be prepared to do everything in their power to obtain for Jews in Palestine complete liberty of settlement and life on an equality with the inhabitants of that country who profess other religious beliefs. I would ask that the Government should go no further.

By the time the Balfour Declaration was signed Montagu was in India as Secretary of State, his advice ignored. But his plea is sufficient evidence that that there were other ways to address anti-Semitism and the suffering of the Jewish people.

Chapter 4
The Aftermath of the Balfour Declaration

The Unravelling of Deceit
Mary Grey

Whatever the motivation of all parties concerned in achieving the Declaration, there is no doubt that its significance remains controversial and is acknowledged as one of the key foundation stones of the on-going Arab–Israeli conflict: it has stirred acrimonious debate among generations of historians on all sides. In his recent writing, 'The Balfour Declaration and its consequences,' Oxford historian Avi Shlaim maintains that Britain's failure as a Mandatory power in Palestine can be at least partly attributed to it, that it was Britain's 'original sin' and that it gave rise to 'one of the most intense, bitter and protracted conflicts of modern times' (Shlaim 2009, pp. 23–24):

> In Arabic there is a saying that something that starts crooked, remains crooked. The Balfour Declaration was not just crooked – it was a contradiction in terms. The national home

it promised to the Jews was never clearly defined and there was no precedent for it in international law.
(Shlaim 2009, pp. 23–24)

According to the pro-Zionist historian Paul Johnson, the final draft, as published on November 2:

> ... no longer equated Palestine with the national home, it had no reference to, [it] was unrestricted Jewish immigration or internal rule, and it safeguarded the rights of the Arabs.... All the same the key piece in the jigsaw, for without it the Jewish state could never have come into existence.
> (Johnson 1987, p. 430)

Arthur Toynbee told an interviewer in 1973 that Balfour was 'a wicked man' (Shlaim 2009, p. 23). This was because the Arabs were robbed of their right to self-determination and were thrown into the most subtle and intricate political situation imaginable and were unprepared.

Of course the historical timing for the signing and subsequent publication of the Declaration were dramatic. As Simon Sebag-Montefiore explains:

> The Declaration was designed to detach Russian Jews from Bolshevism but the very night before it was published, Lenin seized power in St Petersburg. Had Lenin moved a few days earlier, the Balfour Declaration might never have been issued. Ironically, Zionism propelled by the energy of Russian Jews – from Weizmann in Whitehall to Ben-Gurion in Jerusalem – and Christian sympathy for their plight, was now cut off from Russian Jewry until the fall of the Soviet Union in 1991.
> (Sebag-Montefiore 2011, p. 415)

The second dramatic contextual factor was that General Allenby and his army, in the campaign against the Turks, were marching victoriously through Palestine: as he did so, Lloyd George was flamboyantly demanding the capture of Jerusalem 'as a Christmas present for the nation' (Sebag-Montefiore 2011, p. 415). In fact the Declaration was not published in Jerusalem, in *The Jewish Chronicle*, until 9 November and Jerusalem was conquered on 9 December. Allenby – with T.E. Lawrence – entered the city through the Jaffa Gate-on foot, two days later.

But, I hear you say, I am forgetting the jubilation of Weizmann and his followers. And it is true that, despite disappointment that the text did not go as far as he had hoped (in giving the Jews a State and not merely a homeland), Weizmann was overjoyed. As he wrote to Balfour:

> Since Cyrus the Great, there was never, in all the records of the past, a manifestation inspired by a higher sense of political wisdom, far-sighted statesmanship, and national justice towards the Jewish people than this memorable declaration.
> (Segev 1999, p. 50)

But not all shared this jubilation. Indeed, the chickens would now come home to roost in terms of the contradictory promises made to both Jews and Arabs. Weizmann categorically denied to Feisal (son of the Sharif of the Hejaz and key player in the Arab Revolt), that the Zionists intended to set up a Jewish government. (Could he have done otherwise, given that Palestine then consisted of some 700,000 Arabs and 56,000 Jews?) Winston Churchill himself, on an official visit to Palestine, had met with a deputation of Muslim and Christians, who told him that the Arabs had not hated the Turks and trusted the British because of any national prejudices, but because they craved that independence which the former had denied to them and the latter had promised as a reward for shedding their blood in the cause of the Allies. Yet now it seemed that the Arabs' reward was to see Palestine denied independence and 'isolated for a thought-out purpose'. In reply, Churchill insisted that the fulfilment of the Balfour Declaration would be 'good for the Arabs who dwell in Palestine' (Ingrams 1972, pp. 118–119).

It is hard to overstate the complexity of the British position. With promises to both Jews and Arabs, the campaign against the Ottoman Empire by no means won and the Great War apparently carrying on interminably, is it surprising that Brigadier General

Gilbert Clayton, began to suggest that the Balfour Declaration might have been a mistake?

> I am not fully aware of the weight which Zionists carry, . . . and of the consequences necessary of giving them everything for which they may ask, but I must point out that, by pushing them as hard as we appear to be doing, we are risking the possibility of Arab unity becoming something like an accomplished fact and being ranged against us.
>
> (Fromkin 1989, p. 318)

Given all of this, can you justify the Balfour Declaration on moral grounds – *at the time?*

The Problem of Anti-Semitism

Dan Cohn-Sherbok

At the end of Chapter 3 you quoted Edwin Montagu at length. As you pointed out, he was a vociferous opponent of Zionism. In his view, Zionism was a pernicious philosophy which would inevitably lead to increased anti-Semitism. The creation of a Jewish settlement in Palestine, he believed, would prove to be a rallying ground for anti-Semites in every country in the world. According to Montagu, what is required is for Jews to integrate into the societies in which they live. 'Zionism,' he stated, 'has always seemed to me to be a mischievous political creed, untenable by any patriotic citizen of the United Kingdom'. For Montagu, what is required is for Jews to be Englishmen first and foremost. Such an endorsement of assimilation was shared by American Reform Jews who were also opponents of Zionism. At the close of the First Zionist Congress, for example, Isaac Mayer Wise, the spokesman for American Reform Judaism proclaimed: 'We denounce the whole question of a Jewish state as foreign to the spirit of the modern Jew of this land, who looks upon America as his Palestine and whose interests are centred here' (Laqueur 1972, p. 394).

It appears then you are here endorsing such an assimilationist perspective. However, at the end of the First Chapter, you are critical of assimilation as an alternative to a Jewish homeland. You write: 'The problem is that assimilation appears to demand that the minority group suppress its own (unique) identity to "fit in" with the so-called dominant culture.' Yet, this is precisely what Jewish assimilationists such as Montagu and Wise insist must be done. The eighteenth-century Jewish philosopher Moses Mendelssohn was critical of Jewish isolationism. Championing the Jewish Enlightenment, he insisted that German Jews learn the language of the country in which they lived. The Reform movement in Germany and elsewhere altered the traditional liturgy, introducing sermons and prayers in the vernacular, and created schools in which Jewish students would be exposed to Western European culture as well as traditional Jewish sources. At the end of the nineteenth century, Reformers in America issued the Pittsburgh Platform which called for a total revision of Jewish life and thought. The aim was to liberate Jewry from a medieval past in which Jews were subject to discrimination and persecution. Their aim was to modernize the faith and discard ritual trappings which separated Jews from their Gentile neighbours. You will remember that I pressed you in Chapter 1 to provide a solution to anti-Semitism different from Zionism. I asked if you believed that assimilation is the answer. In response you offered a critique of assimilationist ideology, but in Chapter 3 you appear to endorse it. So, I ask you again: are you an advocate or an opponent of assimilationism as a solution to the problem of Jew-hatred?

In Chapter 4 you offer a stinging attack on the Balfour Declaration, quoting a number of writers including Avi Shlaim, Paul Johnson and Arnold Toynbee. But in presenting these views, you are minimising the jubilation felt by world Jewry. Jews everywhere shared the joy expressed by Weizmann in the passage you quoted. The Jewish community in all countries was ecstatic, and the enthusiasm of American and Russian Jewry was expressed in hundreds of resolutions. Henri Bergson, George Brandes and other public figures, alienated from Judaism and Jewish affairs, expressed their approval and willingness to help in the building of a new Palestine. The leaders of German Zionism welcomed the Declaration as an event of world-historical importance, the longest step by far on the road towards the realisation of the Basle programme.

To ensure that a Jewish National Home would be established in Palestine, a Jewish delegation headed by Weizmann addressed the Paris Peace Conference on 27 February 1919. After listening to impassioned speeches by the delegates, the Paris Peace Conference agreed to grant the Palestine Mandate to Great Britain, and accepted the need to establish a Jewish homeland in Palestine as outlined in the Declaration. You declare at the end of Chapter 3 that you are not blind to both Arab and Jewish suffering. This is certainly the case with regard to the Arab situation, and I agree with you that the British did not keep their promises about an independent Arab state. I share your concern about such betrayal. But I am not persuaded that you are sensitive to the plight of Jewry at the end of the nineteenth and early twentieth centuries in Eastern Europe and elsewhere. It appears that your concern for the indigenous Arab population in Palestine has blinded you to the Jewish problem. Again, I stress that the early settlers did not confiscate Palestinian land – they purchased it from Arabs. They were not usurpers, intent on driving Arabs into the sea. Why are you so vociferous in your condemnation? If you had heard the speeches of the Grand Mufti and his followers in the years after the Balfour Declaration, would you have supported their efforts to curtail immigration and drive Jews out of the Holy Land?

Aftermath of Balfour – Buying Up Arab Land

Mary Grey

You repeatedly recall me to what I consider an unfair choice – assimilation (which, as you say, I do not favour), or the solving of Jewish suffering and 2,000 years of anti-Semitism by granting a home for the Jewish people in what was believed to be their ancestral home, Israel/Palestine. I still believe that assimilation demands an unjust suppression of cultural identity, in this case, Jewish identity. May I remind you that

> Cultural assimilation is the process by which a subaltern group's native language and culture are lost under pressure to assimilate to those of a dominant cultural group. The term is used both to refer to colonized peoples when dominant colonial states expand into new territories or alternatively, *when*

diasporas of immigrants settle into a dominant state society. (my italics) Full assimilation occurs when new members of a society become indistinguishable from older members.
(www.wikipedia.org/culturalassimilation)

But, surely this is not the way Jewish people have actually been living? True, as every other faith does, they have built synagogues, and religious Jews have a flourishing distinctive faith life – and in some places, there are Jewish schools; but more than that: Jews contribute to every form of professional life, and excel in many. I do not particularly categorize Yehudi Menuhin as Jewish, rather as an exceptionally gifted violinist. Surely the goal is for every race or ethnic group to maintain its uniqueness which should not be sacrificed for the sake of some imposed dominant state identity?

Secondly, of course Zionists the world over were jubilant, even euphoric over the Balfour declaration – and I do have much sympathy with this. But we cannot gloss over the fact that Balfour's Cabinet had no legal right to give away someone else's land. (The Declaration had no legal status until the time of the British Mandate.) Were the British justified in confiscating land from the Native American Indians, and confining them to reservations? You may not even be aware that Balfour's own attitude to the Jewish people was ambiguous. Yes, he professed his Zionist leanings to Weizmann with genuine great emotion, and even on his death-bed he admitted that this achievement – that is, the Declaration – was what he was most proud of; but in 1905 when Jews – 100,00 were already in England – were fleeing persecution from Eastern Europe, Balfour opposed the Immigration Act allowing them entry to Britain! (Klug 2011, pp. 199–210)

Granted that his attitude was complex and changed when he became a Zionist, let us now consider the position of the Arabs who lived in Palestine. You claim that Jews bought land from the Arabs – but it was more complex. Palestine, far from being an empty land, was densely populated and cultivated, apart from some swampy areas. So of course Zionists found that they had to purchase the land. The Jewish National fund and Keren Hayesod purchased land in the name of the entire Jewish people, which was then restricted to exclusive Jewish use. Much of this land, writes

Lerner (2003, p. 32), was purchased from absentee landlords, who lived in Beirut, Cairo, Damascus and Baghdad, although some came from Palestinian landlords as well as from peasant farmers. And land sometimes included Palestinian villages or 'commons' – lands that had been used for centuries by Palestinian families:

> The land was withdrawn from Palestinian use and the people who lived on it were often forced to move and look for work in an urban economy in which Jewish – only economic institutions were making it hard for Palestinians to find employment.
>
> (Lerner 2003, p. 32)

He continues:

> Imagine yourself living in a village whose agricultural lands have been worked for generations by your family and the families of your small community. Then one day someone arrives to tell you that he holds a piece of paper that indicates that he has bought all the land of your village and that you must move. To where? How will you and your family make a living? ... And you hear that it is happening to others around your country. The Jewish people are throwing you off your land and putting your family and the family of many others into crisis. How would you feel?
>
> (Lerner 2003, 32–33)

What seems tragic – in view of future events – was that former relations between Jews and Arabs were now disrupted. I have heard so many Palestinians tell about these peaceful relations, that were now broken. Indeed, as I have indicated, the British government had realized from the start, that they would need to get rid of the Arab population. As Winston Churchill predicted in 1919:

> There are the Jews, whom we are pledged to introduce into Palestine, and who take it for granted the local population will be cleared out to suit their convenience.
>
> (Qumsiyeh 2004, p. 150)

Small wonder that the Arab inhabitants of Palestine were so distressed. Even General Allenby – now in Jerusalem – dared not read out the Declaration for some time! It is not anti-Semitism that is at issue here, but the deceitful behaviour of the British Cabinet.

The Jewish Problem

Dan Cohn-Sherbok

Your critique of assimilation, I believe, illustrates a profound misunderstanding of the nature of Jewish life. As you know, since the destruction of the Second Temple by the Romans in 70 CE, the Jewish people have been in exile. For nearly 2,000 years we have been mercilessly persecuted and killed in the various counties where we have lived. Under Christendom the Jew has constantly been subject to murderous loathing. Regarded as Christ-killers we have been targeted because of our beliefs and practices. Until the eighteenth century European Jews were compelled to live in ghettos and shtetls (Jewish villages) where we were subject to numerous disabilities. Judeophobia has been a constant feature of daily existence.

At the end of the eighteenth century, however, a number of Christian reformers were deeply troubled by the Jewish problem and pressed for the improvement of Jewish life. In *Concerning the Amelioration of the Civil Status of the Jews*, for example, Wilhelm Christian Dohm argued that a humane society should abolish prejudicial restrictions. All occupations, he stated, should be open to Jews and educational opportunities should be provided. Influenced by such ideas Moses Mendelssohn, the father of the Jewish Enlightenment, sought to modernize Jewish life by translating the Pentateuch into German so that Jews would be able to learn the language of the country in which they lived. Following Mendelssohn's example, a number of Jewish supporters of the Enlightenment – the maskilim – encouraged Jews to abandon medieval patterns of life and thought.

Throughout the nineteenth century Reform Jews sought to modernize Judaism so that Jews would be able to integrate into the societies in which they lived. The synagogue service was transformed by the inclusion of choirs and organs; numerous traditional rituals were abandoned; central principals of religious faith were altered. A leading proponent of such reforms, Israel Jacobson, stated:

> Let me be frank, my brothers, our ritual is weighed down with primitive customs, which are offensive both to our reason and to our Christian friends.
> (Israel Jacobson, in *Short Reader of Judaism*, pp. 131–132)

As time passed other non-Orthodox branches of Judaism – Conservative, Reconstructionist and Humanistic Judaism – championed the reformulation of belief and practice. Such changes paved the way for the integration of Jews into mainstream society. For most Jews assimilation was perceived as a mean to overcome antipathy towards the Jewish people.

At the end of the nineteenth century, however, a number of Jews viewed this quest as fruitless: in their view Jew hatred is inevitable. Leo Pinsker, for example, wrote in *Autoemancipation*:

> For the living, the Jew is a dead man; for the natives, an alien and a vagrant; for property holders, a beggar; for the poor, an exploiter and millionaire; for patriots, a man without a country; for all classes, a hated rival.
> (Leo Pinsker 1932, Autoemancipation, in *The Zionist Idea*, p. 188)

Profoundly affected by the Dreyfus affair, Theodor Herzl in *The Jewish State*, despaired of Western society. In his view, the only solution to the problem of anti-Semitism is for Jews to establish a state of their own in which they will be the majority.

In a post-Holocaust world, Jews remain profoundly troubled by the problem of anti-Semitism with good reason. The Jews of Germany in the 1930s were among the most assimilated in the world, contributing economically, socially and culturally. This did not spare them from the horrors of Nazi rule. Consciously or unconsciously the world-wide Jewish community today subscribes to both of the approaches which I have briefly outlined. The State of Israel is perceived as an indispensable refuge for those who suffer discrimination and persecution. Simultaneously most Jews seek to assimilate and integrate into the societies in which they live. With the exception of the strictly Orthodox who cling to the lifestyle of their ancestors, the majority of Jews seek to discard beliefs and practices which they view as antiquated and irrelevant.

In our discussion you have rejected assimilation as a means of escaping from prejudice and degradation. At the same time you have castigated the British for declaring their support for a Jewish settlement in their ancient homeland. The Jews, you continually stress, have unjustly confiscated land from the indigenous Arab population in Palestine even though the property was legitimately purchased from its owners. (Yet you overlook the fact that although someone has worked land for generations that does not give them the right of ownership.) Repeatedly you express sympathy solely for Palestinians. In doing so, I believe you do not take seriously the tragic history of the Jewish people who have been persecuted, exiled and massacred for nearly twenty centuries. I have asked you repeatedly: what is the solution to the Jewish problem? You have ruled out assimilation. You deny Jews a state of their own in the Holy Land. So I ask you again: what are we Jews to do?

You Cannot Solve One Injustice with Another!

Mary Grey

You have described the history of the assimilationist position very movingly, and I do see the force of your argument. After all, I cited Edwin Montagu's appeal to Balfour in full – an appeal that Balfour and his Cabinet ignored. I also see that assimilation has worked in many countries so that, as I wrote earlier, Jewish people are successfully integrated into society – just consider the influential status of American Jews. But you continue to avoid my insistence that we face both the truth of the complex motivation of the Balfour Declaration and the deceit of the British Government in its avowed intention of ignoring its commitment to the indigenous people of the land. As I cited earlier:

> Balfour wrote to Lord Curzon in 1919: 'in Palestine we do not propose even to go through the form of consulting the wishes of the present inhabitants of the country. . . . The Four Great Powers are committed to Zionism. And Zionism, be it right or wrong, good or bad, is rooted in age-long traditions,

in present needs, in future hopes, of far profounder import than the desires and prejudices of the 700,000 Arabs who now inhabit that ancient land. . . . In short, *so far as Palestine is concerned, the Powers have made no statement of fact which is not admittedly wrong, and no declaration of policy which, at least in the letter, they have not always intended to violate.*
(Ingrams 1972, p. 73)

You are also very one-sided in your awareness of where injustice lies. I am not arguing about the right of the contemporary state of Israel to exist, but about *the morality and legality of the way the country was handed over to the Jewish people in 1917* through a document whose promises to the already-existing inhabitants were never meant to be honoured. I believe that justice can only be attained on the basis of truth. Nor are you fair to accuse me of sympathy only with Arab suffering. In my life's work as a Liberation theologian I have tried to be in solidarity with the victims – and have constantly strived in Christian circles to expose and oppose anti-Judaism in Christian Theology and anti-Semitism in society.

Take the example of Rwanda (Grey 2007). The background to the genocide in 1994 was also colonialism – in this case Belgian, and the struggle for land among two peoples, Tutsi and Hutu. It would be very easy to stick with the position of blaming Hutus as perpetrators (which they largely were) and Tutsi as victims without acknowledging both Tutsi reprisals and moderate Hutus who did not support the massacres and lost their lives because of this. Without considering the wellbeing of both communities there is no possibility of reconciliation in Rwanda.

And this involves looking at historical developments and identifying where mistakes were made that determined future disasters. I believe this also to be the case with Palestine. Of course I long just for a solution to the terrible suffering of Jews in history. You yourself, in any case, favour the assimilationist answer: but imagine if the inhabitants of Palestine had been consulted and involved in discussions with the British government before the Declaration was issued? When you say that working the land for generations does not give the right of ownership, you are not thinking historically: it is only with conquest and Empire that these things became contested. But I do concede that in many cases Arabs were willing to sell the land to Jewish settlers and that their opposition to the new incomers 'was rooted in emotion, in religion, in xenophobia, in the complex of feelings that tend to overcome people when newcomers flood in to change their neighbourhood' (Fromkin 1989, p. 523).

You cannot solve one injustice with another. And the extraordinary postscript to Balfour was that yes, unsurprisingly, the Arabs were upset and felt betrayed, but even the British army in Palestine opposed the Declaration. Churchill estimated that 90 per cent of the army were against it. On 29 October 1921 General W.N. Congreve, commander of the British armies in Egypt and Palestine, sent a circular to all troops, saying that while the Army was officially supposed to have no politics:

> In the case of Palestine these sympathies are rather obviously with the Arabs, who have hitherto appeared to the disinterested observer to have been the victims of an unjust policy forced upon them by the British Government.
> (Fromkin 1989, p. 524)

The troubled history goes on: Balfour Day in Palestine – November 2 – is to this day commemorated in sorrow.

A Clear View of History

Dan Cohn-Sherbok

I want to respond to the various points you make in your last exchange. First, I am glad that you see the force of the assimilationist argument. But you do not indicate whether you have changed your view of assimilationist ideology as far as anti-Semitism is concerned. As I attempted to illustrate, for the last 200 years most Jews have divested themselves of the manifold laws which have separated them from their neighbours in the quest for social, economic and political acceptance. Previously you objected to such a policy. Do you now think this has been an acceptable strategy?

You say that I have avoided your insistence that we face the complex motivations lying behind the Balfour Declaration and the deceit of the British government in its avowed intention of ignoring its commitment to the indigenous population of the land. I accept that Britain's endorsement of the Balfour Declaration was partly motivated by political interests, yet this does not mean that the British government had no sympathy with the Zionist cause. On the contrary, a concern for the welfare of the Jewish people was a crucial element – though not the only element – in the formulation of British policy.

It is also not true to say that Britain had no sympathy for the indigenous Arab population in Palestine. Numerous steps were taken to ensure that their rights were protected. When the British Mandate was confirmed by the League of Nations, the Preamble to the text of the Mandate stated:

> Whereas the principal Allied Powers have also agreed that the Mandatory should be responsible for putting into effect the declaration originally made on 2nd November 1917 by the Government of His Britannic Majesty, and adopted by the said Powers, in favour of the establishment in Palestine of a national home for the Jewish people, it being clearly understood that nothing should be done which might prejudice the civil and religious rights of existing non-Jewish communities in Palestine, or the rights and political status enjoyed by Jews in other countries.
>
> (Laqueur and Rubin 1995, *The Israel-Arab Reader*, pp. 30–31)

When Sir Herbert Samuel became High Commissioner in 1920, he was intent on implementing the Balfour Declaration which aimed to safeguard the civil and religious rights of the Arabs. On 10 August he cautioned Chaim Weizmann: 'It is upon the Arab rock that the Zionist ship may be wrecked.' To the Palestinian Jewish leaders, he stated:

> You yourselves are inviting a massacre which will come as long as you disregard the Arabs. You pass over them in silence. . . . You have done nothing to come to an understanding. You know

> only how to protest against the government . . . Zionism has not yet done a thing to obtain the consent of the inhabitants and without this consent immigration will not be possible.
>
> (Johnson 1987, p. 437)

Throughout his time as High Commissioner, Samuel pursued a policy of even-handedness. Despite Arab unrest, the British were intent on implementing egalitarian principles. Thus in a meeting of the Imperial Council on 22 June 1921 the Canadian Prime Minister Arthur Meighen asked: 'How do you define our responsibilities in relation to Palestine under Mr. Balfour's pledge?' In response, Winston Churchill, the Colonial Secretary, said: 'To do our best to make an honest effort to give the Jews a chance to make a national home for themselves.' Meighen then asked if this meant they would take control of the government, Churchill replied that they could do so if they became a majority in the country. Meighen then asked if this meant pro rata with the Arab population. To this Churchill said: 'Pro rata with the Arab. We made an equal pledge that we would not turn the Arab off his land or invade his political and social rights.' (Johnson 1987, p. 440). Hence, it is not true to say that promises to the already existing inhabitants were never meant to be honoured.

I am aware that throughout your life's work as a liberation theologian you have tried to be in solidarity with victims of oppression and persecution. I acknowledge that you have sought to expose and oppose anti-Semitism in Christian theology and society. Yet, I believe that your sympathy for Arab suffering (which I share) has clouded your analysis of the early history of the Zionism. You cannot avoid the fact that Jewish settlers legitimately purchased land from Arab owners. You continually stress that, as a liberation theologian you have supported the marginalized and persecuted. Surely, this was precisely the predicament of European Jews who were subject to violent pogroms. Was their fate really of no consequence?

I know that you are deeply concerned about what you perceive as the injustices of the Balfour Declaration and its aftermath. Yet, a continual emphasis on the injustice of this document will be seized upon by Palestinian supporters to delegitimize the modern state of Israel. I know that you yourself are concerned with justice for all. But it is naive to suppose that your work in this area will not be used by Jew-haters, and that you yourself will be perceived as sharing their antipathy to the Jewish people.

Chapter 5
The British Mandate

Arab Resistance

Dan Cohn-Sherbok

In 1919 while tension mounted between Jews and Arabs in Palestine, the British military administration clamped down on Zionism: a series of official decisions were made including the prohibition of Jewish immigration, the withholding of authorisation for land transfer, the non-recognition of Hebrew as an official language, and the banning from public performance of the Zionist anthem which incensed Jewish settlers. The Zionists felt that the promise of the Balfour Declaration was being broken, while the Arabs believed that the Jewish National Home might be aborted through resolute action.

In the early months of 1920 Arab anti-Jewish agitation increased. Such activity was organized by the Muslim-Christian Association which had been founded in November 1918. From April 4 to 8, 1920 Arab rioters attacked the Jewish Quarter of the Old City of Jerusalem. The Arab police sided with the rioters and had to be withdrawn and disarmed. The Army did not enter the Old City, and forbade the Jews to organize their own defense. Vladimir Jabotinsky, who tried to do so, was arrested. In the four days of bloodshed, nine people died (five of them Jews), and 244 were wounded (211 Jews). Most of the victims were old men, women and children.

What do you make of these events? In our discussion so far, you have repeatedly pointed out the injustice of the British involvement in Palestine. You have valiantly defended the rights of the indigenous population, and have castigated the British for their duplicity and unwillingness to consult the native population about Zionist aspirations. There is, however, another side to this argument, and I have sought in our dialogue to explain the Jewish perspective. But given your commitment to peace and reconciliation, I am sure you would condemn the violence that was unleashed against the Jewish community in these Arab riots. Is this not so?

In the summer of 1920 Sir Herbert Samuel arrived in Palestine as High Commissioner for Palestine, intent on implementing the Balfour Declaration. In August he authorized a Land Transfer Ordinance that made it possible for Zionists to acquire land, and in the following month an Immigration Ordinance opened Palestine to legal Jewish immigration to those who had obtained visas from the Zionist Organisation. Initially Samuel sought to reconcile Arabs to British policy by pardoning the ringleaders of the Arab riots of 1920, including Haj Amin al-Husseini and creating an Advisory Council with an Arab majority in the unofficial membership. Such actions, however, did not pacify the Arab community. A focus of Arab resentment was the increasing number of Jews who had entered Palestine. By April 1921 nearly 10,000 Jews had come into the country under Samuel's Immigration Ordinance.

In April 1921 an election took place of for the Grand Mufti of Jerusalem as the supreme representative of Muslim Arabs. Haj Amin al-Husseini came fourth despite his notoriety as the principal instigator of anti-Jewish riots of Easter 1920. Haj Amin and his followers declared that the elections had been rigged by the Jews to have a pro-Zionist Mufti. Samuel's major advisor on Arab affairs encouraged him to invalidate the elections, but Samuel made no decision. While this matter remained unresolved, Arab riots took place on 1 May in Jaffa. Jewish shops and a shelter for immigrants were attacked. Twenty-seven Jews and three Arabs were killed, and one hundred and four Jews and thirty-four Arabs wounded. In the next few days, rioting spread to other costal centres. By 7 May forty-seven Jews had been killed and one hundred and forty-six wounded, and forty-eight Arabs killed and seventy-three wounded. What is your reaction to these incidents?

During the years 1920–1922 there were grave doubts about the possibility of establishing a Jewish National Home as proposed by the Balfour Declaration. Although Samuel sought to create institutions in Palestine, Arabs continually resisted his efforts. After the May riots of 1921 Samuel proposed that an Advisory Council be elected as a step towards self-government. At the same time he stated that the Balfour Delectation did not imply that a Jewish government would be formed to rule over the Muslim and Christian majority. Rather, he insisted that the British government would never impose a policy that would be contrary to the religious, political and economic interests of those living in Palestine. Despite these efforts in August 1921 an Arab delegation went to London to meet with British officials. Because the Arabs were not able to secure an assembly with legislative and executive powers to control immigration and to receive a repudiation of the Balfour Declaration, they rejected the offer of an elected assembly. Do you believe such intransigence was justified?

The Impact of Balfour in Palestine

Mary Grey

You are right: the violent attacks by Arabs on the newly arriving *Jewish* people in Palestine, in the wake of the Balfour Declaration, are appalling. I do not support violence anywhere, however justifiable the cause appears to be. But, that was the world in those days, and is the world now that we live in. People *do* take to the sword and gun in retaliation often without consideration of other means. But I have tried consistently to make clear that I do not support the inflicting of suffering and killing on one people as opposed to another. What I also attempt to make clear *are* the issues of justice – for both sides. And to open up the complex motives and responsibilities of the British government in Palestine, post-Balfour.

And what springs to the fore when General Allenby conquered Jerusalem and Herbert Samuel, ardent Zionist, arrived as the first

High Commissioner, is the uncertainty as to what the legal consequences for Palestine ensued following the Balfour Declaration. What seems extraordinary is *the scarcity of official records on the origins of the Balfour Declaration.* As the Colonial Office (responsible for Palestine since March 1921) sought to review the entire problem, it 'discovered' that 'very little is recorded', and Captain William Ormsby-Gore, Under Secretary for Colonies 1922–1924, had to be asked to add what he remembered to the very 'scanty material available'. When Balfour was consulted, the 'official' story asserts that he was unable to help. He was suffering from bad memory, and he regretted the death of Mark Sykes, who, he said, 'had the whole thing at his finger's ends'. From the little material available to him, Sir John Evelyn Shuckburgh was not able to find out what were the 'precise reasons' that led His Majesty's Government to issue the declaration. Furthermore, *he discovered that the correspondence previous to the declaration was not available in the Colonial Office* (Huneidi 1999). This being the case, it is hardly surprising that the Balfour Declaration, in its origins and in its motives, even regarding the identities of those who collaborated in drafting it, remains controversial, even today, now more than ninety-five years since it was published.

This belief is further reinforced when we learn that the Colonial Office was not able to find any material of importance relating to this question in the records of the Foreign Office. Another mystery is: why did General Allenby in Palestine remain silent on the declaration, censoring all mention of it as he launched his great offensive? The best answer to this question can be derived from his biographer, General Wavell, who wrote:

> . . . with the entry into Palestine and capture of Jerusalem political as well as military problems began to occupy Allenby. Palestine presented some very thorny and difficult questions. The awkwardness of reconciling our pledges to the Arabs, our undertakings to our Allies (the Sykes-Picot Agreement), and the Balfour Declaration to the Zionists was already becoming evident to those who knew of them. . . . He refused to allow the Balfour Declaration to be published in Palestine.
>
> (Wavell 1940, pp. 236–237)

It was not promulgated for nine years! Wavell also noted that the declaration had been made on the very day the third battle of Gaza was in full swing, adding that 'few realized its significance or danger at the time' (Wavell 1940).

Thirdly, there was also a motion in the House of Lords, desiring to scrap the Balfour Declaration, mostly on expediency on the grounds that it was too expensive! It was defeated. In December 1922 Shuckburgh defended Britain's policy as justified in a time of extreme danger for the country:

> In spite of the protests of the Arabs, who form much the largest part of the population of Palestine, and of repeated criticisms in the Parliament and the press, His Majesty's Government have consistently adhered to the position that they are bound to give effect to the Balfour Declaration and intend to do so . . . whatever may or may not have been our motives, it must always be remembered that the Declaration was made at a time of extreme peril to the cause of the Allies. The point is that, having cried out to the Jews in our moment of agony (that is how they would put it), we cannot throw them when the peril is past. A Jewish National Home will be founded in Palestine. The Jewish people will be in Palestine as of right and not on sufferance. . . .
>
> (Shuckburgh 1922)

That explains Britain's position but gives no attention to that of the Arabs. How should they have reacted, given the loss of land, the continual racist remarks that 'they were not even real Arabs', the failure of their delegation to Britain, the American-initiated King-Crane Commission, and their own Conferences? Can't you even admit that failure to consult the already-existing population was a fatal mistake, and one that continues to have tragic consequences?

Delegitimizing the State of Israel

Dan Cohn-Sherbok

I want to follow through with the logic of your critique of the Balfour Declaration and the events which followed. Consistently you have criticized the British for their betrayal of Arab interests. I share with you this concern. But we disagree about the British resolve to establish a Jewish homeland in Palestine for refugees fleeing from persecution and oppression. You stress that this is a matter of justice. In your view, the British had no right to determine the fate of the country. The Balfour Declaration, you argue, was a moral travesty. You ask me at the end of your exchange: 'Can't you even admit that failure to consult the already existing population was a fatal mistake.'

I can't agree with you that this was a fatal mistake for the reasons I have already given. But I want to follow the logic of your argument, and draw out its implication. If we were to accept your criticisms of the Balfour Document, where would this lead us? Let me summarize the argument: At the time of the Balfour Declaration, Palestine did not belong to the Britain, nor did Britain have any legal authority in Palestine. At this point, British forces had not so much as set foot on Palestinian soil. Moreover, the Jewish people had no juristic personality in international law – that is, it was not a legal entity, and therefore could not be a party to an agreement in international law. Hence, the British had no justification in 1917 for offering the territory of another country to an ill-defined religious/ethnic group. The Balfour Declaration gained its de facto legal effect only when the Mandate, incorporating the policies of the Declaration was imposed on Palestine. The Palestinian people did not choose to be governed by the British; rather they had the British rule imposed on them. The Palestinians were at this stage merely a subject population in a Middle East carved up between the interests of Britain and France. Is this a fair description of your position?

Critics of Israel who subscribe to this view go further. According to Dawoud El-Alami:

> The creation of the apartheid state that is Israel represents the ultimate victory of the extreme separatist notions propounded by Nazism. Is not the very concept of a Jewish state the ultimate in discrimination? By definition the creation of a state based on religion and ethnicity in an inhabited land can only be achieved by ethnic cleansing. The state built by a people

who have long been victims institutionalises a form of ethic and religious discrimination that would not be acceptable in any other modern state.
> (El-Alami, *The Palestine-Israeli Conflict*, p. 208)

Such a stance delegitimizes the state of Israel, and has served as a basis for continual Arab hostility towards Zionism and the Zionists. It is most forcefully enshrined in the Charter of Hamas. Founded in 1987 during the first Intifada, it was created to liberate Palestine from Israeli Occupation and to establish an Islamic state in the area that is now Israel, the West Bank and the Gaza Strip:

> The Islamic Resistance Movement believes that the land of Palestine has been an Islamic Waqf throughout the generations and until the Day of Resurrection, no one can renounce it or part of it, or abandon it or part of it. . . . Nothing is loftier or deeper in Nationalism than waging Jihad against the enemy and confronting him when he sets foot on the land of the Muslims. . . . Renouncing any part of Palestine means renouncing part of the religion; the nationalism of the Islamic Resistance Movement is part of its faith, the movement educates its members to adhere to its principles and to raise the banner of Allah over their homeland as they fight their Jihad. . . . The problem of the liberation of Palestine relates to three circles: the Palestinian, the Arab and the Islamic. Each one of these circles has a role to play in the struggle against Zionism and it has duties to fulfil. In order to face the usurpation of Palestine by the Jews, we have no escape from raising the banner of Jihad.
> (Hamas Charter 1988, www.thejerusalemfund.org/carryover/documents/charter.html?chocaid=397)

Even if you reject Hamas' endorsement of jihad as a solution to the Middle East crisis, its quest to dismantle Israel and replace it with a Palestinian state is the logical outcome of your (and Dawoud El-Alami's) critique of British policy regarding Palestine following the First World War.

Was This Conflict Avoidable?

Mary Grey

You are rushing ahead! The challenge you pose will emerge later at the founding of the State of Israel. *Hamas* had not even come into being at the time we are discussing, namely the attempts during the British Mandate to achieve acceptance from the local population that Palestine was to be a homeland for the Jews. I will respond to your challenge when the time comes!

Given that our joint aim in this dialogue is for peace and reconciliation, it is crucial that we identify seeds of what was to become – and is now – a seemingly irreconcilable conflict. Historical decisions and actions often need not have been taken *and could have been reversed*. What you rightly describe as an attempt to create a homeland for a persecuted people – even given the complex and sometimes devious motivations of the key actors, which I've attempted to outline – might not have provoked the catastrophic legacy that it has.

To return to our context: the World War situation in which the Balfour Declaration had been issued was now over. The Ottoman Empire was slowly disintegrating. The British Army – 90 per cent of whom were unhappy with having to impose the Mandate – struggled with the situation on the ground which faced them. Churchill did not manifest the same enthusiasm for Zionism as Balfour or Lloyd George, but he tried to be fair with his task, promising the Arabs that the Balfour policy would not be immediately implemented – it might even take two generations. 'The problem of Palestine', wrote Britain's most senior general, Sir Henry Wilson, 'was the same as the problem of Ireland, namely, two peoples living in a small country hating each other like Hell' (Segev 1999, p. 147). It is useful for us now to compare with the long history of bitter conflict in Ireland and how this is at length being resolved – after hundreds of years of tensions.

But there was a time when such bitter conflict in Palestine might have been avoided. Martin Buber, the inspirational Jewish philosopher, scholar and spiritual thinker had already in the early 1920s – then living in Germany – started advocating a *binational* Jewish-Arab state, stating that the Jewish people should proclaim 'its desire to live in peace and brotherhood with the Arab people and to develop the common homeland into a republic in which both peoples will have the possibility of free development' (http://en.wikipedia.org/wiki/Martin_Buber, quotation is from *Jewish Zionist Education*, May 15, 2005).

Rejecting the idea of Zionism as just another national movement, he wanted instead to see the creation of an exemplary society; a society which would not, he said, be characterized by Jewish domination of the Arabs. He thought it necessary for the Zionist movement to reach a consensus with the Arabs even at the cost of the Jews remaining a minority in the country. In 1925 he was involved in the creation of the organization *Brit Shalom* (Covenant of Peace), which advocated the creation of a binational state, and throughout the rest of his life he hoped and believed that Jews and Arabs one day would live in peace in a joint nation. I'm sure you know about contributions of other inspirational people.

As we know, sadly, Buber's ideas did not materialize. Another similar approach is now taken by Rabbi Michael Lerner, editor of *Tikkun*, in *Embracing Israel/Palestine* (Lerner 2011). Lerner calls for strategies of generosity to listen to and embrace 'the other'. He wants recognition that Israel suffers from post-traumatic stress disorder (PTSD) (Lerner is also a psychotherapist), a condition he described in an earlier book (Lerner 2003). This condition is traced back through centuries of persecution and suffering and the experience of homelessness of the Jews. For him this remains an unhealed trauma: *collectively Israelis cannot think outside this box. Survivors of trauma*, he asserts, *Create relationships in which they psychically reproduce the circumstances of the original trauma.'*

His point is that at every point in history when a decisive action was taken, *it might have been otherwise.* Jewish settlers arriving in Palestine post-1917 could have recognized the rights of the indigenous peoples. Palestinian Arabs might have had some sympathy for a homeless people fleeing persecution and been willing to share the land. This did not happen. But in your view, even at this late stage, given Arab hostility at the Balfour Declaration being imposed on them, could the ensuing conflict have been avoided? Might solutions – like Martin Buber's – still offer seeds of hope for future reconciliation between the peoples the land?

Jews and Arabs

Dan Cohn-Sherbok

You are right about Martin Buber and others sought to create a binational state in which Jews and Arabs could live harmoniously together. As you note, it was his aim that both peoples would have the possibility of free development. What he sought to avoid was Jewish domination of the Arab majority. Others, too, were ardent advocates of such a solution to Arab-Jewish hostilities. The organization Brit Shalom was founded by a group of Jewish universalist intellectuals who sought a peaceful co-existence: this was to be achieved by renouncing the Zionist aim of creating a Jewish state. Following the vision of Ahad Ha-Am, it advanced an alternative Zionist conception of creating a centre for Jewish cultural life in Palestine. Brit Shalom supporters and founders included the economist Arthur Ruppin, the philosopher Hugo Bergman, the historians Hans Kohn and Gershom Scholem, the scientist Albert Einstein, and the Reform rabbi Judah Leon Magnes.

A letter from Arthur Ruppin to Hans Kohn in 1930 states:

> In the foundations of Brit Shalom one of the determining factors was that the Zionist aim has no equal example in history. The aim is to bring the Jews as a second nation into a country which already is settled as a nation—and fulfill this through peaceful means. History has seen such penetration by one nation into a strange land only by conquest, but it has never occurred that a nation will freely agree that another nation should come and demand full equality of rights and national autonomy at its side. The uniqueness of the case prevents its being, in my opinion, dealt with in conventional political-legal terms. It requires special contemplation and study. Brit Shalom should be the forum in which the problem is discussed and investigated.
>
> (Flapan 1979, *Zionism and the Palestinians*, pp. 168–169)

In the view of Brit Shalom, a binational state would have been consistent with the Balfour Declaration which called for the creation of a national home for the Jewish people without prejudice to 'civil and religious rights of existing non-Jewish communities in Palestine' but not with the aim of Zionism as conceived by Herzl and other secular Zionists.

As you know, the Jewish community as a whole rejected the proposed binational solution. Arguably, this was a tragedy since in theory it could have provided a peaceful solution to the conflict between Jews and Arabs. But, you must remember that the indigenous population was vociferous in its determination to curtail Jewish immigration and overturn the Balfour Declaration. It was never their intention to accept the presence of a sizeable Jewish population into their midst. As I noted previously, the Arab reaction to Zionism in any form was hostile and violent. You will recall that Haj Amin al-Husseini, as Grand Mufti of Jerusalem, sought to secure the independence of Palestine as an Arab state. Actively opposing Zionism, he led riots against the Jewish community. The intention was to murder Jews and loot their homes. According to the Haycraft Commission, this racial strife was begun by the Arabs and rapidly developed into a conflict of great violence between Arabs and Jews in which the Arab majority, who were generally the aggressors, inflicted most of the casualties. The fundamental cause of these riots was a feeling among the Arabs of discontent with, and hostility to, the Jews due to economic and political causes, the increase in Jewish immigration, and the Arab conception of Zionist ideology.

What you must remember is that the indigenous Arab population was opposed to all forms of Zionism, including the binational conception proposed by Martin Buber and others. You cite Michael Lerner at the end of your last exchange who calls for a generosity and openness. What is required, he states, is a willingness to embrace the other. I would certainly endorse such an approach, but it should not be one-sided. Palestinians too must listen to the Jewish narrative of events, and accept that their intransigence was a fundamental obstacle to peace and reconciliation. From the perspective of the Arab riots which took place after the Balfour Declaration, there is little basis for thinking that Palestinian Arabs might have had sympathy for a homeless people fleeing from persecution and being willing to share the land. On the contrary, there was only hatred and murderous contempt.

A Failure of Empathy

Mary Grey

You write:

> From the perspective of the Arab riots which took place after the Balfour Declaration, there is little basis for thinking that Palestinian Arabs might have had sympathy for a homeless people fleeing from persecution and being willing to share the land. On the contrary, there was only hatred and murderous contempt.

I had appealed to you that we respond to Michael Lerner's appeal to 'enter the mindset of the other' and that we continue to do this as we move towards the present. In other words, let us develop empathy for both parties. What were the impoverished Arab farmers supposed to feel, when 'they were asked to share what little they possessed with foreigners?' (Fromkin 1989, p. 513). How were they supposed to react when the new settlers established good medical and educational resources and institutions, for example, but excluded Arabs from them? (Lerner 2003, pp. 41–42).

What you seem to forget is that this discussion is not simply about 'Jews and Arabs': it is about British Imperialism – and here there are very mixed motives in the wake of the Balfour Declaration. Whereas Lloyd George's Cabinet was (mostly) sincere in promoting the success of the decision to create a homeland for the Jewish people, as I have already argued, the army on the ground in Palestine, conscious of what was happening to the Arab people, was 90 per cent against it. And this influenced opinion back in England. Thus an anti-Zionist official, Ernest T. Richmond wrote to the British High Commissioner that in pursuing Zionism, the High Commissioner and his officials, the Middle East Department of the Colonial office in London and the Zionist Commission in Palestine 'are dominated by a spirit which I can only regard as evil' (Fromkin 1989, p. 518).

> After the end of the Great War, the context had changed. From attaining what appeared to be the zenith of her Empire,

the economic climate had worsened and there were doubts as to whether Britain could financially sustain her policy on Palestine. Yet Churchill, whose overall motivation was to cut costs, struggled valiantly to be loyal to the commitment the Lloyd George cabinet had made. There was no going back on the Declaration, he constantly told the Arab Delegation. It is true that both Churchill and Weizmann had intended to buy up land for Jewish settlers that was unused – a policy that was partially thwarted by rich Arab landowners eager to make a profit from the Jewish settlers – who ended up with some of the most fertile land. (Most Arab peasant farmers struggled to make a living from low-yielding, eroded and poorly irrigated plots.) Three motivations were now in tension: the British desire both to keep its pledges to Zionism and to solve the remaining Turkish presence in the Empire, the Zionist desire to establish affirm presence in Palestine, and the Arab determination to hang onto their land. But the British had failed to understand the roots of Arab opposition to Jewish settlements:

> Arab opposition ... was rooted in emotion, in religion, in xenophobia, in the complex of feelings that tend to overcome people when newcomers flood in to change their neighbourhood. The Arabs of Palestine were defending a threatened way of life.
>
> (Fromkin 1989, p. 523)

Little room for empathy here! Of course this deeper motivation remained unarticulated in discussions with Churchill, where the argument – as the latter understood it – was that the land could not sustain more inhabitants. On 22 July, the League of Nations finally approved the rewritten Palestine Mandate, directing Britain to carry the re-defined Balfour Declaration policy west of the Jordan River. But British enthusiasm for the Zionist project would wane rapidly. Even Lawrence (of Arabia) thought that Britain had discharged its promises to the Arabs creditably: it was his conviction that England was out of the Arab affair 'with clean hands'. (He was mostly referring to the ambiguous promises made to Sharif Hussein with regard to Palestine.)

At the end of this chapter, what we have seen is that the period 1914–1922 'while bringing to an end Europe's Middle Eastern Question gave birth to a middle-Eastern question in the Middle East itself' (Fromkin 1989, p. 563). We will see as our story progresses that the failure of empathy on all sides, the waning of the politics of Empire as a means to solve all conflicts, and the failure of the British to understand the Arab psyche and depth of attachment to the land would have fatal consequences for the future of Palestine.

Chapter 6
Palestine before the Second World War

The Contribution of Women in the Struggle

Mary Grey

You know of course that our story is going to get steadily grimmer, as storm clouds gather. And the context we now enter is illustrative of this. Tensions mount between Jews and Arabs as immigration steadily increases and Jewish life starts to prosper. Arthur Balfour's visit to Jerusalem for the opening of the new Hebrew University illustrates this – as Chaim Weizmann's dream is fulfilled.

But there has been a notable gap in our narrative: the contribution of women. Our characters and leaders have been without exception, male. Let me try to add a certain balance. I first learn of this other dimension – which I suspected must exist – from the Palestinian scholar-activist Mazin Qumsiyeh, who in his life and writing brings this to light:

> How many in the west have heard of the Women's Movements of the 1920s against the British occupation and its support of colonial Zionism?

> From the 1920s and 30s women took the initiative at critical times and also in the post 1967 years, when the national will was debilitated.
>
> (Qumsiyeh 2010, pp. 234–235)

I want to mention one such activist, Tarab Abdul Hadi who was the wife of 'Auni Abdul Hadi, himself active in politics, going on to become a prominent member of the Istiqlal party. It was Tarab Abdul Hadi and other women from well-known Jerusalem families who established the Palestine Arab Women's Congress (PAWC) to make clear their opposition to the Zionist presence in Palestine and their support for the men's national struggle for independence. The first meeting of this Women's Congress was held at Tarab Abdul Hadi's home in Jerusalem on 26 October 1929. The event was recalled later as the 'first time' that Palestinian women entered the political arena. Abdul Hadi became one of the members of PAWC's Executive Committee, which consisted of fourteen women, drawn primarily from among famous Jerusalem families, such as the Husseinis, Alamis, Nashashibis and Budeiris. The women from the Congress wrote letters and sent telegrams to raise awareness of the Palestinian plight: they also engaged in prisoner advocacy, attempting to reduce the length of harsh sentences by appealing to the British authorities and raising money to support families who had lost their sole breadwinners to imprisonment.

Abdul Hadi was also active in the Arab Women's Association (AWA): this also originated in 1929 and became the most prominent feminist organization in Palestine. Founded in Jerusalem at the first Palestine Arab Women's Congress on 26 October 1929, the impetus for its establishment was the 1929 Western (Wailing) Wall riots and violent events that followed. The Riots – at this site sacred for both Jews and Muslims – were provoked by the erection of a screen on the pavement by the wall for the segregation of women. The Palestinians complained to the British who ordered the removal of the screen. The Jews were indignant at what was seen as interference in a Holy Day (Yom Kippur). British efforts to resolve the issue were unsuccessful and riots broke out – and spread all over Palestine in the next few days (Cohn-Sherbok and Al-Alami 2001, pp. 160–161).

The Arab Women's Association had a very large scope for its activities: its goals were to work for the development of the social and economic affairs of the Arab women in Palestine, to endeavour to secure the extension of educational facilities for girls, to use every possible and lawful means to elevate the standing of women. Subsequently the AWA formed branches in most of the major cities and towns in Palestine and became the leading organization of the Palestinian women's movement during the mandate period. Its members were particularly active from 1929 to 1939 in demonstrating against the mandate. Like the members of the Arab Women's Congress, they provided support for the prisoners and rebels of the 1936–1939 revolt – (which we have not yet discussed). They met with, wrote memoranda to, and protested to British government authorities, and they also rallied international and regional support for the Palestinian national movement.

Tarab Abdul Hadi, in her capacity as an AWA organizer, delivered a speech at the Church of the Holy Sepulchre in April 1933, during a visit by General Allenby and declared:

> The Arab ladies ask Lord Allenby to remember and tell this to his government. . . . The mothers, daughters, sisters of the Arab victims are gathered here to make the world witness the betrayal of the British. We want all the Arabs to remember that the British are the cause of our suffering and they should learn from the lesson.

She was also active in the campaign against the veil, an initiative launched by local women encouraging Palestinian women to remove their veils. After the 1948 Arab–Israeli war Abdul Hadi ended up in exile in Cairo, where she died in 1976 (http://en.wikipedia.org/wiki/Tarab_Abdul_Hadi).

I am sure you can also cite Jewish women's activities at this time. In this tragic story of violent conflict, don't you think it important to weave into the narrative these dimensions that give a fuller and more truthful picture?

The Liberation of Women

Dan Cohn-Sherbok

You are right that men played a dominant role in the Zionist movement, yet there were pioneering women as well. Motivated by socialist principles, the founders of a Jewish state were determined to create a society in which women would play a central role. The formal acceptance of women's status as equal to men dates back to the pre-state years when socialist ideals of equality and a challenging new environment provided ample opportunities for women to play important roles.

At the first Zionist Congress, 17 women were present among the 200 participants. In the Second Aliyah, from 1904 to 1913, women accounted for 17 per cent of the mainly Russian immigrants. Many of them were committed to challenging traditional female roles by doing hard physical labour. The kibbutz system promised to liberate women from the yoke of domestic responsibilities. Children were raised communally in special children's houses. All meals were prepared communally with the work shared by men and women; even laundry was done communally.

The women of the Third Aliyah from 1919 to 1923 were from Eastern Europe and made up 20 per cent of the total. In 1920 women were involved in self-defense in the Haganah, the Jewish community's pre-military organization while Palestine was a British mandate. From 1936 to 1939 hundreds of women guarded roads during the Arab rioting. In 1941 the Haganah created the Palmach, a full time-elite military unit. Even though women were not supposed to be members, one commander assembled a small group of women in Jerusalem and taught them to use weapons. During the Second World War (WW II), about 9,000 women joined the British army, serving as radio and radar operators, parachute inspectors and truck or ambulance drivers. A few, like Hannah Senesh, parachuted behind enemy lines in Europe. Women also worked in the illegal immigration movement and fought during the War of Independence. Israel's Declaration of Independence assured all female citizens that they could vote and run for office. In fact, Israel was the first country in the Middle East that gave Arab women the right to vote. Women also participated in the army after Israel became a state. Upon reaching the age of eighteen, all Jewish women were drafted for twenty-four months. In the words of Prime Minister David Ben-Gurion:

> The army is the supreme symbol of duty, and as long as women are not equal to men in performing this duty, they have not yet obtained true equality [and] ... the character of the community will be distorted.
>
> (Rubin, in *Israel*, p. 170)

In describing this quest for women's equality, I have got ahead of myself in recounting the narrative of the establishment of a Jewish state. But I want to highlight the achievements of Zionism in this regard. The question I want to ask you is whether you believe Palestinians have made parallel advances. You cite the examples of notable Palestinian women in the struggle with the British and the Zionists. Clearly their voices were heard. But arguably within Palestinian circles, there has not been the same determination to liberate women from social and religious constraints. Admittedly, in Israel Jewish women have not always been able to attain full equality with men. As one pioneer woman, Zippora Bar-Droma complained: while men were building the country, women took care of everyday matters of the builders. In *Women in the Kibbutz* published in 1975, anthropologists Lionel Tiger and Joseph Shepherd concluded that the majority of women were cooking, cleaning and child-rearing while men were harvesting, planting, guarding and building (Rubin, in *Israel*, p. 69). Nonetheless, the advances in women's liberation in Israel far exceeded the role Arab women were able to occupy in the early years of Zionist development. You have continually castigated the Zionists in their quest to build a Jewish homeland in Palestine. But surely as a feminist theologian you must admire the Zionists' fierce determination to liberate women from inferior traditional roles in society.

Palestinian Women and the Arab Rebellion

Mary Grey

In response to your latest challenge I do not want to jump too far ahead of our story. I absolutely agree with you – strange! – that the 'Zionists' fierce determination to liberate women from inferior traditional roles in society' was really admirable, and that, despite the key role of certain Palestinian women whom I cited in my last letter, that these initiatives were not representative of all Palestinian women, Muslim or Christian. There have been striking developments more recently, but in general, the events we are discussing – the rebellion of 1936, which I want to come to, the expulsions of 1948 and the Occupation (post-1967) have made it extremely difficult for Palestinian women to surmount deeply embedded cultural patterns.

Until the beginning of the twentieth century, the patriarchal relationship of authority and the tribal clan structure of the Arab society have restricted the development and meaningful participation of Palestinian women in society. The significant influences on the rights of women are patriarchy and the teachings of the Quran. Yet, in some matters, the patriarchal tradition of Palestine gives more rights to women than does the shari'a. The Koran demands that women cover their bodies – only the face, hands and feet may be exposed. Palestinian society on the other hand permits women to dress in Western fashion in trousers, tee-shirts, blouses and skirts, to wear makeup and jewellery. One of the main determinants of this role is the family structure which may be a nuclear unit, a transitional unit, or a *hamula* unit (*hamula* means 'extended family', the most common family structure in Palestinian society). In general – as in many traditional societies – (including Jewish) Palestinian parents prefer having boy babies because they 'carry the name of the family' and secures the continuity of the family line its possible future economic stability. (I have seen the same in my work in the traditional villages of rural India.) Of course, women were not expected to earn money, but to adapt to the traditional roles where females were brought up as inferior to men.

Due to the pattern of early marriage it was very difficult for girls to finish secondary or higher education. This was to change after the middle of the 1970s for a variety of reasons. But, like Jewish women in the kibbutz, in farming communities, women were always responsible for a large part of the work in the field such as ploughing and planting crops, taking fruits and vegetables to the cities, as well as – of course – taking full responsibility for home and children. After 1948 with the dispossession and displacement of the Palestinian nation, and the loss of the material basis that sustained the patriarchal family, the need for extra income became paramount – so women as well as men had to go out to work: education for both was essential.

The real point I want to make here is that the increased status of women in Palestine – for example in the refugee camps – occurred through war circumstances. When men seeking work emigrated to the surrounding countries particularly the Arabian Gulf, women were left behind to take responsibility. The new situation gave women more freedom of movement, but not the freedom of full participation in decision-making. The role of women was enhanced without seriously undermining the status of men. So the struggle to live through the hard times that the Palestinian people were going through has denied Palestinian women's that equality and freedom that was being attained in many parts of the world. This would change later, especially at the time of the Intifada.

Of course women's experience in the revolt of 1936 was especially grim. We have not yet described its savagery. Arab anger was fuelled but increasing waves of immigration and the sale of the disappearance of their land. In our dialogue, I have constantly tried to avoid a stark Arab/Jewish polarity by describing the role of British Imperialism. And this is revealed at its starkest by the treatment meted out to the Arabs in this Revolt. In the film *The Land Speaks Arabic* (Maryse Gargour), with a commentary by Nur Masalha, Arab farmers discuss the cruelty of different empires – from the Ottomans to the Israelis: they conclude that the British were the cruellest.

As Mazin Qumsiyeh wrote:

> The Palestinians paid a heavy price for the uprising of 1935–39 in material and human losses. In the first year ... about 1,000 Palestinians were killed, more than half of them unarmed; by the time the uprising ended over 5,000 Palestinians were dead and thousands more injured (per capita these casualties were higher than the intifadas of 1987 and 2000). As collective punishment whole sections of Jaffa and many other places were demolished and the local economy devastated. Approximately

10 percent of adult males were imprisoned. Hundreds were executed and hundreds were exiled.

(Qumsiyeh 2011, p. 85)

You constantly ask me to have compassion for the Jewish people: but in this context have you no compassion of the Arabs? Is this the way the British kept the promises of the Balfour Declaration?

Arab Intransigence

Dan Cohn-Sherbok

It is illuminating to know more about both Palestinian women in the period we are discussing, and encouraging to know that within the Palestinian community a number of discriminatory Muslim restrictions have been eliminated. But I want to turn to the central events of the pre-WW II era. You ask at the end of your last exchange if I have no compassion for Palestinians. I hope that I have made it clear that, in my view, the British are culpable for not keeping their promises about the creation of an Arab kingdom in the post-war period. The Sykes-Picot agreement was a betrayal of previous commitments between the British and the Arabs. Further, I believe the Jewish quest for a one-state solution to the Jewish–Arab conflict proposed by Martin Buber and others would have been a far better starting point for negotiation than mainstream Zionist attitudes. Yet, it is indisputable that the indigenous Arab population never had any inclination to embrace Jewish settlers in the way that you envisage. On the contrary, there was a universal determination on the part of the Arab population to curtail immigration and drive the Jews from Palestine.

I have already cited the role of the Grand Mufti in the early revolts against the Yishuv (the Jewish community in Palestine). At no point were Arabs prepared to participate in any form of representative assembly. Once the League of Nations passed the Mandate for Palestine, the British proposed a Palestinian Constitution which established a Legislative Council. Although such a body would have had an Arab majority, the Arabs adamantly rejected such a plan. Undeterred by the Arab reaction, the British proceeded with elections. In response, the

Palestinian Arab Executive decided on a boycott. With the fall of the Lloyd George government, the Arabs hoped to influence the new British leadership which had not been responsible for the Balfour Declaration. As previously, they were intractable in their opposition to the creation of a Jewish homeland.

In the ensuing years, hostility between Jews and Arabs was a constant feature of life in Palestine. In the view of the Grand Mufti, the Holy Places in Palestine were under threat from the Jewish population. Following an incident that occurred on the eve of Yom Kippur in September 1928 when Jews had placed a screen to separate men and women at prayers near the Wailing Wall, the following year the Grand Mufti initiated a campaign against the Jews in the mosques and the press. On 22 and 23 August 1929 large crowds of Arab peasants made their way to Jerusalem armed with clubs and knives, and the Jewish population was severely attacked. In this conflict, 133 were killed and 339 were wounded among Jews, and 110 were killed and 232 were wounded among Arabs.

Among the Arabs these events led to increased support for the Mufti. In Palestine and throughout the Arab world, he was perceived as the leading figure in the struggle against the Zionist threat. Yet, in time there was a shift in Arab policy from an anti-Jewish to an anti-British stance. In June 1933 the Supreme Muslim Council encouraged Muslims to join in a rebellion against the British. The Jews, they argued, aimed at reconstructing a Jewish Temple in the place of the Mosque of Al-Aqsa. Having refused Muslim demands, Britain was perceived as supporting the Jewish people. Throughout the summer the revolt spread throughout the country. In June, attacks took place among the roads and against the Haifa-Lydia railway line. During the next two months, clashes continued and were accompanied by a general strike. During this period, three Arab princes became involved in the Mandatory government: all three detested Zionism and saw that personal political gains could be made from their participation in the affairs of Palestine.

Throughout these two decades, Arab hostility and murderous contempt for the Jewish population was unrelenting. At no stage were Arabs prepared to find common ground with the Zionists. Let me return to the point you made in your previous correspondence. You refer to Michael Lerner's appeal to enter the mindset of the other. This is precisely what Arabs doing this period were determined not to do: there was simply no empathy for Jewish settlers fleeing from persecution and suffering. Instead, the Arab population rose up in fury against Jews who had come to live in their midst, even if they had purchased land legally and were supported in their quest to create a homeland by the British as well as other nations. You cite the example of Brit Shalom with its emphasis on sympathy for the indigenous Arab population as an example of what Jewish attitudes could have been at the time. I agree with you, and I would have been a supporter. But amongst the Arab community there was no similar empathetic response to the Jewish problem. Instead, there was only antagonism and hatred.

Gandhi and the Issue of Justice for Palestine

Mary Grey

We have now both chronicled the rebellion and tragic killings of this period. Is it surprising that, as you say, that at no stage were Arabs prepared to find common ground with the Zionists? That there was only 'hatred and contempt'? What should we expect? As our former colleague, Dawoud El-Alami wrote:

> You blame the Palestinian for putting up resistance to an incoming population with colonial ambitions, but who is the aggressor here and who is the victim? In any other context the Palestinians would be 'freedom fighters', defending their homeland. One day they are Palestinians living on their ancestral land, and the next, their land is taken away by Europeans and, if not expelled, they become 'the Arabs of Israel'.
> (Cohn-Sherbok and El-Alami 2001, p. 257)

Yes, we agree, it would have been ideal if it had been possible to come to an understanding on sharing the land: if we do not agree, we can at least understand why that did not happen. But, rather than continue to blame the Arabs for hatred and contempt, listen to someone who had peace and non-violent resistance as his deepest motivation, Gandhi, of course.

You cannot say that Gandhi did not love and respect Zionism: but his was more a spiritual than a territorial view:

> Zionism in its spiritual sense is a lofty aspiration. By spiritual sense I mean they should want to realise the Jerusalem that is within. Zionism meaning reoccupation of Palestine has no attraction for me. I can understand the longing of a Jew to return to Palestine, and he can do so if he can without the help of bayonets, whether his own or those of Britain. In that event he would go to Palestine peacefully and in perfect friendliness with the Arabs. The real Zionism of which I have given you my meaning is the thing to strive for, long for and die for. Zion lies in one's heart. It is the abode of God. The real Jerusalem is the spiritual Jerusalem. Thus he can realise this Zionism in any part of the world.
>
> (Gandhi 1921)

But, he realized, as you do, that this spiritual conception would not go down very well in the context we speak about. He knew about the promises Britain had made and the sentiments that the Jewish people had with regard to Palestine. But he was firm as to the ethics of taking the land away from Muslims. (He did not seem to be aware of the Christian population in Palestine at the time):

> The Jews, it is contended, must remain a wandering race unless they have obtained Palestine. I do not propose to examine the soundness or otherwise of the doctrine underlying a moral breach. Palestine was not at stake in the War. The British Government could not dare to have asked a single Muslim soldier to wrest control of Palestine from fellow-Muslims and give it to the Jews. Palestine, as a place of Jewish worship, is a sentiment to be respected and the Jews would have a just cause of complaint against Mussulman idealists if they were to prevent Jews from offering worship as freely as themselves. *By no canon of ethics or war, therefore, can Palestine be given to the Jews as a result of the War*. Either Zionists must revise their ideal about Palestine, or, if Judaism permits the arbitrariment of war, engage in a 'holy war' with the Muslims of the world

with the Christians throwing in their influence on their side. But one may hope that the trend of world opinion will make 'holy wars' impossible and religious questions or differences will tend more and more towards a peaceful adjustment based upon the strictest moral considerations.

(My emphasis – see www.gandhiserve.org)

Gandhi, who condemned anti-Semitism, and very much wanted to visit Palestine himself, thought that

> that does not mean that the Jews and the Christians cannot freely go to Palestine, or even reside there and own property. What non-Muslims cannot do is to acquire sovereign jurisdiction. The Jews cannot receive sovereign rights in a place which has been held for centuries by Muslim powers by right of religious conquest. The Muslim soldiers did not shed their blood in the late War for the purpose of surrendering Palestine out of Muslim control.
>
> (see www.gandhiserve.org)

Of course he made comparison with India's 70 million Muslims – it would be analogous to giving India to the Hindus, and Gandhi struggled against the partition of India, eventually losing his life over it. He considered the giving away of a 'sacred possession' as treacherous. So, even if you cannot agree with 'hatred and contempt' you must at least try to understand the reasons for it and have some kind of empathy for the Arab position.

Misunderstanding Zionism

Dan Cohn-Sherbok

Gandhi was a great figure in Indian history, but I feel he completely misunderstood the nature of Zionism in the passage you quoted. For Jews, Zionism was not an internal conception, or a state of mind. It was a concrete political reality, a solution to the problem of Jew-hatred. It never was a spiritual idea divorced from earthly concerns; it had no connection with religious ideals. Instead it was a secular idea based on a careful analysis of power relations.

Let me return to the central tract of nineteenth-century Zionistic thought – Herzl's *The Jewish State*. Here he stresses that the concept of a Jewish state is not a utopian ideal: it is a vital political solution to the problem of Jewish deprivation, persecution and suffering.

Gandhi clearly deplored political Zionism, and maintained that it was immoral for Jews to seek to create a homeland in Palestine. 'By no canon of ethics or war . . . can Palestine be given to the Jews as a result of the War,' he wrote. Yet, the early Zionists did not intend to seize land through warfare; on the contrary, as I have continually stressed, these pioneers purchased land from Arab owners. You have denounced these Arab landowners (some of whom were absent from Palestine) for selling their lands. But, the key point is that at no stage did Jews seek to conquer the native population and drive them forcefully from their homes. It is a pity that Brit Shalom was not more successful. Mainstream Zionists regrettably often failed to perceive the distress they caused to the native inhabitants. Ahad Ha-Am and other Jews sympathetic to Arab Muslim and Christians were right to attempt to sensitize their coreligionists to the feelings of those who had been settled in the country for generations. There were certainly Jewish failings. But you should not ignore the murderous intentions of Arabs who consistently sought to thwart the British and slaughter the Jews who had come to live in their midst.

Do you justify the Arab revolts of the 1920s? You have consistently condemned the Zionists; you castigate the British; you denounce the Balfour Declaration. Your support is for the Arab cause. Should I conclude, therefore, that had you been present during this period of history, you would have joined forces with the Grand Mufti and his followers. Would you have played a role in the massacre of Jewish settlers? It would have been unrealistic at the time to endorse a Gandhian stance of non-violence. Such an attitude is not consonant with Muslim culture. Islam was spread by the sword, and the notion of a holy war is an indelible feature of Muslim culture. Arabs have been waging a holy war against Zionism and Zionists for over nearly a century. Do you seek to be part of this jihad?

It is naive to assume that the Middle East crisis can be solved by condemning the Jews for their Zionists aspirations, seeking that

Britain apologizes for the Balfour Declaration, and appealing to Gandhi's vision of an internal Jerusalem as a blueprint for a Jewish future. As I have stated in previous exchanges, it is clear that you seek to delegitimize the state of Israel, and seek instead an apology from the British and the Jews for what you perceive as a grave moral mistake. I appreciate that you believe that the Arab population in Palestine has been deprived of their land and subject to discrimination and deprivation; I share your concern in this regard. But such sympathy should not blind you to the horror of the events of the period we are discussing and the Jewish distress caused by Arab terror and attack, as well as the festering Judeophobia that is universal in the Arab world.

Chapter 7
Between the First and Second World War

Jewish Extremism

Dan Cohn-Sherbok

During the 1920s streams of Jewish immigrants entered Palestine. By 1922 they made up 11 per cent of the overall population that had risen to 750,000. By 1928 Jews amounted to about 16 per cent of Palestine's population. During this time Jews owned 4.2 per cent of Palestinian land, much of which was in fertile areas suitable for agriculture. Land purchases were done legally; as we have noted, much was bought from absentee Arab landlords. During the 1920s the Jewish community established the embryonic apparatus of a distinctively Jewish state: a Jewish National Assembly, trade unions, schools, industrial enterprises and a university as well as a defense force (Haganah). As we noted, the growth of the Yishuv (Jewish community in Palestine) caused deep alarm amongst the indigenous Arab population and led to a series of riots.

By 1929 both communities blamed each other for the violence that had taken place. The Jews and the British criticized the Grand Mufti and a journalist, Arif al-Arif, for stirring up anti-Jewish feeling among the Arabs. The Arabs argued that they were responding to the aggressive stand taken by the Zionist extremists intent on bringing about a massive Jewish immigration necessary to create an all-Jewish state in Palestine. During the 1930s the situation in Palestine became even more complex and intractable. Palestinian Arabs believed their land was threatened by growing Jewish immigration: by 1931 Jews made up 16.9 per cent of the population of over one million inhabitants. A British committee report blamed excessive Jewish immigration for the 1929 bloodshed, and suggested that only another 50,000 Jews should be allowed to enter the country.

These events led to a split amongst Palestinian Jewry. The majority followed the more moderate Labour leaders of the World Zionist Organization including David Ben-Gurion in Palestine and Chaim Weizmann in London. These Zionists sought to create a Jewish state in Palestine separate from an Arab state. In their view the Haganah should be a defense force. Jabotinsky, on the other hand, adopted a more extreme line. He and the World Union of Zionist Revisionists had established a militant security force, the Irgun. Their policy was based on four principles: (1) The Jews were standard-bearers of a superior Western civilization in the Middle East; (2) Greater Israel should comprise both banks of the Jordan; (3) the Arabs would never voluntarily accept this notion of Zion; (4) The only solution to the Arab–Jewish conflict is force – Zionists had to carve out their state and secure it behind an iron wall (Ross 2007, *The Israeli-Palestine Conflict*, p. 44).

This rift between right-wing and left-wing Zionists has continued from the 1930s until today, and has resulted in the growth of an expansionist ideology promoted by various political parties within the Knesset. It is a tragedy that such a political stance has gained a substantial following over the years, and has fueled hatred and violence against the Palestinian population. In the period we are discussing, the bombing of the King David Hotel was a particular instance of the dangers of such extremism. This attack was carried out on 22 July 1946 by the militant right-wing Zionist underground organization of the Irgun on the British administrative headquarters for Palestine (which was housed in the King David Hotel in Jerusalem). Ninety-one people of various nationalities were killed and forty-six were injured. Initially the attack had the approval of the Haganah (the principal Jewish paramilitary group in Palestine). It was conceived as a response to Operation Agatha (a series of widespread raids, including one on the Jewish Agency conducted by the British authorities in the British Mandate of Palestine). The Irgun planted a bomb in the basement of the main building of the hotel; warnings were sent by telephone, including one to the hotel's own switchboard, which the hotel staff decided to ignore. The explosion caused the collapse of the western half of the southern wing of the hotel. Some of the inflicted deaths and injuries occurred in the road outside the hotel and in adjacent buildings.

Not surprisingly the bombing inflamed public opinion. After the event, editorials in British newspapers argued that the bombing deflated statements by the government that it had been winning against Jewish paramilitaries. Speaker after speaker in the House of Commons expressed outrage. Ex-Prime Minister Winston Churchill who was an enthusiastic supporter of Zionism, criticized the attack. Prime Minister Clement Attlee commented in the House of Commons:

> Hon. Members will have learned with horror of the brutal and murderous crime committed yesterday in Jerusalem. Of all the outrages which have occurred in Palestine, and they have been many and horrible in the last few months, this is the worst. By this insane act of terrorism 93 innocent people have been killed or are missing in the ruins.
> (en.wikipedia.org/King_David-Hotel_bombing)

Clement Attlee and others were right to condemn such violence. Jewish violent extremism has eroded the spiritual values of our tradition. And what applies to the Zionists is relevant to a judgement about Arab extremism: an unwillingness to embrace the other in a quest for peace has been a failure of both sides in this bloody conflict.

Seeking Justice for Both Sides

Mary Grey

You continually push me into a polarized position which is untrue and I utterly reject it.

For example, you wrote in Chapter 6 (section 'Misunderstanding Zionism'):

> Your support is for the Arab cause. Should I conclude, therefore, that had you been present during this period of history, you would have joined forces with the Grand Mufti and his followers. Would you have played a role in the massacre of Jewish settlers? It would have been unrealistic at the time to endorse a Gandhian stance of non-violence. Such an attitude is not consonant with Muslim culture. Islam was spread by the sword, and the notion of a holy war is an indelible feature of Muslim culture. Arabs have been waging a holy war against Zionism and Zionists for over nearly a century. Do you seek to be part of this jihad?

Of course I do not! Let me be very clear: at every point I am looking for where the justice issue lies. I was very sympathetic to the position of the Jewish people before the First World War and deeply regret the long history of anti-Semitism (and its contemporary occurrences), but sharply criticized the British government for its contradictory promises manifested in the Balfour Declaration (1917); at the same time I continually look for movements and figures who offered an alternative to the violence that, as we know, began to escalate until the end of the Mandate and beyond. That is why I remain very interested in the contribution of Martin Buber and Mahatma Gandhi.

In your last letter, you described the bombing of the King David Hotel in 1946. Not only was this disastrous in terms of killing, but it set a pattern for Jewish extremism in the coming years as well as being influential in the development of international terrorism. Yet, in the aftermath of the bombing, Buber wrote words that are still relevant today:

> To win a truly great life for the people of Israel, a great peace is necessary. Not a fictitious peace, the dwarfish peace that is not more than an intermission, but a true peace with neighbouring peoples, which alone can render possible a common development of this portion of the earth as a vanguard of the awakening of the Near East.
>
> (Mendes-Flohr 1984)

Like Buber, Gandhi had much more to say – and I think you are short-sighted to dismiss his contribution – to which I will return. Gandhi had many Jewish friends – dating from his days in South Africa. And his closest friend in his Ashram was a Jewish, namely Hermann Kallenbach. Gandhi wrote to the latter:

> And now a word to the Jews in Palestine. I have no doubt that they are going about it in the wrong way. The Palestine of the Biblical conception is not a geographical tract. It is in their hearts. But if they must look to the Palestine of geography as their national home, it is wrong to enter it under the shadow of the British gun. A religious act cannot be performed with the aid of the bayonet or the bomb. They can settle in Palestine only by the goodwill of the Arabs. *They should seek to convert the Arab heart*. The same God rules the Arab heart who rules the Jewish heart. They can offer *satyagraha*[1] in front of the Arabs and offer themselves to be shot or thrown into the Dead Sea without raising a little finger against them. They will find the world opinion in their favour in their religious aspiration. There are hundreds of ways of reasoning with the Arabs, if they will only discard the help of the British bayonet. *As it is, they are co-sharers with the British in despoiling a people who have done no wrong to them.* (My italics)

> I am not defending the Arab excesses. I wish they had chosen the way of non-violence in resisting what they rightly regarded as an unwarrantable encroachment upon their country. But according to the accepted canons of right and wrong, nothing can be said against the Arab resistance in the face of overwhelming odds.
>
> (Gandhi 1937)

You can detect a note of resignation in Gandhi's tone. He saw that the situation before the Second World War was becoming intractable. For the Arabs there were two enemies – the Jews and

---

[1] Non-violent resistance.

the British authorities in Palestine. For the Jews equally there were also two enemies – the Arabs and the British. It would appear that the British were pushed into the middle of a conflict they had little control over as the two other sides involved were so driven by their own interests. In an effort to end the violence, the British put a quota on the number of Jews who could enter Palestine in any one year. They hoped to appease the Arabs in the region but also keep good relations with the Jews by recognizing that they could keep entering Palestine in restricted numbers. But they failed on both counts.

Given this degree of escalation, was there any way of preventing, at this stage, a conflict we now know would roll on for more than six decades?

The Grand Mufti and the Jews

Dan Cohn-Sherbok

You quote Gandhi advising Jews that they should seek to convert the Arab heart. Surveying the pre-WW II period, was this ever a possibility? At every stage, the Arabs were intractably opposed to the notion of a Jewish homeland. At no point were their hearts moved by the suffering of Jewry in Eastern Europe or elsewhere. With one voice they cried out against Jewish immigration. This protest manifested itself in violence in the 1920s and in the years that followed. With the rise of Nazism in the early 1930s as Jews were murdered in the most horrific way under the Third Reich, the Arabs turned their face from this tragedy.

Let me remind you of the actions of the Grand Mufti, the leader of the Palestinian Arabs. During this period, the British feared that the Arabs under the influence of Haj Amin, who was living in exile, might again stage a revolt. In October 1939 the Grand Mufti left Beirut for Baghdad where he was welcomed as a hero. Working on behalf of a pro-Axis war effort which culminated in a coup headed by Rashid Ali, he issued a fatwa on 9 May 1941 which was broadcast over Iraqi and Axis radio. Proclaiming a jihad against the British, he declared that they had profaned the Al-Aqsa mosque and had been waging a war against Islam. When the British defeated Rashid Ali's forces, nearly 200 Jews living in Baghdad were killed by the Grand Mufti's followers.

Escaping from Baghdad along with Rashid Ali, Haj Amin fled to Tehran. However, when Soviet and British forces occupied Iran in September 1941, the Mufti made his way to Berlin. There he met with Adolf Hitler, Heinrich Himmler and Joachim Von Ribbentrop and other Nazi leaders – his aim was to persuade them to extend the Nazi's anti-Jewish programme to the Arab world. The Mufti sent Hitler 15 drafts of declarations he wanted Germany and Italy to make concerning the Middle East. One called on the two countries to declare the illegality of the Jewish home in Palestine. Further, he wished Germany and Italy to accord to Palestine and to other Arab countries the right to solve the problem of the Jewish elements in Palestine and other Arab countries.

In a meeting in November 1941 the Mufti met with Hitler who told him the Jews were his foremost enemy. He stated:

> Germany stood for uncompromising war against the Jews. That naturally included active opposition to the Jewish national home in Palestine . . . Germany would furnish positive and practical aid to the Arabs involved in the same struggle. Germany's objective [is] . . . solely destruction of the Jewish element residing in the Arab sphere . . . In that hour the Mufti would be the most authoritative spokesman for the Arab world.
> (www.jewishvirtuallibrary.org/ source/History/muftihit.html)

For the rest of the war the Grand Mufti continued to reside in Germany, but once Germany was defeated he escaped again to Beirut, via Berne and Paris, and proclaimed a jihad against the new State of Israel.

You say that at every point you are looking for where justice lies. Does it lie here? Can it be found in the Grand Mufti's plea to Hitler? If you are truly critical of anti-Semitism, then what justification can you give for the Arab quest to side with the Nazis in this war against world Jewry including the Jews of Palestine?

Let me remind you that six million Jews were slaughtered in the Nazi quest to rid the human race of a Jewish presence. It is clear that the Mufti and his followers would have gone along with this programme of extermination enthusiastically. In the name of human values, we should condemn all forms of terrorist extremism, hatred and violence. This applies equally in the Arab world as in the Jewish community. I deplore the activities of the Irgun, and similarly condemn the Arab violence unleashed against Jewish settlers in Palestine. Do you join me in such revulsion?

Increasing Radicalisation on All Sides – Revolt against the British

Mary Grey

We have now entered upon one of the most tragic periods of our subject and the darkest days of the history of the Jewish people. The Nazi evil policy of extermination of the Jews in Germany is now the backcloth to the events we describe. I was born in the midst of the Second World War, and looking back, it is hard at this point to understand why Britain should find herself again in the same position as at the century's beginning. As a child I was so caught up in the post-war period of austerity and rationing (there were acute food shortages) that I did not discover until much later what had been the plight of the Jews during the war. Like many other Christians I was – and still am – horrified, still asking myself could the Churches have done more at the time. Bishop George Bell of Chichester was an exception in the efforts he made to alert the world. The memory of this appalling policy and the loss of European Jewry is still a very strong dimension of the contemporary conflict.

So I utterly condemn the moves made by the Grand Mufti, Amin al-Husseini, to forge an alliance with Hitler. But, for a start, it has to be understood that his appointment was a disaster. It was the result of an intrigue by a violently anti-Zionist official, Ernest T. Richmond, a member of the British High commissioner's secretariat. He was said to be 'a declared enemy of Zionist policy' (Fromkin 1989, p. 518). Richmond through this appointment believed he was striking a blow against Zionism:

> As time would show, he had struck a crueller, more destructive blow against Palestinian Arabs, whom the Grand Mufti was to lead into a bloody, blind alley.
>
> (Fromkin 1989, p. 518)

Al-Husseini's views were virulently anti-Semitic – I have absolutely no defense for them. He boasted that he supported the Nazis 'because I was persuaded and still am that if Germany had carried the day, no trace of the Zionists would have remained in Palestine' (Sebag-Montefiore 2011, p. 456). Yet, Peter Wien, in *Arab Nationalists, Nazi-Germany and the Holocaust: an Unlucky Contemporaneity* argues that you have to understand the way that the Grand Mufti's actions were later interpreted in the light of post-1948 events:

> To sum up, the Arab nationalist efforts and the anti-Zionist atrocities had nothing to do with German Nazi barbarity except for a parallelity of time.

Later in his essay he shows how German sources manage to create artificially a link between German anti-Jewish policy and Arab anti-Zionism which had nothing in common (www.hist.net/kieser/aghet/Essays/EssayWien.html). Yet, lest you think there is now too much agreement between us (!), I argue that it is a mistake to assume that all Arab nationalists were Hitlerite anti-Semites. For example, Wasif Jawhariyyeh, who was very sympathetic to the Jewish plight, wrote in his diary that Arab Jerusalemites, loathing the British for their injustice, dishonesty and the Balfour Declaration, hoped Germany would win the war.

> They used to sit, listening to the news, waiting for the headlines of victory, grieving over good news for England.
>
> (Fromkin 1989, p. 456)

Nor was this wartime escalating situation helped by British moves. In the 1939 White Paper, Britain curtailed immigration to Palestine and showed a lack of sympathy to Jewish refugees. In fact she turned back shiploads of desperate refugees. The story of the SS

Exodus in 1947 is a particularly shocking incident. The SS Exodus was a ship that carried Jewish emigrants from France to Palestine on 11 July 1947. Most of the emigrants were Holocaust survivors who had no legal immigration certificates for Palestine. Following wide media coverage, the British Royal Navy seized the ship and deported all its passengers back to Europe. The passengers ended up in internment camps in Germany:

> By the time they had docked at Hamburg, many of the refugees were in a defiant mood. When they first set out on their historic quest, they had believed they were days away from arriving at a Jewish homeland. The prospect of being sent to camps in Germany represented a pitiful failure of their original mission and for many of the Holocaust survivors, it was almost impossible to bear.
>
> (http://www.wikipedia.org/wiki/Exodus_(ship))

In your exchanges, you refrain from criticizing the British (mostly). But surely you see that British policy in Palestine was ultimately untenable, to be tolerated by neither side? The stage was set for the Jewish revolt against the British, declared by Menachem Begin, who enters the scene for the first time. It was also the dying days of the Mandate.

Nazism and the Zionist Cause

Dan Cohn-Sherbok

From the vantage point of the twenty-first century, it is difficult to perceive the rifts that existed in the Jewish world in the early twentieth century regarding Zionism. As I noted previously, Orthodox Jews in Palestine, Eastern and Western Europe and elsewhere were bitterly opposed on religious grounds to the creation of a Jewish state in the Holy Land. Reform Judaism adamantly rejected the mass immigration of Jewry to Palestine. Similarly, Jewish socialists regarded a Jewish state as a retrograde step in their determination to build a world community based on universalist principles. Only a small minority of Jews sought to advance the Zionist cause. Amongst the early Jewish settlers in Palestine, there were deep ideological divisions. As we noted, the Revisionists led by Jabotinsky broke away from mainstream Zionism and formed their own movement.

Yet the events of the Second World War profoundly altered Jewish consciousness. As the Nazis unleashed their campaign against Germany Jewry and later the Jews of Europe, it became increasingly clear that the Zionist analysis of the precariousness of Jewish existence was true. If assimilated European Jews were not safe in the countries where they lived, then Herzl's analysis of the Jewish predicament was correct. Jews were destined to suffer at the hands of non-Jews in lands where they were in the minority. This was the obvious lesson of modern history, and throughout the Jewish world a homeland in the Middle East was perceived as the only solution to the threat of anti-Semitism. Orthodox and non-Orthodox Jews joined together in support of Zionism as the Nazis advanced across Europe. In Palestine itself the various political factions united in the face of the Nazi threat. The Palestinians, led by the Grand Mufti, however, regarded Hitler as their saviour. In the mind of Palestinian Arabs, Britain had betrayed Arab interests, and with the rise of the Third Reich they turned to Germany for support. At his meeting with Hitler in November 1941, the Grand Mufti was told that after the war it would be left to him to deal with the Palestinian problem.

I appreciate what you say about Nazism and the stand of the Grand Mufti. But I want to explore your own position. Throughout our discussion, you constantly castigate British policy concerning the Middle East. You are particular harsh about the Balfour Document and subsequent British support for the Zionist cause. You argue that the Zionists – with support from the British and others – essentially stole land from the Arabs. In your view, the Arab uprising is understandable in the light of such betrayal of their interests. You frequently cite critics of Zionist policy in making your case against the creation of a Jewish homeland in Palestine.

At the same time you say you are adamantly opposed to anti-Semitism in any form. But at no point do you concede that in the face of persecution and massacre, the Jews were right to press for a country of their own. Even at the point when we are discussing the Nazi policy of extermination, you focus on the iniquity of the establishment of a Jewish homeland in Palestine and what you perceive as the iniquitous role of the British government. If you are truly sympathetic to the plight of Jewry in the face of the Nazi onslaught, why are you unwilling to concede that there is a place for Jews in their ancestral home? Why do you not see that the British were fighting to protect Jews from their enemies by supporting the Zionist project? The holocaust united world Jewry in support of the creation of Israel. Why did it leave you behind?

Anti-Palestinian Propaganda

Mary Grey

Your challenge is a serious one, but your arguments are one sided. You want me to agree that 'the British were fighting to protect Jews from their enemies by supporting the Zionist project'. But the British during the Mandate years had their own imperial interests in trying to keep peace in Palestine: ultimately fighting both Jews and Arabs proved too much and they were relieved when the Mandate came to an end. It is an inglorious period of British history.

You say that 'The Holocaust united world Jewry in support of the creation of Israel. Why did it leave you behind?' I agree absolutely with you that the tragedy of the Holocaust united world Jewry in favour of the creation of Israel – something Chaim Weizmann had wanted from the beginning. It also united many countries of the world – as well as the Churches – when the horrors of the camps were uncovered.

Again, I return to my argument, that, yes, it might have been the right solution, were it not for

- the treatment meted out to the Arabs, and
- the way the fact of the Holocaust has come to be used to justify any future unjust actions of the Israeli government.

But here is a further point. Yes, the Grand Mufti's agreement with Hitler and his subsequent actions are beyond justification, but there is evidence to suggest that to accuse all Palestinians of being pro-Nazi because of one man, is a travesty of the truth.

As Benny Morris argued:

> Unfortunately, to the Palestinian people this question implies that they should pay the prices for the collaboration of a single person with the Nazis! Although there were a minority of Palestinians who collaborated with the Nazis, a whole nation cannot pay the price for the choices of the few. It's not just that the Palestinian people (and most of the Arab countries as well) aided the allies with men and logistical support, they also ignored the call for Jihad against the allies, that was declared by al-Hajj (the Grand Mufti).
>
> (Morris 2001, p. 165)

What is more, there is evidence that in the Second World War both sides looked for allies with who would be the winner. Tom Segev writes (Segev 1999, p. 464) that at the same time that the Mufti was asking for Nazi help, Avraham Stern, the Lechi commander – a freedom movement also known as the Stern Gang – suggested establishing a Jewish alliance with Nazi Germany to end British rule: 'He was guided by the same principle: my enemy's enemy is my friend'. According to the pro-Israel historian, Martin Gilbert:

> Avraham Stern . . . tried to make contact with Fascist Italy in the hope that, if Mussolini were to conquer the Middle East, he would allow a Jewish State to be set up in Palestine. When Mussolini's troops were defeated in North Africa, Stern tried to make contacts with Nazi Germany, hoping to sign a pact with Hitler which would lead to a Jewish State once Hitler had defeated Britain. After two members of the Stern's Gang had killed the Tel Aviv [British] police chief and two of his officers, Stern himself was caught and killed. His followers [chief among them Yitzhak Shamir who led the Stern Gang after Stern's death] continued on their path of terror.
>
> (Gilbert 2008, pp. 111–112)

So, whereas nothing should be allowed to diminish the memory and significance of the Holocaust, I criticize the way certain memories of the Holocaust are being exploited to suggest that all Palestinians were Nazi sympathizers. Yet such propaganda tactics are now being fed to many Israeli school children and especially upon visiting the Holocaust museum at Yad Vashem (www.palestineremembered/story420.html). As I've written earlier, the truth is what we seek to uncover and at times, it's elusive, especially when overlaid with propaganda. And we'll see this again and again in our story – not least in the coming chapter.

Chapter 8
Post War Developments 1946–1948

Zionist Systematic Planning

Mary Grey

We enter an even more painful period that has set the scene for on-going conflict. You are aware that after the war, United Nations Committee on Palestine (UNSCOP) proposed as a solution to the conflict to divide Palestine. But the UN was inexperienced – having only existed since 1945 – and the Palestinians boycotted the discussion. As Walid Khalidi explained:

> The native people of Palestine, like the native people of every country in the Arab world, Asia, Africa, America and Europe, refuse to divide the land with a settler community.
> (Pappé 2006, pp. 34–35)

Essentially, nothing had changed for the Arabs since the Balfour Declaration. The final map that UNSCOP proposed meant Palestine being divided into three parts. On 42 per cent of the land, 818,000 Palestinians were to have a state that included 10,000 Jews, while the state for the Jews was to stretch over almost 56 per cent of the land, which 499,000 Jews were to share with 438,000 Palestinians. The third part was a small enclave around the city of Jerusalem which was to be internationally governed and whose population of 200,000 was equally divided between Palestinians and Jews. What was felt as very unjust for the Arabs was that the Jewish state incorporated the most fertile land. What was to mean further tragedy was that the Jewish state included 400 Arab villages.

Now the leadership of David Ben Gurion – who would be Israel's first Prime minister – swung into play.[1] It was he who persuaded his associates, known as the Consultancy, simultaneously to accept and reject the partition proposal. The Palestinian boycott was his justification to ignore the terms of the partition, claiming that the borders would be secured by force. Israel would determine its own borders. And now began the planning of what became known as Plan Dalet, the forcible removal of the Palestinians from their villages.

It is important to note the degree of planning of this exercise. The definition of genocide of Raphael Lemkin in his book *Axis rule in Occupied Europe* (1944) is now widely accepted in Genocide Studies. He emphasizes the degree of planning – that nothing was spontaneous. Thus Pappé combines oral and archival sources to produce an account of the Zionist 1947–1949 genocide of the Palestinians as systematically planned. A young historian from the Hebrew University, Ben-Zion Luria, proposed that the Jewish National fund carry out a detailed registry of all Arab villages (Docker 2012, pp. 12–13). A topographer, photographers and Orientalists were all recruited:

> By the late 1930s, precise details were recorded about the topographic location of each village, its access roads, quality of land, water springs, main sources of income, socio-political composition, religious affiliations, the names of its mukhtars, relationships with other villages and the age of individual males between sixteen and fifty.
> (Docker 2012, citing Pappé 2006, pp. 15–19)

---

[1] I cited him earlier in terms of his use of the Bible.

A sinister element was listing all those who had participated in the revolt of 1936, and particular attention was paid to those who had killed Jews. This would fuel some of the worst atrocities. What greatly saddens me is to read that infiltrating Arab villages was easy, as the investigators benefited from traditional Arab hospitality. By 1943 this research had become even more systematic – including all details of trees and cultivated land, the living rooms of important people and what arms were available to the villages. The final update was in 1947 and focused on creating lists of wanted people. All this meant that when on the 10 March 1948, veteran Zionist leaders put the final touches to Plan Dalet and military orders were dispatched to units on the ground: these included detailed descriptions as to the methods to be employed:

> Laying siege to and bombarding villages and population centres; setting fires to homes, properties and goods; expulsion, demolition and planting of mines among the rubble to prevent any of the expelled inhabitants from returning.
> (Pappé 2006, pp. xi–xiii, 28, 49)

Each unit was equipped with its one list of villages and neighbourhoods as the targets of the master plan.

How is it possible to defend such orders and the violence that would now follow?

Plan Dalet: The Controversy

Dan Cohn-Sherbok

The period following the Second World War in Palestine was for many reasons one of the most tragic. As you note, UNSCOP proposed a solution to the conflict between Jews and Arabs in Palestine which involved partitioning the country. You cite Walid Khalidi's, General Secretary of the Institute for Palestine Studies, explanation why such a plan was bitterly resisted by the native population. What became crucial in subsequent developments was the Arab determination to resist United Nations policy. It was the recognition of such a stance that led to the formulation of Plan Dalet. This plan was worked out by the Haganah in March 1948 – it was the fourth and final version of less substantial plans that had outlined what the Zionists would do in the face of Arab attack. Essentially it was a set of guidelines, the stated purpose of which was to take control of the Jewish state and to defend its borders and peoples, in expectation of an invasion by regular Arab armies.

What you do not mention is that Plan Dalet is subject to much controversy. According to some writers, it was aimed at an ethnic cleansing of Arab villages. In the view of Walid Khalidi, this plan was designed to bring about the conquest of Palestine. In his book *The Ethnic Cleansing of Palestine*, Israeli historian Ilan Pappé argues that Plan Dalet was a blueprint for removing the native population. According to Pappé, the general section of the plan which was distributed to politicians disguised the real intentions of the Haganah. The true plan was handed down to brigade commanders as clear-cut operational orders for action. Each brigade commander received a list of the villages or neighbourhoods that had to be occupied, destroyed and their inhabitants expelled. This is how you have interpreted Plan Dalet. If you are correct, then you would be right to condemn such a scheme.

Yet, as you will know, other historians have reached a different interpretation of Plan Dalet. According to the Israeli historian, Yoav Gelber, Plan Dalet was a defensive plan:

> Although it provided for counter-attacks, Plan Dalet was a defensive scheme and its goals were (a) protection of the borders of the upcoming Jewish state according to the partition line; (b) securing its territorial continuity in the face of invasion attempts; (c) safeguarding freedom of movement on the roads; and (d) enabling continuation of essential daily routines.
> (Gelber, *Palestine*, 1948, 2006, pp. 303–306)

Again, military historian David Tal asserts that although the plan did provide the conditions for the destruction of Palestinian villages and the deportation of the dwellers, this was not the reason for the plan's composition. Rather, its aim was to ensure full control of the territory assigned to the Jews by the partition resolution thereby placing the Haganah in the best possible strategic position to face an Arab invasion (Tal, *War in Palestine*, 1948, 2004, p. 87).

In assessing the events of 1948, it is important to bear in mind that there are two diametrically opposed interpretations of the intentions of the Haganah. What is clear, however, is that the Yeshuv was under threat from Arab invasion. The tragedy, I believe, was not that partition was recommended by the United Nations Committee on Palestine, but that the indigenous population and surrounding Arab states were determined to thwart any attempt to divide Palestine into a Palestinian and Jewish state. Both of us believe that peace and reconciliation is of primary importance. This could have been achieved if partition had been accepted by both sides of the conflict. This was not to be. From the 1920s on, Palestinian Arabs were determined to reject any attempt to provide a homeland for the Jews in the Holy Land. It is this intransigence which is at the heart of the seemingly insoluble conflict between Arabs and Jews. The great pity is that Palestinians have throughout their history been unwilling to compromise about the creation of a Jewish homeland in the Middle East.

Al Nakba – The Catastrophe

Mary Grey

You often repeat that 'the great pity is that Palestinians have throughout their history been unwilling to compromise about the creation of a Jewish homeland in the Middle East' – to which I have to reply: do you have any example from history of an indigenous people freely giving up their lands to incomers without their being consulted? You also replied to me that Plan Dalet had no sinister motivation – and was meant to be a defensive measure. To which I can only reply: look at what happened . . .

Following the period of preparation, a series of massacres began. The first and most horrific was Deir Yassin – and was a contributory factor to the exodus of Arabs from their villages. On 9 April 1948 between 120 and 254 unarmed villagers were murdered, including women, the elderly and children. There were also cases of rape and mutilation. As Nur Masalha writes:

> Most Israeli writers today have not difficulty in acknowledging the occurrence of the Deir Yassin massacre and its effect, if not its intention of precipitating the exodus. However, most

of these writers take refuge in the fact that the massacre was committed by 'dissidents' of the Irgun.

(Masalha 2007, pp. 62–63)

Other massacres followed, apparently also geared towards precipitating the evacuation of the villages. Eventually, in a massive 'clearance' of the Galilee, around 530 villages were emptied, their inhabitants forced to flee. Massacres occurred in at least 16 villages (Masalha 2007, p. 65). Nearly 800,000 Palestinians were forced into becoming refugees – in Bethlehem, the West Bank, the Gaza strip, Lebanon and other parts of the world. There are approximately 7 million Palestinian refugees in the world – one in three refugees in the world is a Palestinian: 4.5 million are comprised of the original 'Nakba' refugees and their descendants.

I have travelled with Palestinians who have experienced 'Al Nakba' to their original villages and it is a very poignant experience to hear their stories. Canon Naim Ateek, Director of Sabeel, was, as a boy, himself driven out of the village of Beisan, now Bet She'an. The Archbishop of Galilee, Elias Chacour, has told his story of being driven out of Biram – again as a young child. Yet he works ceaselessly for peace and reconciliation.

Possibly the worst story is of the massacre at Al Tantura, yet it can be told as a story of forgiveness. At a Conference in Jerusalem organized by Sabeel (an organisation working for the liberation of Christians in Israel/Palestine), I met one of the perpetrators of the massacre of Al Tantura. (I had visited Al Tantura the day before – a beautiful seaside village near Acre.) According to the thesis of Teddy Katz of Haifa University up to 250 men died. (Katz, supported by Ilan Pappé, paid a severe price for sticking to the truth of his story.) Joseph Ben Eleazar, one of those responsible for the massacre, was present at the Sabeel Conference with his son and daughter-in-law. Himself a Holocaust survivor, he had fled to Israel, and joined the Irgun, one of the groups responsible for the early massacres dispossessing Palestinians from their villages. Involved in the rounding up of the Arabic men of the village of Al Tantura, he suddenly experienced a moment of *déjà-vu*, as he remembered his own experience of being rounded up in a square in Germany. Years of seeking his own spiritual pathway ended in conversion to Christianity and his joining the Bruderhof, a Peace Group now based in Hastings, in England.[2] Later, through searching internet, he discovered the names of the sons of the men killed at Al Tantura and journeyed to Israel to beg forgiveness. His journey seeking forgiveness and reconciliation carries on (Grey 2010, pp. 83–84). Ben Eleazer died in 2013.

I have also visited refugee camps in Bethlehem, where the walls are decorated with frescoes depicting the dispossessed villages. In Dheishe camp, I met a grandmother who still sleeps with the key of her front door under her pillow in the hope of returning to her house.

So many stories, so many memories. But one of the greatest difficulties for the Palestinian people who have been 'ethnically cleansed' (and space has prohibited by telling more stories in greater detail), is that the visible remains of their homes has been removed:

> By the end of the 1948 war, hundreds of entire villages had not only been depopulated but obliterated, their houses blown up or bulldozed. While many of the sites are difficult of access, to this day the observant traveller of Israeli roads and highways can see traces of their presence that would escape the notice of the casual passer-by: a fenced-in area, often surmounting a gentle hill, of olive and other fruit trees left untended, of cactus hedges and domesticated plants run wild. Now and then a few crumbled houses are left standing, a neglected mosque or church, collapsing walls along the ghost of a village lane, but in the vast majority of cases, all that remains is a scattering of stones and rubble across a forgotten landscape.
>
> (Khalidi 1948)

If the truth is obliterated, unacknowledged, how can there be reconciliation between Israelis and Palestinians?

---

[2] See Joseph Ben-Eleazar, *The Search*, www.ploughbooks.com

The War of Independence

Dan Cohn-Sherbok

You have provided a robust interpretation of what Palestinians refer to as the Nakba (catastrophe). There is no doubt that the suffering, deaths and destruction of Arab villages during the War of Independence is a tragic chapter in the history of modern Israel. Yet, you have omitted the background to this conflict. From 1947 the political climate in Britain underwent a transformation. For some time the opposition had urged that the Mandate be rescinded. Churchill recommended that the United Nations take over control of Palestine. On 18 February 1947 the British government announced that it had no power under the Mandate to determine whether Palestine belonged to the Arabs or the Jews. As a result, the only course open was to submit the problem to the United Nations. To facilitate this transition, Britain requested that a Special Session of the General Assembly consider this issue.

This meeting, which took place from 28 April to 15 May 1947 resolved to set up an investigating eleven-member body – UNSCOP which was to report by the autumn. During the summer, members of this Committee went to Palestine. On 31 August UNSCOP completed its report in Geneva, unanimously recommended the end of the British Mandate. A majority report – with a vote of seven to three with one abstention – stated that Palestine should be partitioned into an Arab and Jewish state with an international zone for the Holy Places. On 29 November 1947 the General Assembly formally considered the report. Thirty-three delegates voted in favor; thirteen were opposed, including the eleven Muslim states. There were also ten abstentions. Early in December the British government made it clear that it would continue to rule in Palestine until 15 May 1948 at which time the Mandate would come to an end.

From what you have previously written, it is clear that you strongly disapprove of the United Nations intervention, and that you repudiate UNSCOP's recommendation that Palestine be partitioned. Further, I assume that you disapprove of the General Assembly's vote on 29 November 1947. I find it hard to believe, however, that you would have sided with the Arab nations who began preparations for war against the new state of Israel. If you think the Palestinians should not have resorted to violence, then surely they should have been less intransigent and have compromised with the Zionists. Yet, this is what they have continually failed to do. I am also puzzled by your attitude towards the United Nations itself. Surely those countries who voted against UNSCOP's recommendation should as members of the UN have accepted the decision reached through democratic processes. Am I to think that you believe countries should ignore United Resolutions if they disagree with them?

Let me turn to the assault against Deir Yassin. In the months following the General Assembly vote in favor of partition, Arab attacks against Jews commenced; in response, the Haganah and Irgun engaged in acts of reprisal. In general, the British forces remained aloof from this conflict. As you noted, on 9 April an attack on the Arab village of Deir Yassin was carried out by the Irgun killing 250 Arab civilians, including women and children. According to Menahem Begin, this assault was part of a strategy to keep open the lines of communication between Jerusalem and the rest of the Yishuv. Recalling this event in his book, *The Revolt*, Begin asserted that an advance warning was given by loudspeakers to civilians encouraging them to leave. The Arab account of this incident, however, records that the civilians were deliberately massacred. Once news of what occurred at Deir Yassin was broadcast on Arab radios the Arab population fled from Jewish areas. By mid-May nearly 300,000 Arabs left their homes seeking refuge in neighbouring countries. What you leave out of your account of the evacuation of villages is that these terrible events took place because of the Arab determination to reject the United Nations vote in favor of partition and the creation of a Jewish state. Had partition been accepted by the Arabs, this conflict would not have taken place and the Palestinian refugee problem would not have existed.

You are right to point out the terrible suffering of the Palestinians in this conflict, yet you ignore the dangers facing the new Jewish state. On the day of independence, Egyptian planes bombed Tel Aviv. The next day began the intervention of five Arab states. In your view, should Israel not have sought to defend itself? In this context, I want to return to an earlier question I asked about the existence of a Jewish state. You continually stress that it was unjust of the Jewish people to establish a homeland in Palestine. You ask at the outset of your last exchange whether any example can be cited from history where indigenous people have freely given up their lands to incomers without being consulted. The implication of this question is that a Jewish homeland should not been created without the consent of indigenous Palestinians. And of course, if their consent had been solicited, they would not have given it. You have criticized the Balfour Declaration as an illegitimate imposition of British policy. In essence, your position is that despite Jewish suffering in Eastern Europe and elsewhere, the Jewish state should never have been established in Palestine. Yet, at times you state that you believe the State of Israel should exist. I simply cannot understand your view. If Israel should not have been created in the first place; if Britain should no have issued the Balfour Declaration; if Jewish settlers had no right to the land they obtained; then surely modern Israel should not have existed in the past, and should not exist now. To say anything else is illogical.

Let the Truth Be Known!

Mary Grey

For one exchange that's a lot of accusations! Let me offer some clarification. I suspect our attitudes to history are very different.

First, of course I approve and respect the UN – I wish the contemporary Israel government did the same – but that is still to come! You criticize the Arabs for rejecting the UN Partition plan, but, as I explained earlier (in section 'Zionist Systematic Planning'), this was a hugely biased partition in favour of the Jews, who would own all the fertile land. The Arabs would be left with scarce water resources, desert, stony lands and barren hills. Why would they want to agree?

Secondly, I look at historical decisions in their context: suppose they had not been made, would the outcome have been different? Let me give the example of Pakistan. It has become a new country since 1947 and the decision to divide India and Pakistan cost the lives of thousands, created an immense displacement and refugee problem – and the consequences of that fateful decision are still troublesome. *But that decision did not have to be made –* Gandhi consistently opposed it. But because I criticize it and lament its consequences – does not mean I want to delegitimize Pakistan! Similarly, the decision to give Palestine to the Jews did not have to be made – and I have criticized it on the grounds of injustice to the indigenous people. But it has been made and since Israel has become recognized as a State by the UN, I accept this. All my efforts at reconciliation are based on the acceptance of Israel: at the same time I strive for justice for both sides. In our interchange, we are trying to explore these decisions in the contexts in which they arose.

Thirdly, I cannot really believe you defend the Deir Yassin massacre as Begin does, 'as a strategy to keep open the lines of communication between Jerusalem and the rest of the Yeshiva' and that advance warning was given. According to Rabbi Michael Lerner, Deir Yassin was a village which had gone out of its way to establish good relations with its Jewish neighbourhoods of western Jerusalem, and refused to let Arab Units use the village as a base for an attack. It's true that one of the motives was to secure the road to Jerusalem:

> But Deir Yassin stands out in the memory of the Palestinians because of the atrocities committed there against Palestinians . . . Benny Morris quotes an *Israeli commander* who reported on April 12: The conquest of the village was carried out with great cruelty. Whole families – women, old people, children – were killed and there were piles of dead.
>
> (Lerner 2003, p. 60)

It was this – and similar massacres that had the greatest impact on demoralising and terrifying the Palestinians, becoming a major factor in their flight from their homes. Menachem Begin and Yitzhak Shamir openly advocated that Palestinians should be terrorised into flight (Lerner 2003, pp. 60–61).

Is it any wonder that the Arab nations tried to come to the rescue? It doesn't matter whether I approve or not, the fact is that it is wholly understandable – and largely unsuccessful. As Musa al Alami wrote:

> We approached it (the conflict) in an ad hoc manner, with no unity, no comprehensive strategy and no overall leadership. . . . The Jews conducted the war with a unified strategy, unified leadership and general conscription. Our weapons were poor and defective, while those of the enemy were good and powerful.
>
> (Cohn-Sherbok and El-Alami 2001, p. 182)

Within three months of the conflict, a quarter of a million Arabs were living as refugees in neighbouring countries. Is it any wonder that the memories of Nakba are seared into Palestinian consciousness? And that this is resisted by the Israelis? A gesture of reconciliation was attempted in the formation of 'Zochrot' (Remembering), which is an Israeli non-profit organization founded in 2002. Based in Tel Aviv, its aim is to promote awareness of the Nakba and the 1948 Palestinian exodus. Its slogan is 'To commemorate, witness, acknowledge, and repair.'

Zochrot organizes tours of Israeli towns, which include taking displaced Palestinians back to the areas they fled or were expelled from in 1948 and afterwards. The group erects street signs giving the Palestinian history of the street or area they are in. Zochrot sees this as causing 'disorder in space,' raising questions about naming and belonging. A key aim is to 'Hebrew-ise the Nakba' by creating a space for it in the public discourse of Israeli Jews (http://www.wikipedia/zochrot).

But, in contrast with this hopeful story, I have to report that on 23 March 2011, the Knesset[3] approved, by a vote of 37 to 25, a change to the budget, giving the Israeli Finance Minister the discretion to reduce government funding to any non-governmental organization (NGO) that organizes Nakba commemoration events. This is memoricide – killing of memories – and banning of any commemoration of what had happened. If the founding of the

---

[3]The Israeli parliament.

Delegitimizing Israel

Dan Cohn-Sherbok

First, I must stress that I am appalled by the massacre of Palestinian villages whatever the reason. I am not in a position to determine the validity of Menahem Begin's explanation of the attack on Deir Yassin – but whatever the motive, it was a terrible tragedy. Nonetheless, I am certain that the Arab unwillingness to accept the presence of a Jewish homeland in Palestine was the cause of the war against the Jewish state. You state that you approve and respect the United Nations. Yet, you disapprove of the UN Partition plan because you say that it would favor the Jews. Yet partition was approved by a democratic vote at the UN, and as a result Israel was immediately attacked. I am still unclear whether you approve of the Arab response. You say it was understandable. But were they right to go to war?

I want to turn next to your comparison of the situation in India with Palestine. I acknowledge that Gandhi opposed partition, and arguably it has cost thousands of lives and caused immense suffering. However, the division of India into two states is not a parallel case. You continually argue that Palestinian land was taken unjustly from the indigenous Arab inhabitants and given to the Jews. You are adamant that this was immoral. In the case of India and Pakistan, however, there is no suffering minority which has been disenfranchised and persecuted due to partition.

You write: 'The decision to give Palestine to the Jews did not have to be made, and I have criticized it on the grounds of injustice to the indigenous people. But it has been made and since Israel has become recognized as a state by the UN, I accept this.' There is, I believe, a fundamental error in the logic of your argument. You believe that land belonging to the Palestinians was stolen. In your view, it did not belong to the Jews, and Palestine should never have been partitioned. But surely if the land was stolen; if the division of Palestine should not have taken place, if the Palestinians have been victims of a fundamentally immoral act, then it makes not sense to say that Israel should exist. You state that you do not want to delegitimize Israel, but that is precisely what your arguments do. In this regard, the Palestinian Liberation Organization and Hamas are far more consistent. There are unrepentant in their wish to wish to see Israel disappear. In June 1974, for example, the Palestinian National Council, the legislative body of the Palestine Liberation Organization, referred in its Ten Point Plan to the central principles of the movement: the denial of the existence of the State of Israel, the demand of the return of all Palestinian refugees to their original homes, and the establishment of an Arab-Palestinian state in the entire region of Palestine within the pre-1948 borders. The Hamas Covenant, issued in 1988, is also uncompromising in its aims. The Charter states that the struggle against the Jews is very great and very serious and calls for the eventual creation of an Islamic state in Palestine in place of Israel and the Palestinian Territories and the obliteration or dissolution of Israel.

From the early nineteenth century, Palestinian critics of Zionism have put forward the same arguments that you have used: Zionists have trampled on the rights of the indigenous population; the British acted out of imperialistic and colonialistic motives and acted irresponsibly by not consulting the native population regarding Zionist aspirations; the Balfour Declaration should never have been issued; Jewish settlers had no right to the land they purchased given the suffering of Arab farmers who had cultivated the land for many generations; the United Nations should never have approved the partition plan. As a result of this stance, surrounding Arab nations have attacked Israel in a series of wars and have sought Israel's destruction. You embrace the Arab critique of modern Israel, yet you say you do not seek to delegitimize the Jewish state. I believe you are muddled.

Chapter 9
The War of Independence and Aftermath

The War of Independence

Dan Cohn-Sherbok

The State of Israel was announced on 14 May 1948 in the City Hall of Tel Aviv. The Declaration of Independence outlined the history of Israel from ancient times to the present, and included a call to Arab neighbours for peace and coexistence. The United States and the Soviet Union as well as other countries recognized the new state; David Ben-Gurion became the first prime minister, and a broad multi-party government was established. The Arab world, however, was determined to drive the Jews into the sea. The moment the British mandate ended, the armies of Iraq, Syria, Jordan, Egypt and Lebanon crossed into the territory of the former mandate and attacked Jewish-held sectors. It initially appeared that Israel would be destroyed by the long-established, better-equipped Arab forces. Surrounded by hostile enemies, there was a real danger that the Jewish state would be obliterated in the struggle.

The Arab campaign in the north, conducted largely by the Syrians, made no gains. In the south, Egyptian forces advanced, but they were finally halted on 29 May, just 16 miles from Tel Aviv. The greatest Arab successes came to the British-officered Jordanian army which captured Jerusalem's Old City and expelled the entire population. The Jewish army continued to hold Jewish-populated west Jerusalem.

On 11 June the United Nations (UN) imposed a ceasefire. Two days earlier, the Israel Defense Force (IDF) finished constructing a steep circuitous route (the Burma Road) which bypassed Jordanian-held territory, to transport supplies to Jerusalem. During the ceasefire, Israel obtained weapons from Czechoslovakia. Thousands of Jewish immigrants also arrived, many of whom were immediately sent to the front line with little or no training.

During the 10-day interval between the breakdown of the first ceasefire on 8 July and the imposition of a second ceasefire on 18 July, the IDF captured Galilee as well as Lod and Ramle. A UN diplomatic effort failed when both sides rejected a proposal to maintain international control that would establish an Arab state and only a very small Jewish state. At this time Jewish extremists assassinated Count Folke Bernadotte, a UN mediator who had proposed major Jewish concessions. Once the Egyptians shelled an IDF supply envoy, Israel launched an offensive on 14 October, capturing Beersheba in eight days and drove the Egyptian forces back across the border except in the Gaza Strip.

During the War of Independence Israeli losses had been great: the 6,000 killed were 1 per cent of its population. Yet Israel had fulfilled the goal of establishing itself as an independent state. Moreover, it now governed 21 per cent more territory than had been available under the UN Partition Plan. On 11 March 1948, Israel was admitted to the UN as a member. As far as the Arabs were concerned, neither the Palestinians nor the Arab states had created a new state in the former British mandate. In 1950 Jordan's King Abdullah annexed the West Bank; Egypt ruled in the Gaza Strip. Within Israel, military control was established over areas of the Galilee, which was populated by 150,000 Arabs. Arab rule prevailed in east Jerusalem and the West Bank and the Gaza Strip.

You refer to the War of Independence as the Nakba. You are right, it was a catastrophe. The war against Israel saw the destruction of 360 Arab villages and 14 Arab towns. About

70 per cent of the indigenous Arab population had become refugees. Some were evicted from their homes; others fled from the area because of the conflict. The number of these refugees is disputed: Israel records 520,000; the British 600,000–700,000; the United Nations 720,000. Whatever the number, the scale of the exodus was immense. An entire society was dispersed. Over 200,000 were crammed into the Gaza Strip; more than 300,000 lived in the West Bank; about 100,000 fled to Lebanon; another 100,000 to Syria and around the same number to Transjordan. You will blame the British and the Jewish settlers for this tragedy. In your view a Jewish state should never have been created in Palestine. Yet, the fact is that had the Arabs compromised with the Jews in the years leading up to and following the Holocaust, this tragedy would never have taken place.

A Crucial Moment in Our Story

Mary Grey

You are consistently blaming the Arabs for the lack of peace in the Holy Land. You say, referring to the Nakba, and the forcing of most of the Arab population into becoming refugees:

> Yet, the fact is that had the Arabs compromised with the Jews in the years leading up to and following the Holocaust, this tragedy would never have taken place.

So, whereas you blame me for 'muddled logic' I could say the same for you! Yet, I won't, because I do not want this conversation to degenerate into mudslinging. My purpose in this increasingly painful exchange is to exert every effort towards reconciliation. You constantly forget that we are trying to stick with decisions made in a certain context and the choices available to both communities in this context. So, whereas I have criticized the British for not fulfilling its promises to the Arabs, criticized them for the partition of India and the creation of Pakistan (it was Lord Mountbatten who made the key decisions) – and despite what you say, there are obvious parallels – and the decision to create an apartheid state in South Africa, I do believe in respecting international law in recognizing the legitimacy of the State of Israel. Yes, I would have preferred different decisions to have been made prior to 1917, but that time has passed. Yet, as I have said, the partition of territory was unjust to the Arabs. The criterion at every point in this process is: where is justice? (I will come later to the formation and policies of Hamas and the PLO.)

But you forget that this never was, never has been, a level playing field. The Palestinians had very poor representation in the UN – and the terms of partition gave them a very unjust deal. Look at the struggle they have had recently (2011) into simply achieving observer status in the UN! Your accounts of the Nakba underestimate the number of destroyed villages and the number of refugees – but let us not quarrel with the figures you give. The catastrophe the Arabs went through almost destroyed them as a people. Why would you even wonder that the Arab nations tried to come to their rescue? The Palestinian people at this point, dispersed as they were into various refugee camps, were incapable of doing much to help themselves.

I think we should acknowledge that our story has reached a crucial significant moment. The longed – for state has now been created. Chaim Weizmann's dream has been realized and he has now become the first President. A new capital is built in Tel Aviv and King Abdullah of Jordan has control of Israel – even if his rule would be short-lived. For the Arabs, *al nakba*, the catastrophe, however terrible, was the event that set them on a downwards spiral that is ever worsening, whereas Israel's fortunes would now continue to prosper. At that point, no one would have imagined what would be the terrible future of the Palestinian people.

And now, for the newborn state, the hero of the day is David Ben-Gurion, Israel's first prime minister. I have quoted him earlier in connection with his controversial use of the Bible. At this point, it would have been vital to establish good relations with what Arabs were left in Israel and initially, Ben-Gurion's attitude was encouraging:

> Ben-Gurion believed in the equal rights of Arabs who remained in and would become citizens of Israel. He was quoted as saying, 'We must start working in Jaffa. Jaffa must employ

> Arab workers. And there is a question of their wages. I believe that they should receive the same wage as a Jewish worker. An Arab has also the right to be elected president of the state, should he be elected by all.'
>
> (http://en.wikipedia.org/wiki/David_Ben-Gurion)

But, whereas he recognized the strong attachment of Palestinian Arabs to the land, in an address to the United Nations on 2 October 1947, he doubted the likelihood of peace:

> This is our native land; it is not as birds of passage that we return to it. But it is situated in an area engulfed by Arabic-speaking people, mainly followers of Islam. Now, if ever, we must do more than make peace with them; we must achieve collaboration and alliance on equal terms.

In contrast with this positive approach, Nahum Goldmann criticized Ben-Gurion for what he viewed as a confrontational approach to the Arab world:

> Ben-Gurion is the man principally responsible for the anti-Arab policy, because it was he who molded the thinking of generations of Israelis. Simha Flapan quoted Ben-Gurion as stating in 1938: 'I believe in our power, in our power which will grow, and if it will grow agreement will come . . .'
>
> (http://en.wikipedia.org/wiki/David_Ben-Gurion)

But, as I argued earlier, Ben-Gurion's ambition for the land was his driving motivation. In his War Diaries in February 1948, Ben-Gurion wrote: 'The war shall give us the land. The concepts of "ours" and "not ours" are peace concepts only, and they lose their meaning during war.' Also later he confirmed this by stating that, 'In the Negev we shall not buy the land. We shall conquer it. You forget that we are at war' (http://en.wikipedia.org/wiki/David_Ben-Gurion).

The name of the game has changed: in acquiring a new state, the concept of sharing land has been lost, and the language of conquest has taken over. You cannot now lay the blame completely at the doors of the vanquished Arabs who have now lost everything.

The Nakba

Dan Cohn-Sherbok

If you believe I am guilty of muddled thinking, you must tell me so. Our debate should never degenerate into mud-slinging (as you call it), but for the sake of truth we must be frank with one another. So let me turn to the issue of war and peace. I do reiterate my claim that had the Palestinian Arabs sought some form of compromise with Jewish settlers prior to, during and after the Holocaust, the terrible events of 1948 would not have happened. In saying this, I do not seek to excuse or justify the massacres and destruction of Arab villages that took place then. Nor do I wish to challenge your assertion that the terms of partition were weighted against the indigenous Palestinian population. Yet, what you and other critics blindly ignore in the analysis of the ways in which you believe Arabs were mistreated in the creation of a Jewish homeland in Palestine is Arab responsibility for violence and war.

One of the most distorted perceptions of the conflict between Arabs and Jews in 1948 has been given by the well-known Israeli historical revisionist, Ilan Pappé (whom you have previously referred to). In a recent essay, 'The State of Denial: The Nakba in the Israel Zionist Landscape,' he writes that the Nakba was the worst chapter in the history of Jewish abuses. Jews, he writes, expelled, massacred, destroyed and raped in that year and generally behaved like the other colonialist movements operating in the Middle East and Africa since the beginning of the nineteenth century. Repeatedly he asserts that the Jews had adopted a policy of ethnic cleansing which they were able to put into practice before, during and after 1948, and he argues that there has been since this date a deliberate attempt to erase from memory the evil of this crime. In his view there were three stages in the implementation of this programme of ethnic cleansing: (1) the period from December 1947 to the end of the summer of 1948 when the coastal and inner plains were destroyed and their populations evicted, (2) the autumn and winter of 1948 which included the Galilee and the Negev and (3) the period until 1954 when dozens of additional villages were destroyed and villagers were expelled (Pappé, in Lowenstein and Moor, pp. 23–42).

What is missing from this searing diatribe against Israel and its political leaders is any recognition that the new Jewish state was under siege from its surrounding Arab neighbours. It was not Israel who waged war against the Arabs. It was the Arabs who were intent on destroying the state of Israel and driving the Jews into the sea. It was they, not the Jews, who were the aggressors. Had the Palestinian Arabs pursued a policy of reconciliation with the Jewish settlers during the first, second and third aliyah, this terrible history of violence could have been avoided.

You say you believe in respecting international law regarding the legitimacy of the State of Israel. Yet this is what the Arab nations were determined not to do in 1948. Instead they ignored the UN vote for partition and attacked Israel immediately following the reading of the Declaration of the State of Israel. I have asked you before, and I ask you again, do you believe they were right to do so? Would you have joined them in their determination to eliminate Israel from Palestine? Where does your pursuit of justice lead you? It led the Arabs to war. Where would it have led you?

You are right that atrocities do occur during wartime. The destruction of Arab villages, the flight of refugees, and the suffering and misery of Palestinians in refugee camps are the tragic consequences of the War of Independence (or the Nakba as the Palestinians call it). But you must imagine what would have happened if the Israelis had lost the war. The Arabs made no secret of their desire to massacre them and drive them into the sea. You argue that the Arabs in the surrounding countries defended the Palestinians from the Jewish settlers, but their sympathy did not extend to offering homes to the refugees. Quite the reverse. The refugee camps have been preserved despite the vast surrounding Arab lands in order to ferment as much trouble and difficulty as possible for Israel.

Seeking the Truth about al Nakba

Mary Grey

I am sorry if I have not been clear. As my goal is reconciliation, I grieve over actions on both sides that have created what seems to be an irrevocable chasm.

When you say, 'I have asked you before, and I ask you again, do you believe they were right to do so?' meaning the Arab countries waging war on Israel – of course I don't! But, as I said in my last letter, I understand why they came to the rescue in the face of the tragic way the Arab population was being driven from their lands. Would I have joined them in their determination to eliminate Israel from Palestine? Of course I wouldn't. I believe there is always space for mediation and conflict resolution in the most difficult of situations. I have tried to be consistent in telling you that my stance is one of empathy, trying to understand the story from all aspects.

'Where does your pursuit of justice lead you? It led the Arabs to war. Where would it have led you?' I would have joined with any peace-making efforts at the time. My experience in the last 20 years of worrying over British interventions in the Balkans, Iraq and Afghanistan has only confirmed this view. But, at the same time, efforts for mediation don't stop me from trying to understand why people have acted as they did, and what was the underlying truth that drove their actions.

So I worry about your critique of Ilan Pappé's account of the Nakba which you say is biased. You say, 'It was not Israel waging war against the Arabs.' No, but it certainly was Israel's policies to drive out the Arabs from their lands and villages. What I find surprising in your critique is that this is firmly contradicted by the Oxford professor of International Relations, Avi Shlaim (Shlaim 2009, pp. 59–61). He critiques Palestinian historian Nur Masalha for overstating the case of Zionist aggression in a 'selective and tendentious use of the evidence' (Shlaim 2009, p. 59). But then he continues:

> For a broader, more balanced and more searching analysis of the causes of the Jewish triumph and the Arab defeat in the struggle for Palestine, one must turn to Ilan Pappé.

Yes, Shlaim acknowledges that he is a revisionist Israeli historian but his work is based on the most thorough research – and he has paid the price for his discoveries in having to leave the country. Shlaim continues:

> Based on deep knowledge of the primary and secondary sources in English Arabic and Hebrew, it – (his work) – provides a

powerful synthesis of the revisionist literature on the causes and consequences of the first Arab–Israeli war. Pappé sets out to investigate the way the two communities, the Jews and Arabs of Palestine, prepared themselves for the trial of strength that was bound to come.

(Shlaim 2009, p. 60)

The outcome of the war was determined even before a shot was fired, and he admits that the Jewish success in building the infrastructure of a state and in winning the diplomatic campaign was decisive. And yes, he admits that the inadequacy of Palestinian leadership was a decisive factor – as we shall see it continues to be.

But the research of Pappé – and others – reveal much more. These scholars show us that the expulsion of the Arabs was not a policy that suddenly emerged in 1948 but had already been embedded in the very origins of Zionism. Theodor Herzl, whose dreams of a Jewish State we discussed in Chapter 1, was already writing in his diary in 1895:

> We shall try to spirit the penniless population across the border by procuring employment for it in the transit countries, while denying any employment in our own country.

And he was not alone. One of the movement's most liberal thinkers, Leo Motzkin, wrote in 1917:

> Our thought is that the colonization of Palestine has to go in two directions: Jewish settlement in eretz Israel and the resettlement of the Arabs outside the country. The transfer of so many Arabs may seem at first unacceptable economically, but is nonetheless practical. It does not require too much money to resettle a Palestinian village on another land.
> (Ilan Pappé, *The Ethnic Cleansing of Palestine*, p. 6)

This colonialist view – comparable with the ethnic cleansing in many other parts of the world that accompanied colonialist enterprises – was held by most leading Zionists in the British Mandate period, as well as by some British. As soon as the Zionists secured the land in 1948, they acted on this plan by expelling as many Palestinians as possible, leading to the – as yet unsolved – refugee situation.

Now we come up against a problem of interpretation. Pappé thinks that the failure to reach a settlement at the end of this war – fatal in terms of future developments – was due to Israeli intransigence. Others – traditional Israeli historians – put it down to Arab intransigence. And this is the line you seem to take. Yet Pappé shows that at the Conference at Lausanne in 1949 – convened by the Arab Conciliation Commission – the Arabs were prepared to negotiate on the basis of the UN partition resolution that they had rejected 18 months earlier:

> Israel, however, insisted that a peace settlement should be based on the status quo without any redrawing of the borders or readmission of the Palestinian refugees. It was therefore Israeli rather than Arab inflexibility which stood in the way of a peaceful settlement.
>
> (Shlaim 2009, p. 61)

Are you prepared to admit that there is another interpretation of this tragic period?

Revisionist History

Dan Cohn-Sherbok

I am glad we both appear to agree that the Arab response to the creation of a Jewish state in Palestine was misguided. From what you have written about accepting the legitimacy of the new state of Israel in the light of the vote at the United Nations General Assembly, it seems we also agree that Arab nations should not have taken up arms against the Jewish state. Instead, they should have accepted partition even if they were unhappy about its terms. You go on to say that instead of supporting Arab attack, you would have joined any form of peace process that existed at the time. The problem with such an approach, however, is that from the Palestinian side, there never were efforts to achieve peace and reconciliation with the Jewish settlers. Instead, from the 1920s until the creation of the state of Israel, the Palestinians rose up against the Yishuv, and did everything in their power to curtail immigration and end Jewish nation-building. It is a pity there was no peace movement for you to join. Instead, the Grand Mufti – the leader of the Palestinian Arabs – urged violence and massacre. When he met with Hitler in Germany, he was intent on driving the Jews out of Palestine. Reconciliation was never on his mind.

Now, I want to be clear about your stance. To sum up your answers to the questions I put to you in my last exchange: am I right in thinking that despite your critique of Zionist aspirations, you believe (1) the Palestinians and the surrounding Arab nations should have accepted the UN vote about partitioning Palestine, (2) the Arabs should not have initiated war against Israel and (3) the Palestinians and the Arabs in general should have pursued a policy of peace and reconciliation with the Jews. If I have misunderstood your view, I hope you will correct me. I reiterate my assertion: it was the Arabs, not the Jews, who were intransigent in this conflict. At no point in the history of the Palestinian–Arab conflict up until 1948 did they seek peace. From the first decades of the twentieth century they sought to oust Jewish settlers from their midst. The War of Independence was an Arab initiative to drive Jews from the Holy Land. The failure of Ilan Pappé's view is that he presents the policy of ethnic cleansing as the driving force of the war itself. He implies that the Israeli leadership welcomed this conflict so Israel would be able to destroy Arab villages and expel the Palestinian population. In presenting this thesis, he makes no reference to the fact that the Jewish state was facing Arab attack and the possibility of extinction. The War of Independence was a catastrophe for both sides. Historical revisionists have rightly called attention to the suffering of the Palestinians in this conflict, but in doing so they have overlooked the anguish, pain and grief of the Israeli population as the faced the threat of annihilation.

I want to turn finally to the Conference at Lausanne in 1949 which was convened by the Arab Conciliation Commission. You point out that the Arabs were prepared to negotiate on the basis of the UN partition resolution that they had rejected 18 months earlier. As Avi Shlaim notes, the Israelis insisted that a peace settlement should be based on the status quo. You cite this as evidence (based on Pappé's interpretation) that it was the Israelis, not the Arabs, who were intransigent. What is omitted from this interpretation of events is context. The Arabs had lost the war that they had waged against the Jews. At no point prior to this conference had they sought any form of peace agreement. Imagine what the situation would have been if the Arabs had won. They would have massacred the Jewish settlers and driven them from Palestine. If the Jews had convened a conference of conciliation, seeking some form of partition, do you honestly believe the Palestinians would have made any concessions to their demands?

Revisionist History and Misinterpretations

Mary Grey

Not so fast! While I agree that if the Arabs have accepted the partition plan by the UN, if the Arab nations had not initiated war against the Jews, if the Palestinians had pursued a policy of peace and reconciliation, etc., all would have been well. But they didn't and there was no peace. But if they had, there could have been no peace with justice, since they had lost their land and homes.

Secondly, whereas I have plenty of sympathy for the fear the Jews must suffered at the Arab invasion, so soon after the tragedy of the holocaust, we have to avoid being 'economical with the truth' as to why the Arab nations invaded.

The Arab League came into existence in 1945 and was the highest forum for the making of pan-Arab policy on Palestine. It had unanimously rejected the UN partition plan and was bitterly opposed to the establishment of a Jewish state.

Before partition the Arab League had affirmed the right to the independence of Palestine, while blocking the creation of a Palestinian government. Towards the end of 1947 the League established a military committee commanded by the retired Iraqi general Ismail Safwat whose mission was to analyse the chance of victory of the Palestinians against the Jews. His conclusions were that they had no chance of victory and that an intervention of the Arab regular armies was mandatory. The political committee nevertheless rejected these conclusions and decided to support an armed opposition to the Partition Plan excluding the participation of their regular armed forces.

This is what was contained in a cable to the UN in a sub-clause:

> *Peace and order have been completely upset in Palestine, and, in consequence of Jewish aggression, approximately over a quarter of a million of the Arab population have been compelled to leave their homes and emigrate to neighbouring Arab countries.*

Noting that the British would now take no responsibility for the Mandatory territories, the statement declared that

> *the Arab Governments find themselves compelled to intervene for the sole purpose of restoring peace and security and establishing law and order in Palestine.*

According to Yoav Gelber, the Arab countries were drawn into the war by the collapse of the Palestinian Arabs and the Arab Liberation Army and the Arab governments' primary goal was preventing the Palestinian Arabs' total ruin and the flooding of their own countries by more refugees. According to their own perception, had the invasion not taken place, there was no Arab force in Palestine capable of checking the Haganah's offensive (http://en.wikipedia.org/wiki/1948_Arab%E2%80%93Israeli_War).

I agree with you that the Yishuv perceived the peril of an Arab invasion as threatening its very existence and took Arab propaganda literally. But here we both fall victim to misinterpretations as to how many troops, how many casualties on both sides, whether 'ethnic cleansing' was pre-planned (you challenge this and I have cited both Herzl and Pappé to show that the transfer of the Arab population was always part of the plan) how many villages were dispossessed and so on.

One further difficulty is that we need to be careful as to the historicity of certain belligerent phrases. For example, three times you declare that the 'Arabs wanted to drive the Jews into the sea.' And

I've heard you repeat this in different historical contexts. But where did this phrase originate? Some sources say:

> This is a commonly propagated myth, especially in relation to justifying Israel's massive military aid. Supporters often state it as fact that the Arabs have a desire to push the Jews into the sea.
>
> The matter of the fact is that this statement is a total fabrication by the Zionist propaganda machine. No Arab, or Palestinian leader has ever stated that they wanted to push the Jews into the sea. *In fact, the usage of this term originated in a speech by Israeli prime minister, Ben-Gurion.* In his speech, he states that the Arab armies intended to 'push all the Jews into the sea, dead or alive'. This statement has been attributed to many Arab leaders, specifically the former PLO leader, Yasser Arafat. I challenge anyone to actually find any reference to this statement by any prominent Arab leader in the early years of Israel's existence.
>
> The Arabs never intended to 'push the Jews into the sea', and they never did. Ironically, the Zionist forces of early Israel did what they claimed the Arabs wanted to do to them. They **literally pushed the Palestinians into the sea.** There are documented cases of Jewish forces literally driving Palestinians into the sea, by forcing them onto boats after they were expelled from their homes.
> (http://news.sky.com/story/1148934/israel-will-not-let-iran-get-nuclear-bomb?plckFindCommentKey= CommentKey:eb337c80-2f59-4eb7-87e1-d057f06dc888)

Let's at least agree that the use of this phrase at this time is historically unjustified!

Chapter 10
Suez and Beyond

Aftermath of 1948

Mary Grey

My first reaction on addressing this topic is a sense of shame that I had never looked at the Suez crisis from an Arab–Israeli perspective. As a child it dimly entered my world as being a disaster for Britain. I did not then connect it with the period of the collapsing British Empire. Later, on marrying Nicholas, I became more aware of the event as a personal disaster for Anthony Eden, the then Prime minister of Britain – whose brother Timothy was Nicholas's godfather. But now I engage with it in terms of Arab–Israeli relations.

The official version is straightforward enough. The attack followed the President of Egypt, Gamal Abdel Nasser's decision of 26 July 1956 to nationalize the Suez Canal, after the withdrawal of an offer by Britain and the United States to fund the building of the Aswan Dam. This was in response to Egypt's new ties with the Soviet Union and recognizing the People's Republic of China during the height of tensions between China and Taiwan. The aims of the attack were primarily to regain Western control of the canal and to remove Nasser from power. The crisis highlighted the danger that Arab nationalism posed to Western access to the Middle East oil.

Less than a day after Israel invaded Egypt, Britain and France issued a joint ultimatum to Egypt and Israel, and then began to bomb Cairo. Despite the denials of the Israeli, British and French governments, allegations began to emerge that the invasion of Egypt had been planned beforehand by the three powers. Anglo-French forces withdrew before the end of the year, but Israeli forces remained until March 1957. In April the canal was fully reopened to shipping, but other repercussions followed.

The three allies, especially Israel, were mainly successful in attaining their immediate military objectives, but pressure from the United States and the USSR at the United Nations and elsewhere forced them to withdraw. As a result of the outside pressure, Britain and France failed in their political and strategic aims of controlling the canal and removing Nasser from power. Israel fulfilled some of its objectives, such as attaining freedom of navigation through the Straits of Tiran (http://en.wikipedia.org/wiki/Suez_Crisis).

But let us take a step back and try to understand Israel's involvement. After 1948 the Palestinian Arabs have been crushed and driven out. The new-born state of Israel is victorious over the surrounding Arab states though understandably fearful of their continuing opposition. After the 1948 war according to Israel, many Arabs tried to infiltrate the country abetted by Arab governments (Shlaim 2009, pp. 85–86). The propaganda was that this was Arab guerrilla warfare designed to weaken the infant state. But Benny Morris suggests that the motives were more economic and social rather than political. Many refugees returned, looking for relatives, returning to homes, recovering possessions and tending their fields. Although there were acts of terror, Morris thinks – on the basis of meticulous research – that 90 per cent of these 'infiltrations' were economically motivated. Between 2,700 and 3,000 people, mostly unarmed, were killed by Israeli soldiers.

Each Arab country dealt with these cross-border forays in their own way. But Israeli reprisals were severe. For example, there was a raid on the West Bank village of Qibya in October 1953, commanded by a certain major called Ariel Sharon – who will become a key player in our story. He blew up 45 houses and killed 69 Jordanians.

But a key moment in the relations between Israel and Egypt came when Ben-Gurion ordered a raid on the Egyptian army camp in Gaza city in which 38 Egyptian soldiers were killed and many wounded. Before this Egypt had a consistent policy of curbing border raids into Israel, but this incident changed their attitudes towards the Palestinians.

It seems to me that this could have been a decisive moment for reconciliation after the events of 1948, but it became the opposite, largely because of the warlike disposition of Ben-Gurion. According to Shlaim (2009, p. 91), Ben-Gurion failed to understand the impact of the Gaza raid on Egypt and Nasser and it was now downhill all the way. There were indeed moderate influences within his government, notably Moshe Sharrett, who was sensitive both to Arab feelings and world opinion. Moderates like Sharrett advocated peaceful co-existence. And apparently Nasser respected him. But he was no match for the ambitions of Ben-Gurion who emerged from his desert retreat to take over and authorize the Gaza raid and oust Sharrett from his position. What had begun as local scuffles escalated into an international war – thereby stoking the fires of Arab hatred.

Do you now agree that this outcome could have been averted?

Obstacles to Reconciliation

Dan Cohn-Sherbok

Before turning to the post-war period, I want to go back to your observation in the last chapter about the claim that the Arabs wished to drive the Jewish settlers in Palestine into the sea. You may be correct that this phrase was not actually used by any Palestinian leader, but there is no doubt that the Palestinians sought to drive the Jews from Palestine. This was the clear aim of the Arab armies that invaded the newly created the Jewish state in 1948. You will remember that the Grand Mufti during the Second World War sought to persuade the Axis powers to eliminate the proposed the Jewish state from the Holy Land. Hence, even if the expression 'drive the Jews into the sea' is simply hyperbole, there is no question that the Palestinians were intent on destroying the newly created State of Israel.

Throughout our discussion we have lamented the failure of the Jews and Arabs to compromise. I reiterate my claim that this was primarily due to Arab intransigence. The history of Arab aggression in the years leading up to the War of Independence (or Nakba as you call it), and the determination of the Arabs to thwart partition through invasion and war is testimony to this fact. You assert that if the war had not taken place, there would have been peace with no justice. Perhaps so. But in my view this would have been preferable to armed conflict with its horrendous consequences for both the Palestinians and Jews.

Yet despite Arab intransigence during the early history of modern Israel, in the following years decisions taken by both Israel and the Palestinians made reconciliation even more difficult. In this both the Arabs and Jews are to blame. Let me begin with the aftermath of the War of Independence. On 27 June 1948 Count Bernadotte the chief negotiator appointed by the UN, submitted a plan providing for a union involving the whole of Mandate Palestine in a partnership between the kingdom of Jordan and the Jewish state. Jordan was to be in possession of its West Bank territory including East Jerusalem. The Arabs would thereby acquire the whole of the Negev, and Israel was to be allocated western Galilee. Unlimited Jewish immigration would be allowed for two years. Subsequently it would be controlled by a United Nations Agency. Finally, all Arabs would be allowed to return to their former homes. Unfortunately, such a plan was unacceptable to both the Jews and Arabs. From the Israeli side, the lack of sovereignty was a fundamental obstacle; for the Arabs, such a proposal was perceived as granting too many concessions. This failure to agree to the terms of this plan undermined the possibility for future stability in the region. On 8 July, the day before the truce was to expire, fighting broke out in the Negev which continued for 10 days. As a consequence of this conflict, the Israelis succeeded in widening the Jerusalem corridor; in addition they captured large areas of Lower Galilee. All this could have been avoided if an agreement had been made by both sides.

The situation deteriorated further by Israel's policy concerning Palestinian refugees. When the second truce was established, more than half a million Arabs had fled from Israeli territory. From the earliest stage, the Israeli government was opposed to their return. On 16 June Prime Minister David Ben-Gurion declared to his

Cabinet that those who had taken up arms against the Jewish state would have to bear the consequences. Given the Arab onslaught against the Jewish nation during the war, such a policy was understandable, yet it laid the foundations for future conflict and the evolution of the Palestinian refugee problem.

On 5 July 1950 the Israel government enacted the Law of Return which exacerbated these difficulties. This legislation guaranteed the right of every Jew, regardless of where he or she lives, to enter Israel as an immigrant and become a citizen on arrival. This new law, Ben-Gurion explained, established that not only does the state accord the right of settlement to the Jews living abroad, but that this right is inherent in every Jew by virtue of being a Jew. In the light of the Holocaust, it is understandable why the Jewish community was anxious to provide a place of refuge to the Jews world-wide. Yet, it led to bitter resentment on the part of Arab refugees who were denied a similar right, and it is this issue – perhaps more than any other – which poses a fundamental stumbling block to a negotiated settlement. At this early point in Israel's history, it is a great pity that more thought was not given to finding a way forward for the Jews and Arabs to live together in the land of their ancestors.

The Right to Return – Still a Burning Issue

Mary Grey

For the first time I agree with almost all the points you make, (!) and I think it is right to flag up that in this tragic tale that this, the post-1948 period, was one of the moments when there might have been reconciliation or uneasy co-existence. But, as I said in my last exchange, sadly, it became the opposite, largely because of the warlike disposition of Ben-Gurion (Section 1 'Aftermath of 1948').

It is also true that in 1948 the international community felt a deep sense of responsibility for this mass dispossession, the flight of refugees and the Zionist transfer policy that began at this time. The United Nations mediator, Count Folke Bernadotte, who – as you related – was later assassinated by a Zionist terrorist hit squad, had himself stated that it would be **an offence against the principles of elemental justice** if these innocent victims of the conflict were denied the right to return to their homes, while Jewish immigrants flow into Palestine.

But it was the United Nations Resolution 194 that remains critical: Article 11 of the resolution reads:

> (The General Assembly) Resolves that the refugees wishing to return to their homes and live at peace with their neighbours should be permitted to do so at the earliest practicable date, and that compensation should be paid for the property of those choosing not to return and for loss of or damage to property which, under principles of international law or in equity, should be made good by the Governments or authorities responsible.

As you know, since the late 1960s, this article has increasingly been quoted by those who interpret it as a basis for the 'right of return' of Palestinian refugees. But, Israel has always contested this reading, pointing out that the text merely states that the refugees 'should be permitted' to return to their homes at the 'earliest practicable date' and this recommendation applies only to those 'wishing to . . . live at peace with their neighbours' (http://www.wikipedia/wiki/Palestinian_right_of_Return#UnitedNations_General_Assembly_resolution194).

In particular, it was David Ben-Gurion, the first Prime Minister of Israel, who insisted in an interview with the members of the Conciliations Commission that as long as Israel could not count on the dedication of any Arab refugees to remain 'at peace with their neighbours' – a consequence, he contended, of the Arab states' unwillingness to remain at peace with the state of Israel – resettlement was not an obligation for his country.

As you are aware, the flow of refugees dramatically increased after the 1967 war. But today, the problem has escalated into the third generation and is an even more burning issue – given the sheer numbers involved. Even if today's Palestinians were not alive when these events took place, the issue is a passionate one for them. When I visited Dheishe refugee camp in Bethlehem recently, a young girl pointed out the significance of the symbol of the key: many of the survivors of the 1948 exodus still sleep with the key of their front door under the pillow! This girl then introduced me to her grandmother, forced to flee from a village outside Jerusalem – who showed me her key!

It is as if these events are still live in the present. Nakba day was celebrated in Bethlehem with the key symbol still holding central

During the period 1950–1955 only 10 per cent of cross-border Arab infiltrations were by military bands. The bulk of the early border troubles were cases of the Palestinians sneaking back to collect possessions, harvest crops or simply see the homesteads they had lost. In some cases the incursions were Bedouin tribesman wandering across unmarked borders. Yet, whatever the motives of those making these raids, the Israel Defense Force responded with ferocity. Borders were mined and suspects shot. The bodies of those who were slain were booby-trapped to kill relatives coming to collect them. Over six years about 5,000 Palestinians were killed. It must be remembered, however, that semi-military incursions did take place by independent groups of Palestinian fedayeen. In 1953 for example, with Egyptian backing, young Palestinians launched regular, planned attacks on Israeli civilians. This led to the creation by Israel of Unit 101 to wipe out these terrorists under the command of Major Ariel Sharon. Israeli defenders of Unit 101 argue that it kept Israel safer than it otherwise would have been. Critics of Israel, however, maintain that it provoked further anger and increased the chances of other attacks. Moreover, they point out that Unit 101 was responsible for two incidents that the Palestinians labeled massacres.

Following the Suez War, Israel was perceived in the West as an important power in the Middle East. Ben-Gurion remained as Prime Minister until his resignation in 1963. The Suez setback had ended any hopes that he might once have had about Israel living at peace with its neighbors within secure borders. In 1961 fresh waves of immigrants had swelled the population to around 2.2 million. Despite such growth, the Palestinians remained determined to create their own state. President Nasser of Egypt set up a Voice of Palestine radio station, a Palestinian newspaper and convened the first Arab summit to create the Palestine Liberation Organization (PLO) in 1964, and two years later, the Palestinian Liberation Army (PLA). He selected Ahmad Shukayri to lead the PLO which had been created as a response to Israel's completion of the National Water Carrier scheme, a canal (Beit Netopha) that took water from Lake Tiberias to the Negev Desert. This development infuriated Syria, and on several occasions disputes between the two countries over the use of water from the River Jordan flared into border conflicts. In 1963 Syria called for all-out war against Israel. Previously in 1959 the place. And of course, many murals in the camps depict the village from which the people have been forced to flee.

But the central question, with which I ended my last exchange, is still: in the development post-1948 and the build-up to the Suez war and after, was there ever a chance for the moderate voice in Israeli politics to prevail?

The Palestinian Struggle

Dan Cohn-Sherbok

You have discussed Ben-Gurion's role in the creation of the State of Israel. After the war of 1948–1949 he was convinced that no Arab state would accept peaceful co-existence with Israel. Thus, in his view Israel was obliged to adopt a policy of aggressive defense, responding to every threat with retaliation and if necessary pre-emptive strikes. Such a policy might appear extreme, but for Ben-Gurion and others this stance was the result of the bitter lessons of history. According to these Zionists, for almost 2,000 years the Jews had been a despised and persecuted people. Such attitudes had culminated in the Nazi's deliberate attempt to annihilate Jewry. Yet, due to Jewish resistance and determination, the Jews had survived. Now that the nation had a state of its own, a secure haven where they would be free from destruction, it would be folly not to defend such new-founded security. If there would be lasting peace between Israel and its neighbors, it would have to be on Israel's terms.

As you noted, not all Israelis subscribed to Ben-Gurion's viewpoint. Foremost among those who took a less hawkish position was Moshe Sharrett who played a key role in the armistices of 1949. Although he accepted that security was of primary importance, he believed that in the long term this could be established only by reaching some permanent settlement with Israel's neighbors. Such a position might call for a land-for-peace arrangement. As we will see, these two views – Ben-Gurion's and Sharrett's – have dominated Israeli politics from the 1950s until the present day. Arguably, it is a pity that Sharrett's vision has not predominated and that there has been unwillingness to accept the UN resolution you quoted about repatriation. As we will see, the Law of Return has become possibly the most crucial issue in subsequent negotiations between Israel and the Palestinians.

Palestinians exiles living in Kuwait formed a nationalist organization of their own, Fatah (conquest).

Fatah's founders, including Yasser Arafat, were discouraged by the failure of fellow Arabs to help the Palestinians. Consequently, Fatah initially rejected the PLO as an empty gesture by Arab states. Fatah's claim was that by force of arms the Israelis had created a state that had no right to exist. Its aim was to destroy Israel and replace it with a single, secular Arab–Jewish Palestine. Its tactics included bombings and hijackings. Its weaponry and explosives were communist-supplied and Syria was identified as the state most likely to shelter Fatah's fighters. With the creation of the PLO and Fatah, the stage was set for an unending struggle against Israel. Throughout our discussion we have stressed the failures of both Zionists and Israelis to find a way to live in peace and concord. From the early decades of the twentieth century Arabs had rejected the creation of a Jewish homeland. Once established, they had fought to destroy it, and this quest became the hallmark of all future dealings with the Zionists and their supporters.

The Persistence of Non-violence

Mary Grey

I agree that, at this difficult period, attitudes have hardened and the stage seems set for escalating violence. As Benny Morris wrote:

> If the destruction of Israel was not Arab policy before, after 1956 it most certainly was. While border clashes and terrorist infiltration remained rare during 1957–1962, the political will to belligerence had vastly increased in the Arab world as a result of Israel's collusion with the ex-imperialist powers and the onslaught against Egypt.
>
> (Morris 1999, p. 301)

We have already noted that the military and expansionist policies of David Ben-Gurion prevailed over those of the moderate leader, Moshe Sharrett. And steadily, in the background, the Hebraicisation of Arab villages progressed – their original names being wiped from the map. In the Negev, for example, the committee assigned Hebrew names to 561 geographical features including mountains, valleys, springs and waterholes, using the Bible as a resource.

(Masalha 2007, p. 68)

Many Arab sites were disguised by the planting of conifer forests – yet this tree is not native to Palestine.

As you describe, the PLO was founded with its stated goal as the 'liberation of Palestine' through armed struggle. It also called for a right of return and self-determination for the Palestinians. The Palestinian statehood was not mentioned. And from this Fatah developed.

But to follow this track of violent tactics is to miss the non-violent trajectory among the Palestinians. The first dimension of non-violence resistance is the way of *sumud* – which means steadfastness, resilience, staying in the land. After the shock of the *nakba* – which took some years – writes Mazin Qumsiyeh, the Palestinians started mobilizing and founded a poets' committee, *rabita,* in 1952 (Qumsiyeh 2011, pp. 100–101).[1] Many Arabs in Israel joined the communist party – there being no acceptable alternative: the party's cultural programmes gave voice to poets and writers.

There were various attempts to set up a Popular Front – to work for the return of Refugees and end land confiscation – and this in fact sent a 13-page memorandum to the United States on the status of the Palestinians within Israel. But the authorities reacted by disbanding the movement and sentencing one member to 10 years' imprisonment. Progressive elements of society – including Arab students at the Hebrew University established the 'Arab–Jewish committee' in 1961 to end military rule. In fact the Arab activism at Israeli universities would mushroom over the decades.

Thus did 12 per cent of the Palestinians within Israel struggle to survive and resist by civil methods – as did Palestinian refugees beyond the Green Line in the West Bank, Gaza and other Arab countries (Qumsiyeh 2011, p. 104). An impressive focus on education and training for leadership was embarked on. (For example,

---

[1]This was largely unnoticed until a book by Ghassan Kanafani, *Literature of Resistance in Palestine* was written in 1968. He was murdered by a car-bomb in Beirut 1972.

Yasser Arafat studied engineering at King Fuad I University.)[2] A period of non-operation and direct resistance intensified and culminated in a crackdown on Palestinian resistance in 1956. This in turn led to the founding of the PLO – which actually accomplished little initially, due to the fact that it had side-stepped traditional Palestinian leadership, viz., the Al-Husseini and Al Nashashibi families. Fatah would address this issue.

But I want to end this letter with two profound reflections on the violent nature of military action, one by the retiring Archbishop of Galilee, Elias Chacour, and the other by Moshe Dayan in the course of the Suez war. Elias Chacour as a young child had been driven out of his village of Biram with his family and wrote later:

> I could not help but view the Zionists as victims too – victims of something far worse than death camps. Beyond the hurling of bombs, the murder of innocents and bearing to the world false witness against their neighbour, the Zionists were stricken with a disease of the spirit. It was as if some demon of violence had been loosed and it whispered cunningly, *Might is right. Achieve your own ends by whatever means necessary – all in the name of God* ... For the first time I saw the face of my true enemy and the enemy of all who are the friends of God and of peace. It was not the Zionists but the demon of militarism.
> (Chacour 1984, pp. 126–127)

My second example is perhaps more surprising: an Egyptian ambush had killed a security officer of a kibbutz, Ro'i Rothberg and Dayan delivered the eulogy:

> Yesterday at dawn Ro'i was murdered. The quiet of the spring morning blinded him, and he did not see those who sought his life hiding behind the furrow. Let us not today cast blame on the murderers. What can we say against their terrible hatred of us? For eight years now they have say in the terrible refugee camps of Gaza, and have watched how before their very eyes, we have turned their lands and villages, where they and their forefathers previously dwelled, into our home. It is not among the Arabs of

---

[2]This would become the University of Cairo.

Gaza, but in our own midst that we must seek Ro'is blood. How did we shut our eyes and refuse to look squarely at our fate, and see, in all its brutality, the fate of our generation?

(Morris 1999, pp. 187–188)

It is such clear and courageous thinking from both sides of the conflict that means that violence – and I realize we are going to face much worse – need not have the last word.

The Plight of the Refugees

Dan Cohn-Sherbok

You are right to point out the terrible situation that refugees faced after 1949; as I noted, I have great sympathy for their plight. The Palestinian refugees beyond Israel were gathered together by relief and other agencies and settled in vast tented caps. There were four on the East Bank of the River Jordan, 19 on the West Bank; 15 in Lebanon; eight in the Gaza Strip; and nine in Syria. Some of these temporary camps were later emptied and their occupants moved on. In the eyes of Israelis, these camps were a ring of hatred around the newly founded the Jewish state. In just a few months after the war the inhabitants had become stateless, Arab refugees without a home. Some of those marooned in the camps were illiterate or semi-literate farmers; others were unskilled laborers.

Those who moved into Lebanon fared better than elsewhere. From the six camps scattered around Beirut, there were prospects of employment. Conditions were worst in the Gaza Strip where population density was the highest. Few facilities existed for employment. The camps in Syria and Jordan were better, but life was still deplorable. In Jordan the large number of refugees was a problem for King Abdullah. The native Jordanians were outnumbered by these immigrants. Abdullah responded by claiming to be their true leader in the hope that he would be able to rule over a Pan-Arab country that included his own state incorporating the West Bank as well as Syria, Lebanon and possibly even Iraq. The refugees were given citizenship and opportunities for education. To support this programme of Jordanization, Palestinian nationalist organizations, political parties and the media were banned.

On the West Bank, however, attempts at Jordanization were less successful. Local services were strained and there was constant conflict between the original inhabitants and the refugees. Dismayed by the situation, the Palestinians were encouraged by Nasser's attempt to revive Arab nationalism. The Arab nation, he declared, would drive out the imperialists and the Zionists, and the people of Palestine would be able to return home.

The question I want to put to you is why 60 years later the refugee camps are still there: hotbeds of hatred, homelessness and dreams of a better life. Why did the Arab nations who were intent on driving the Israelis out of Palestine not seek to integrate the Palestinians into Arab lands, build them homes, provide educational opportunities and insure that their suffering would end? You stress the importance of non-violence in dealing with human tragedy – it is in this spirit that I ask this question. In the last few exchanges, you highlight the injustices perpetrated against the Arabs who fled from Palestine and were refused repatriation in their native land. You are dismayed by what you describe as the Hebricisation of Arab villages and the disguise of Arab sites. Your quotation from Elias Chacour portrays the Zionists as diseased in spirit; they are, in his view, the enemy of all who are the friends of God and of peace. No doubt Dayan in his eulogy of Ro'i Rothberg was right in pointing to the causes of Arab hatred of Israel as a result of life in the camps. But, in making your case against Israeli militarization, I am puzzled why you say nothing about the attitudes of Arab nations concerning the plight of the refugees. Why did they leave their Palestinian brothers and sisters to suffer deprivation. Why did they not close down the camps? Why did they not come to their aid?

Since the State of Israel was founded, the Israeli government has done everything possible to rescue the Jews who were in situations similar to the Palestinian refugees or worse. There were massive airlifts to rescue the Jews from Yemen in Operation Magic Carpet; in addition, enormous resources were poured into airlifts (Operation Solomon) to rescue the Jews of Ethiopia who were facing dangerous political destabilization in the country. Many of the surrounding Arab nations with their enormous oil revenues could have organized a similar plan for the Palestinians. Yet, apparently to make a political point, they left them where they were.

Chapter 11
The Six-Day War and Its Aftermath

Continuing Aggression

Dan Cohn-Sherbok

Despite the armistice agreements between Israel and its neighbours, attacks against the Jewish state continued, including the conflict over Suez in 1956. As we noted, Fatah was founded by Yasser Arafat and bases were established in most Arab countries. The same year Nasser summoned Arab leaders to a summit in Cairo to discuss Israel's action to divert water from the River Jordan to the Negev desert. The central concern was that this was being done to strengthen Israel's capacity to absorb large numbers of immigrants. At this meeting, Arab representatives delegated a Palestinian leader, Ahmed al-Shukairy, to explore ways to create a representative body of all Palestinians. This ultimately became the Palestine Liberation Organization (PLO). Later, an assembly of Palestinians from throughout the world met an assembly in Jerusalem.

At this time the leadership of Fatah wanted to exhibit its strength. One group proposed launching attacks on Israeli targets.

Egypt wanted restraint, but Syria encouraged the idea of immediate assault and opened training camps. Later, Fatah launched several operations, but they were not effective. By the end of October 1966 Syria had given full support to Fatah, but Egypt was not involved. On 4 November, however, Egypt signed a new defense alliance with Syria, thereby committing itself to the liberation of Palestine. By early 1967 both Egypt and Israel were accusing one another of troop build-up on the Syrian front. The Six-Day War began on 5 June 1967, ending with a massive Arab defeat. Israel thereby became the dominant power in the Middle East. Israeli troops were stationed in the Suez Canal, the Red Sea and the River Jordan and held a line on Syria only thirty miles from Damascus. They controlled the whole of the country, including the banks of the Jordan and Jerusalem, along with one million Palestinians in the West Bank and Gaza Strip. Further, they occupied the Sinai Peninsula and a thousand square miles of Syrian territory on the Golan Heights. Approximately one million Arabs had been displaced. Some 350,000 Palestinians fled from the West Bank to the Bank of the Jordan. For at least 150,000 Palestinians, this was the second time they had been refugees. A further 160,000 people were refugees in Syria from the villages and farms of the Golan Heights. All this was the result of the Arab determination to destroy the newly created State of Israel.

Following Israel's victory, Egypt continued to launch a campaign of attacks, aimed at bolstering Arab morale and at the same time disrupting Israeli life. Undeterred in their determination to rid Palestine of the Jews, Palestinian representatives discussed what their next step should be. Yasser Arafat was convinced that the struggle should continue. Trips were made to the West Bank to encourage fellow Palestinians. Yet, Fatah's attempt to create an armed revolution in the West Bank was ineffective. Despite these obstacles, the leaders of Fatah continued to launch attacks on Israel. At this stage the various Palestinian movements failed to unite under one main group and the PLO was discredited in the eyes of many Palestinians and Arabs. Eventually on 3 February 1969 Arafat was elected Chairman of the Executive Committee of the PLO. In the same year the American administration proposed a peace settlement. The Secretary of State, William Rogers, put forward a plan for an agreement between Israel on one side, and Egypt and Jordan on the other. The proposal included Israeli withdrawal as part of a package settlement, cessation of the state of war, secure and recognized borders, demilitarized zones and special arrangements in Gaza and Sharm al-Sheikh, freedom of navigation through the Straits of Tiran, Israel's use of the Suez Canal and settlement of the refugee problem. When the Egyptians agreed in principle to a modified revised peace agreement, the Palestinians unleashed a storm of protest among the resistance organizations in Jordan. Arafat and Fatah attacked Nasser. Yet, again peace and reconciliation between Israel and its Arab neighbours became a distant hope.

Triumph and Tragedy

Mary Grey

You again judge this tragic war in terms of Arab aggression. Superficially I agree this is one way to look at it. Indeed, the Biblical scholar the late Michael Prior, speaks for many of us in the west who at that point failed to understand the bigger picture:

Halfway through my undergraduate theology the Israeli–Arab war broke out on 5 June 1967, arousing my first interest in the region. Although not matching the Nintendo-like portrayal of war during the Gulf War of 1991, the television, pictures, reports and commentary portrayed a classic David versus Goliath conflict, with diminutive, innocent Israel repulsing its rapacious Arab predators. The comprehensive victories over several Arab States . . . produced surges of delight in me. I was to learn much later that the 1967 war inaugurated a new phase in the Zionist conquest of Mandated Palestine, one which brought theological assertions and biblical interpretations to the very heart of the ideology which propelled the Israeli conquest (Prior in Macpherson (ed.) 2006, p. 202).

The triumph of Israel is beyond question, with heavy Arab casualties: between 10,000 and 15,000 Egyptians were killed – to mention only one country. The tragedy lies both in the consequences for the Palestinians, some of which you have described; but also that an opportunity for clemency and understanding was lost between Israel and the Palestinians. As Rabbi Michael Lerner writes:

> I too hoped that Israel would use that triumph to show generosity toward the Palestinian people who had offered no resistance to the IDF and who had previously been under the rule of the Jordanian army. If ever there was a moment when generosity by Israel – building up the Palestinian economy and creating a peace-oriented and demilitarized Palestinian state – could have led to security for Israel, that was it.
>
> (Lerner, 15 June 2013)

Many writers dispute the origins of the war, claiming that Arab aggression has been exaggerated: the Palestinians had been quiescent for more than a decade (Morris 1999, p. 303). I think also that you characterize the PLO solely as an aggressive violent organization. You omit its other important activities. As Canon Naim Ateek writes:

> The PLO is best known for its military wing ... but very few realize the extent of the civilian services the PLO provides. It employs thousands of people who run schools, hospitals and health clinics, publish books and periodicals. Promote literacy programs, operate radio stations, work at economic development and so on.
>
> (Ateek 1989, p. 39)

But it is the way that the military triumph of the Six-Day War has come back to haunt Israel today that prompts the writer, Uri Avnery, to call this war a tragedy. Undoubtedly, he writes, victory was announced looked immense – 'so immense, indeed, that many believed it an act of God':

> Israeli public reaction was stupendous. The entire country was in delirium. Masses of victory-albums, victory-songs, victory-this and victory-that amounted to national hysteria. Hubris knew no bounds. I cannot claim that I was entirely untouched by it.
>
> (Avnery, *Tikkun*, 15 June 2013)

But, he continues, just as in a Greek tragedy, hubris did not go unpunished. The gold turned to dust. The greatest victory in Israel's history turned into its greatest curse. *The occupied territories are like the shirt of Nessus, glued to our body to poison and torment us* (My italics) (Avnery, *Tikkun*, 15 June 2013).

Avnery relates that, slowly, the Israeli government got used to the astonishing fact that there was no real pressure on Israel to withdraw from the occupied territories. So, not only was one quarter of the West Bank driven into exile; not only did General Dayan evict the inhabitants of the three Arab villages and eradicate any sign that they ever existed. (They have been replaced by a national park financed by the government of Canada and well-meaning Canadian citizens.) The writer Amos Kenan wrote a heart-rending report on this horrible eviction of the villagers, men, women, children and babies, who were made to march on foot under the scorching June sun all the way to Ramallah. Not only have the Palestinians been subject to an ever-increasing harsh Occupation since 1967, but as both Lerner and Avnery write, a historic opportunity was missed. The vast majority of today's Israelis, anyone less than 60 years old, cannot even imagine an Israel without the occupied territories.

Would you agree that there is an element of tragedy at this period of Israel's history and that an opportunity was missed?

Arab Aggression against Israel

Dan Cohn-Sherbok

The Six-Day War was a victory for Israel over the Arab states that sought its destruction. Its cause was the determination of these surrounding nations to wipe Israel off the map. In January 1964 at a summit meeting of Arab countries, Syria proposed using the 75,000 Palestinian refugees in the country as well as an even greater number in other Arab lands to destabilize Israel. At the Arab summit, it was formally accepted that Palestinians throughout the Arab world should seek to liberate their homeland and determine their destiny. Subsequently the Jordanian government allowed an Assembly of Palestinian Arabs to meet in East Jerusalem. As a consequence of these deliberations, the PLO was created: its aim was to attain the objective of liquidating Israel and a Palestine Liberation Army was created. This organization was to receive financial support from the Arab world and Nasser placed both Sinai and the Gaza Strip at its disposal.

On 8 April 1966 a Fatah squad crossed into Israel from Syria, planting a mine which killed an Israeli farmer. Another farmer was killed by a mine on 16 May. On 12 and 13 July more Fatah units crossed the border from Syria planting more mines. In the ensuing months more Fatah cross-border attacks were launched. On 4 November 1966 Syria signed a mutual defense pact with Egypt. It was Nasser's aim to rally the Arab States to a final assault against Israel. During the first three months of 1967 Syrian artillery bombardments and cross-border raids were launched on Israeli settlements in the north. On 7 April 1967 Syrian mortars on the Golan Heights were fired against kibbutz Gadlot.

Eventually Nasser emerged as the pivotal figure in this conflict. On 13 May Egyptian troops moved into the Sinai from which Israel had withdrawn its troops. In order to stem the rumour that Israel was preparing for war, an Israeli Independence Day parade was held on 15 May without the usual large numbers of tanks and weapons. Alarmed by the lack of heavy armour, the Egyptians accused Israel of having sent the missing equipment to the north, predicting that Israel would invade Syria. On 16 May Nasser ordered the United Nations to remove its forces from Sinai. On 20 May Israel reserves began a partial mobilization. The same day the Egyptian Minister of War travelled to Gaza to inspect the troops that had replaced the United Nations force. Alongside these soldiers were members of the Egyptian sponsored Palestinian Liberation Army. In Israel military leaders and politicians pressed for a pre-emptive strike against Egypt and Syria. However, the Chief of Staff, Yitzhak Rabin and the Prime Minister, Levi Eshkol, were reluctant to take this action. On 22 May Nasser declared that Egypt was reimposing her blockade of the Straits.

On 24 May U Thant, the Secretary General of the United Nations, flew to Egypt in an attempt to persuade Nasser not to precipitate a war. Nasser, however, would not agree. On 25 May American President Johnson declared that the blockade was illegal. Yet, despite such international pressure, Egyptian armoured units crossed the Suez Canal and took up positions inside Sinai. On 27 May the Israeli War Cabinet met to discuss whether to take action. At that stage opinion was divided. On 29 May Nasser spoke to the members of the Egyptian National Assembly. It was not simply the issue of the closure of the Straits which was the central problem, he stated. It was the aggression of Israel against the Palestinians in 1948. The following day King Hussein of Jordan flew to Cairo; at a meeting with Nasser he added Jordan to the Syrian–Egyptian defense pact. On 31 May troops from Iraq arrived in Egypt. On 2 June Nasser warned that if any power dared to make declarations on freedom of navigation in the Straits of Tiran, Egypt would deny that power oil and free navigation in the Suez Canal. Approximately 100,000 Egyptian troops and 900 tanks were deployed in Sinai. On the Golan Heights there were 75,000 Syrian soldiers and 400 tanks. In addition, the Jordanians had assembled 32,000 troops and 1,600 tanks. A further 150 tanks were travelling from Iraq through Jordan. A further 140,000 Egyptian troops and 300 tanks were also available if needed. There were also approximately 700 Arab combat aircraft. Surrounded by these hostile forces determined to wipe out the Jewish state, Israel launched an attack on 5 June.

This is the background to the Six-Day War. It is undeniable that Israel's future was at stake. Its Arab neighbours were determined to destroy the Jewish state. The PLO was created for this explicit purpose. Israel's crushing victory was met by relief and rejoicing throughout the Jewish world. You criticize Israel for its lack of magnanimity for the Palestinians who suffered as a result of this conflict. But you must consider what the consequences would have been for the Israelis if they had been defeated. Do you truly believe the Arab nations would have been concerned for Jewish welfare after having successfully destroyed Israel? The whole security of Israel was at stake. The Jews won the war; the last thing they were likely to do was to give opportunities for further Arab aggression.

Those who should have come to the aid of the Palestinians were not the Jews but the Arab nations who had joined together against Israel. Let me return to the question I asked you at the end of the last chapter: why did oil-rich Arab states not rescue the refugees from suffering and degradation? Why did they not offer them homes and integrate them into the countries where they had fled? Or at the very least why did they not provide adequate resources to ensure that the refugees could live with dignity?

Palestinian Refugees and Their Host Arab Countries
Mary Grey

Sometimes I think you have not read my answer to you! You write of the Arab States as 'wanting to wipe Israel off the map'; of the PLO wanting to liquidate Israel – ignoring my attempt to highlight the humanitarian and social side of the organization. And why would Palestinians not need an organization to protest at having lost their country? Conceived by the Arab states at the first Arab summit meeting, the 1964 Arab League summit (in Cairo), the stated goal of the PLO was indeed the 'liberation of Palestine' through armed struggle. The original PLO Charter (issued on 28 May 1964) stated that 'Palestine with its boundaries that existed at the time of the British mandate is an integral regional unit' and sought to 'prohibit . . . the existence and activity' of Zionism. It also called for a right of return and self-determination for Palestinians. Palestinian statehood was not mentioned, although in 1974 the PLO called for an independent state in the territory of Mandate Palestine. So the group has used multi-layered guerrilla tactics to attack Israel from their bases in Jordan (including the West Bank), Lebanon, Egypt (the Gaza Strip) and Syria. *But remember how weak they were compared with the forces of Israel.*

But let me not fall into the same trap and avoid your question. You have asked more than once: 'Why did the Arab countries not settle the refugees in their countries – meaning Lebanon, Jordan and Syria – rather than leaving them in camps?' I have been asking this question of Palestinians who remember the Nakba of 1948. First of all, they say that the Palestine refugee problem arose as a result of a pre-determined Zionist plan – as I have already described in referring to Ilan Pappé's work. Whereas you see Israel as being hospitable and welcoming to Jews under persecution in different parts of the world, the Palestinians see them as settling these groups in Palestinian homes, *their homes*, fully furnished and stocked with food, homes from which about 750,000 Palestinians had been driven.

Secondly, have you forgotten that Israel was accepted as a member state at the UN after it promised to repatriate the refugees, a promise Israel later reneged upon? In fact, Count Folk Bernadotte, UN envoy to Palestine, was assassinated by a member of the Stern gang because he called for the repatriation of Palestinian refugees as soon as possible.

But perhaps the most important point is to be aware that the Palestinian people are of course Arabs, a distinct people – but who are not Jordanians or Lebanese or Egyptian or other. Their country is Palestine. Their land is Palestine. They were to be hosted in those Arab countries only until UN resolution 194 calling for the repatriation and compensation of Palestinian refugees was passed. To become absorbed into Jordan, Lebanon or Syria would be to lose their identity as Palestinians. Maybe that is not fully understood.

Also, it must be noted that the Palestinian refugees created a great burden on the host countries – economically, demographically and otherwise. These host countries have regularly stated that they are willing to allow the Jews who left their homes in the Arab countries to return home if they so wished. I cannot stress enough how much it would mean to the Palestinians to return to their own homes, the villages they love and the trees they have planted.

But you would be right in asserting that consequences of the Six-Day War would radicalize the Palestinians and significantly weaken Nasser's influence. In fact, the resounding defeat of Syria, Jordan and Egypt in the War destroyed the credibility of Arab states that had tried to be defenders of the Palestinian people and their nationalist cause. Now the way was opened, particularly after the Battle of Karameh in March 1968, for Yasser Arafat to rise to power. He advocated guerrilla warfare and successfully sought to make the PLO a fully independent organization under the control of the *fedayeen* organizations.[1] At the Palestinian National Congress meeting of 1969 Fatah gained control of the executive bodies of the PLO and Yasser Arafat was appointed PLO chairman at the Palestinian National Congress in Cairo on 4 February 1969.

You will say that the PLO is now organized to attack Israel: but how could the Palestinians not fight to regain possession of their land?

---

[1] *Fedayeen* means literally 'redeemers' or 'those who sacrifice'. Not normally connected to an organized government or military, they often operate in areas with little or no government control and are associated with the role of resistance against occupation or tyranny.

The PLO and the Jews

Dan Cohn-Sherbok

I read your last exchanges with care. You stress the humanitarian activities of the PLO. I do not dispute that the PLO had these social concerns. But the PLO's main objective was to wipe Israel off the map. Its primary goal was to destroy the Jewish state. It was a liquidation – not a welfare – organization. It endorsed and encouraged violence as the means of achieving its end. You frequently stress that you are an advocate of peace. That you deplore war. But it is clear that you value justice as a higher goal, and that you support the Palestinian cause. You perceive Israel as the aggressor with expansionist aspirations. You clearly believe the PLO was justified in its aims. Despite your alleged concern for peaceful reconciliation, what you in fact endorse is violence in the name of justice. You write: 'How could the Palestinians not fight to gain possession of their land?' It is not the dove of peace that you bring to this conflict but rather violence and warfare.

You argue that the Zionists deliberately sought to evacuate the Palestinians from Palestine and settle Jewish refugees in their homes. This you believe was an intentional plan devised by Zionist leaders such as David Ben-Gurion. What such an interpretation fails to note is that the Palestinian refugee problem was primarily the result of a war unleashed by Arab states against Israel. It is inconceivable that Israel would have welcomed such an attack so that it could drive out the Palestinians and take their homes. On the contrary, when David Ben-Gurion read out the Declaration of Independence on 18 May 1948 he explicitly stated Israel's hopes for peaceful coexistence with its Arab neighbours. These were not pious, empty words but the expression of a real desire for harmony and peace. Yet even as these words were uttered in Tel Aviv, Jews in Israel and beyond knew that they would be followed (as they were the next day) by a massive Arab attack.

You are right that it has always been a central feature of Zionism that Israel would welcome Jews experiencing persecution in other parts of the world. It is perverse to believe, as you seem to, that Zionism helped Jewish refugees merely to colonize Palestine. The whole point of Zionism is to protect Jews from aggression. This, however, should not have been at the expense of Palestinian refugees, and I (like you) deplore Israel's unwillingness to follow UN Resolution 194 which calls for the repatriation of Palestinian refugees. Yet, it is naive to believe – as you clearly do – that Arab states currently seek to welcome Jews who previously left these countries and would now treat them as equal citizens. Aware of the intense hostility of these states to Israel and the growth of Jew-hatred, these Jewish refugees were fearful for their future in these Arab lands and fled in terror. There is no evidence that such antipathy to Jews has dissipated.

Your answer to my question concerning the seeming lack of concern for the Palestinians in the countries where they reside is that their absorption would undermine and destroy Palestinian identity. You write that the Palestinians are a distinct people; they are not Jordanians or Lebanese or Syrians. They were therefore to be temporary residents in the host countries until they could return to their native homeland. This may be so. Yet, I do not believe it is a sufficient justification for the poverty, hardship and suffering they have endured for sixty years in refugee camps. Of course these refugees pose a significant economic and demographic problem for the countries where they reside. But surely more could have been done by the governments of Egypt, Jordan, Lebanon, Syria and elsewhere to ease their suffering and provide them with decent housing and welfare facilities. If Jews in any country had found themselves in such terrible circumstances, there is no doubt that the world Jewish community would have come to their aid. Indeed, the primary aim of the Zionists was to rescue Jews from precisely such adversity, and it is the triumph of Zionism that this aim has been repeatedly accomplished since the Jewish state was founded.

Ben-Gurion and 'Peaceful Coexistence' – Confronting the Truth

Mary Grey

Sometimes I wonder whether we inhabit the same universe! Your dismissal of my motives of peace with justice is both cruel and unjustified. You write:

> It is not the dove of peace that you bring to this conflict but rather violence and warfare.

I do not and never will advocate violence. But I recognize I am saying this from a context which is not threatening my life and home and know I'm really fortunate in this. (Yet my mother's ancestors fled the Irish famine in the nineteenth century, arriving impoverished in England.) I don't condone Palestinian violence but understand why it happened. They had lost everything and been driven into becoming refugees for the second time. Did you realize that after the Nakba in 1948 male Palestinians for the age of 10 were caged in large pens – after Israeli 'search and arrest' operations before being moved to prison camps where they languished for most of 1949? That they were punished if they tried to come back to their homes and that soon a law was passed forbidding the sale of land to 'non-Jews'? (Ilan Pappé 2006, pp. 200–202)

It is hardly surprising that the Palestinians, finding all their country under Israeli occupation and its entire people either expelled or under alien rule, lost faith in the world community and came to realize that,

> even in this era of so-called civilization, International Law and U.N. Charter, might is right and what is lost by force can be regained only by force. They intensified, therefore, their resistance by guerrilla attacks against Israeli military personnel and objectives. The Israelis retaliated by ruthless bombardment using Phantom jets and napalm against the defenseless men, women and children in their refugee camps in Jordan, Lebanon and Syria. The Palestinian resistance was vilified by Zionist propaganda and their captured members were savagely tortured in Israeli hands.
>
> (www.palestinehistory.com/issues/refugee/ref1967)

Secondly, you refer to David Ben-Gurion's famous speech in 1967, *The Declaration of Independence,* where he says:

> We appeal – in the very midst of the onslaught launched against us now for months – to the Arab inhabitants of the State of Israel to preserve peace and participate in the upbuilding of

the State on the basis of full and equal citizenship and due representation in all its provisional and permanent institutions.
(www.mideastweb.org/bg1947)

I agree that this is a call for peaceful coexistence and also that it was – rightly – a momentous occasion for the worldwide Jewish community. But there is a lot of evidence that Ben-Gurion did not actually mean what he said. For example, a leading Zionist, Nahum Goldmann – President of the Jewish congress 1948–1977 – criticized Ben-Gurion for what he viewed as a confrontational approach to the Arab world. Goldmann wrote:

> Ben-Gurion is the man principally responsible for the anti-Arab policy, because it was he who molded the thinking of generations of Israelis.

Ben-Gurion – who had already said in 1948 – 'I believe in our power, in our power which will grow, and if it will grow agreement will come . . . ' believed a peaceful solution with the Arabs had no chance and began preparing the Yishuv for war. In his *War Diaries* in February 1948, he wrote:

> The war shall give us the land. The concepts of 'ours' and 'not ours' are peace concepts only, and they lose their meaning during war. Also later he confirmed this by stating that, 'In the Negev we shall not buy the land. We shall conquer it. You forget that we are at war'
> (http://en/wikipedia/wiki/David_Ben-Gurion)

So the picture is not a clear as you describe. I already cited Ben-Gurion in section 'The Bible is Our Mandate!' of Chapter 2 in his recourse to the Bible to justify conquest and confiscation of Arab land. But at this point of our story it is important to mention the influence of two other figures, the Rabbis Kook, father and son. Particularly Rabbi Zvi Yehuda HaCohen Kook was prominent in the newly energized National Religious Party (NRP) which saw the conquests of 1967 as part of the Divine redemptive plan (the first peal of deliverance (Morris 1999, pp. 331–332) and along with Ben-Gurion's appeal to the Bible, were responsible for the justification of growing expansionism and of the new settler movement (Gush Emunim). For Kook and his disciples, as Nur Masalha writes,

> Israel must continue the ancient biblical battles over settlement of the 'Land of Israel' to be won by a combination of religious faith and military might.
>
> (Masalha 2007, p. 139)

As you know, initially Zionism was a secular movement, but this new development changed everything. The belief of the NRP was that the beginning of the 'final redemption', which would end in the coming of the Jewish messiah, had been ushered in.

At the end of this period, Israel's status in the region as a military power has been established; the policy of confiscation and conquest of Arab land is well underway with a dual justification of military might and biblical underpinning. I cannot see how you can argue with any truth for Ben-Gurion's supposed policy of 'peaceful coexistence'.

Chapter 12
Renewed Conflict between Israel and the Arabs

Yasser Arafat and the Battle of Karameh

Mary Grey

We now enter on a period of escalating violence – as the conflict between the Arab States and Israel continues, as well as Arab–Israeli conflict within Israel and the West Bank. We have alluded to Yasser Arafat briefly but he now becomes a key figure in this period.

Arafat was born in Cairo in 1929. He became an Arab nationalist at Cairo University, when he began procuring weapons to be smuggled into Palestine. During the 1948 War, Arafat left the University and, along with other Arabs, sought to enter Palestine to join Arab forces fighting against Israeli troops. However, instead of joining the ranks of the Palestinian Fedayeen (guerrillas) Arafat fought alongside the Muslim Brotherhood, although he did not join the organization. In early 1949 when Israel was winning the war, Arafat returned to Cairo from a lack of logistical support.

Returning to the University, Arafat studied civil engineering and served as president of the General Union of Palestinian Students from 1952 to 1956. Called to fight with Egyptian forces during the

Suez Crisis, he never actually fought on the battlefield. Following this, Egyptian president Nasser agreed to allow the United Nations Emergency Force to establish itself in the Sinai Peninsula and Gaza Strip, causing the expulsion of all guerrilla forces there – including Arafat. After settling in Kuwait, Arafat worked as a school teacher.

As Arafat began to develop friendships with Palestinians he and the others gradually founded Fatah – a word used in early Islamic times to refer to 'conquest'.

As we have both written, Fatah dedicated itself to the liberation of Palestine by an armed struggle carried out by Palestinians themselves – different from other Palestinian political and guerrilla organizations, most of which firmly believed in a united Arab response. Arafat's organization never embraced the ideologies of the major Arab governments of the time, generally refusing to accept donations to his organization from major Arab governments, to preserve his independence. While in Kuwait, he built the groundwork for Fatah's future financial support.

In 1962 Arafat and his closest companions migrated to Syria. Now Fatah had approximately three hundred members but none were fighters. In Syria, he recruited members by offering them higher incomes to enable his armed attacks against Israel. He led several unsuccessful raids from Syria – his followers were poorly trained and badly equipped.

After the Six-Day War although Nasser and his Arab allies had been defeated, Arafat and Fatah could claim a victory, in that the majority of Palestinians, who had up to that time tended to align with individual Arab governments, now began to agree that a Palestinian' solution to their dilemma was indispensable. Barely a week after the defeat, Arafat crossed the Jordan River in disguise and entered the West Bank, where he set up recruitment centres in Hebron, the Jerusalem area and Nablus (http://en.wikipedia.org/wiki/yasser_arafat).

Throughout 1968 Fatah and other Palestinian armed groups were the target of a major Israeli army operation in the Jordanian village of Karameh, where Fatah headquarters were located (Karameh is the Arabic word for 'dignity').[1] The operation was in response to

---

[1] Benny Morris says 'honour' (Morris 1999, p. 368).

attacks, including rockets strikes from Fatah and other Palestinian militias. Though advised by a pro-Fatah Jordanian divisional commander to withdraw his men and headquarters to the nearby hills, Arafat refused, stating, 'We want to convince the world that there are those in the Arab world who will not withdraw or flee.'

On the night of 21 March, the IDF attacked Karameh with heavy weaponry, armoured vehicles and fighter jets. Fatah held its ground, surprising the Israeli military. As Israel's forces intensified their campaign, the Jordanian Army became involved, causing the Israelis to redeploy in order to avoid widening the conflict. By the end of the battle, nearly 150 Fatah gunmen had been killed and a similar number captured. At least 84 Jordanian soldiers and 28 Israelis were also killed. Despite the higher Arab death toll and the fact that the battle was decided in Israel's favour, Fatah considered themselves victorious because of the Israeli army's withdrawal. Some have alleged that Arafat himself was on the battlefield, but the details of his involvement are unclear. However, his allies – and Israeli intelligence – confirm that he urged his men throughout the battle to hold their ground and continue fighting.

I mention this incident because of its symbolic significance. Morris writes:

> For the first time in decades, the Arabs had stood up to the IDF armor and routed it. Karameh was to serve a generation of Palestinian fighters as a symbol of heroic resistance and proof of the IDF's vulnerability.
>
> (Morris 1999, p. 369)

But there are two other reasons. First, I want to be clear that I condemn the anti-Semitism against Jews living in Arab countries experienced at this time that led to a mass exodus from these countries. Michael Lerner thinks that a case can be made of irrational Arab anti-Semitism (Lerner 2003, p. 79). But I also grieve over the fact that Arab resistance at the massive loss of their homes and identity is so heavily criticized and misunderstood.

And that is partly the reason for citing Arafat at this point. For many he remains a deeply flawed character and this judgment would increase as our narrative progresses. But Kofi Annan, former UN Secretary General, in his recent autobiography, gives a nuanced opinion. Yes, he says, Arafat was a problem, but so was Sharon and Israel's settlement policy – as we shall see (Annan 2012, pp. 252–253). I hope you will agree.

Mounting Aggression

Dan Cohn-Sherbok

You are right that the years following the Six-Day War led to escalating violence and instability in the region despite initial steps towards peace. Following the Six-Day War the government of National Unity, led by Lev Eshkol, prepared to give up large areas of the occupied territories in exchange for peace. On 19 June 1967 the Israeli Cabinet agreed upon a four-point resolution stating that Israel was willing to withdraw to the international border with Egypt in exchange for a peace treaty. The resolution also stated that Israel was prepared to withdraw to the international border with Syria as long as the Golan Heights were demilitarized. No mention was made of the West Bank and the Gaza Strip – these were to be dealt with at a later stage.

Despite Israel's flexibility concerning these various territories, the Arab states were unwilling to engage in negotiation. At the first meeting of Arab nations after the war – the Khartoum Conference from 19 August to 1 September 1967 – the Arabs declared that there would be no peace with Israel, no recognition of Israel and no negotiation with Israel regarding any Palestinian territories. The Arab defeat in the war led to widespread resentment against the Jewish state. The loss of the Golan Heights and the West Bank and the continued presence of Israeli troops along the east bank of the Suez Canal evoked outrage among Arab leaders. Throughout 1968 Egypt carried out bombardments against Israeli positions along the canal. This war of attrition between Israel and Egypt posed a serious problem: Israel could not afford to sustain constant casualties along its border. In response to this Egyptian initiative, Israel embarked on a sustained policy of retaliation.

By this stage the Soviet Union was deeply involved in Egypt, re-equipping its forces. The situation was complicated by the fact that Israel was receiving mixed signals from the United States. The

Secretary of State, William Rogers, was pressing for a ceasefire and negotiated peace; Henry Kissinger, the National Security Adviser, however, appeared to encourage increasing Israel's military activity. On 29 October 1969 Rogers offered an interpretation of Security Council Resolution 242, proposing an international frontier between Egypt and Israel as a security border. On 17 November Israel indicated that it would not agree to the State Department's proposal, and on 7 January 1970 the Israel Air Force made its first deep penetration strike on Egypt.

Two weeks later Nasser flew to Moscow to obtain effective air-defense, surface-to-air missiles operated by Russian crews. Eventually the Kremlin agreed with Nasser's request. Fearing further conflict, the United States put pressure on Israel to accept a ceasefire and negotiate peace agreements. Reluctantly Prime Minister Golda Meir agreed with Washington's demands, and on 31 July the government of Israel accepted a ceasefire and the application of Resolution 242. The following months Secretary of State William Rogers commenced with his plan to create a negotiated peace between Israel and Egypt. Once plans for the Israeli withdrawal from Sinai had been proposed, Rogers put forward a further plan for the withdrawal from the West Bank. Despite these developments, the Arabs persisted in their unwillingness to negotiate with Israel. However, in February 1971 there was a significant change of policy.

On 4 February 1971 Nasser's successor, Anwar Sadat, addressed the Egyptian Parliament, stating that if Israel were to withdraw her forces in Sinai, he would be willing to reopen the Suez Canal, have his forces cross to the East Bank, approve a ceasefire, restore diplomatic relations with the United States, and sign a peace agreement with Israel. In a draft response to the Sadat initiative, Abba Eban formulated several principles:

(1) Israel welcomes Egypt's readiness to conclude a peace agreement.

(2) It proposes to discuss with Egypt all points contained in her reply to Ambassador Jarring (special representative of the Secretary-General of the United Nations), as well as all topics mentioned in Israel's memorandum 'Essentials of Peace' and any additional questions mutually agreed upon.

(3) In these negotiations to be held on the level of Foreign Ministers and under the auspices of Dr Jarring, both sides will present their detailed positions on the territorial, demographic, military and other outstanding issues.

The memorandum 'Essentials of Peace' was an Israeli Foreign Office document communicated to Jarring on his visit to Israel on 8 January 1971 which endorsed the withdrawal as well as all the other provisions of Resolution 242. Yet, on the day after Jarring's departure from Israel, Golda Meir took over all aspects of the negotiation. In an amendment to the 'Essentials of Peace, Israel stated that it would not withdraw to the pre-June 1967 lines. This meant in effect that if Sadat were prepared to negotiate a peace treaty with Israel, this would leave Israel in possession of Egyptian territory. For Egypt such a situation was intolerable, and war now became inevitable. At 2 pm on the afternoon of Yom Kippur, 6 October 1973, the Egyptians and Syrians launched an attack on Israel.

You Cannot Kill a People's Memory!

Mary Grey

On the brink of the Yom Kippur war you are right to highlight the escalating violence of the Palestinians. I cannot deny it and find it very painful to discuss. I have told of the rise of the PLO and especially Fatah, with Yasser Arafat's leading role in this. But after the 1967 war a number of actively violent Palestinian groups became active:

> Beneath the PLO umbrella there appeared an impossibly large number of *fedayeen* groups: in 1970 there were perhaps 30 operating in Jordan alone. Some were independent; most were backed by an Arab state or a communist power, primarily the USSR and China. Many were infiltrated by the Israelis, the CIA or both.
>
> (Ross 2007, p. 136)

But the most startling way that the Israel–Palestinian conflict leapt into the consciousness of the world – and would remain there – was in the bombing of 1972, during the Summer Olympic Games in Munich. This outrage was the work of the Black September Organization. This was a Palestinian organization, founded in 1970. It was responsible for the kidnapping and murder of eleven Israeli athletes and officials, and the fatal shooting of a West German policeman, during this event. I am old enough to remember the international shock this caused – especially given the Olympic traditions of and hopes for peace.

This was an attack on 11 members of the Israeli Olympic team, who were taken hostage and eventually killed, along with a German police officer. Shortly after the crisis began, they – members of Black September – demanded the release of 234 prisoners held in Israeli jails, and the release of the founders (Andreas Baader and Ulrike Meinhof) of the German Red Army Faction, who were held in German prisons. Black September called the operation 'Ikrit and Biram', after two Christian Palestinian villages[2] whose inhabitants were expelled by the Haganah in 1948. These events led to the creation of permanent, professional and military-trained counter-terrorism forces of major European countries.

The attackers were apparently given logistical assistance by German neo-Nazis. Five of the eight members of Black September were killed by police officers during a failed rescue attempt. The three surviving attackers were captured, but later released by West Germany following the hijacking by Black September of a Lufthansa airliner. Israel responded to the killers' release with Operation Spring of Youth and Operation Wrath of God, during which Israeli intelligence agency Mossad and special forces systematically tracked down and killed Palestinians suspected of involvement in the massacre (http://en/wikipedia/wiki/munich_massacre.org).

I cannot forget the horror of this event. Also that – our family lived in Belgium at the time – that the capture of the Baader – Meinhof terrorists figured in our lives, with the need to travel through roadblocks between Belgium and Germany at the time, to the excitement of our children!

What possible justification would I have for such violence? I hear you asking. Again, I have to go back to 1948 and the dispossession

---

[2]Biram is the village where Elias Chacour, Melkite Archbishop of Galilee, was born and from where his family was driven out in 1948.

of the Palestinians, their sense of loss, loss of home, land, identity and nation. What they found intolerable, and I sympathize with this, was

> The categorical refusal of the Israelis to acknowledge the Nakba and their absolute unwillingness to be held accountable, legally and morally, for the ethnic cleansing they committed in 1948.
> (Pappé 2006, pp. 236–237)

Israel's insistence that nothing prior to 1967 will be included in any negotiations totally removes the right of return of the Palestinian refugees from any Peace Negotiations. The Israelis seem unable to acknowledge the trauma they inflicted on the Palestinians in 1948 and the ongoing effect this would have, and that their version is in stark contrast with the Palestinian narrative which the people live to this day *as ongoing affliction*. The denial of this traumatic memory – or *memoricide,* as Pappé calls it – is an insidious form of persecution. Yet it should be realized that it is impossible to kill a people's memory. As Philippe Gaillard, head of the Red Cross delegation in Kigali, wrote, in the context of the Rwandan genocide (1994):

> You may kill as many people as you want, but you cannot kill their memory. Memory is the most invisible and resistant material you can find on earth. You cannot cut it like a diamond, you cannot shoot at it, because you cannot see it; nevertheless it is everywhere, all around you, in the silence, unspoken suffering, whispers and absent looks.
> (Gaillard in Rittner *et al* (eds.) 2004, p. 111)

All the attempts to remove evidence of the ancient Palestinian villages, to re-name them,[3] to forest the area in order to conceal them and to forbid any reference to Al Nakba in school textbooks, cannot eradicate its memory. Murals of their old villages are painted on the wall of the refugee camps. Survivors of Al Nakba

---

[3]For example, Saffuriya (Roman Sepphoris), became Hebrew Zippori.

still sleep with the key of the front door under their pillows, in hope of return to them. But to have the truth of the past denied publicity is affliction indeed. Would acknowledgment of this be a first step towards reconciliation?

Justifying Horror

Dan Cohn-Sherbok

You are right to highlight the bombing that took place at the Summer Olympic Games of 1972 as an inhuman act of brutality. The kidnapping and murder of eleven Israeli athletes and officials as well as the fatal shooting of a West German officer caused international shock. As you noted, before this crisis began, Black September demanded the release of 234 prisoners held in Israeli jails as well as founders of the German Red Faction Army held in German prisons. You ask what possible justification would there could be for such violence. In response, you highlight the dispossession of the Palestinians and their sense of loss. You say what the Palestinians found intolerable – and you sympathize with this view – is the refusal of the Israelis to acknowledge the Nakba and what you refer to as the ethnic cleansing that took place in 1948. You go on to say that the Israelis seem unable to acknowledge the trauma they inflicted on the Palestinians in 1948. You refer to the denial of this traumatic memory as 'memoricide'. All attempts to remove evidence of Palestinian villages by planting forests where they once stood, as well as forbidding any reference to the Nakba in school textbooks you regard as acts of historical violence against the Palestinian people.

In the last chapter you said that I was cruel. You stated that I had misinterpreted your views. You stressed that you do not nor ever will advocate violence. Yet, what I find disturbing is your continual and insistent criticism of Israeli policy. Even here – when you discuss the Munich massacre – you seek to provide a justification for Palestinian aggression. If you are critical of Israel for violence done to the Palestinians (including the act of what you call memoricide), then surely you would wish to criticize the Arabs for their attack on Zionists during the first few decades of the twentieth century, the Arab determination to wipe Israel off the map during the War of Independence (or Nakba), the Arab quest to destroy Israel during the Six-Day War and the Arab attack on Israel during the Yom Kippur War.

You ask at the end of your last letter: 'Would acknowledgment of this (memoricide) be a first step towards reconciliation?' I do believe that peace and reconciliation between Israel and the Palestinians may be possible, and we will explore such steps at the end of this book. But you seem to suggest that reconciliation is only possible if the Jewish people confess that they are responsible for Palestinian suffering, that they have stolen their land and have oppressed them for over a century. You highlight what you believe are acts of Zionist and Israeli injustice. You castigate the British for their support of the Zionist cause, and believe Britain should apologize for the Balfour Declaration. When it comes to Arab or Palestinian acts of aggression and violence, however, you seek to understand the motives involved, and provide a psychological, sociological and economic justification. To continually excoriate one side and find excuses for the other looks very much like prejudice.

You stated at the outset of our discussion that you deplore anti-Semitism and regard the history of Christian antipathy to Jews as a disgrace. You emphasize that you are sympathetic to the plight of the Jews of Eastern Europe at the end of the nineteenth century and understand why they sought to have a homeland of their own. Yet, as you examine the history of Zionism and the creation of a Jewish state in Palestine, you seem incapable of recognizing Palestinian and Arab atrocities. In my view, reconciliation can only occur if truth is told about the totality of evil. This includes both Israeli and Palestinian inhumanity and the suffering of both peoples.

Mounting Violence – Yet a Chink of Hope

Mary Grey

That's a lot of accusations in one exchange! I would have hoped by now we had a degree of understanding. You write:

> You castigate the British for their support of the Zionist cause, and believe Britain should apologize for the Balfour Declaration.

If you really *heard* what I have been saying you would understand that I do not call for an apology *tout court* for the Declaration but **recognition and repentance** for the fact that Britain did not honour her promises to the indigenous peoples of Palestine, the Arabs (though they are not named as such) – as stated in the second half of the Balfour declaration – neither immediately nor through the Mandate years (www.balfourproject.org).

Secondly, you accuse me of criticizing Israel and Israeli policies: but when it comes to Arab or Palestinian acts of aggression and violence, I seek to understand the motives involved, and provide a psychological, sociological and economic justification. *To continually excoriate one side and find excuses for the other looks very much like prejudice.*

It is neither fair not true to accuse me of being incapable of recognizing Palestinian and Arab atrocities. I condemned the murder of the Olympic athletes and do criticize violence on both sides – and will continue to do so. I agree totally that reconciliation can only occur if truth is told about the totality of evil on both sides. That does not prevent me from trying to understand the motives for violence. I asked 'what possible justification?' – but never condoned it.

But I think your hounding me in this way is blinding you from admitting an obvious fact: there is an imbalance of power in the situation. *There is no equal playing field:* Israel since the Six-Day War has been recognized as an international player. Palestine has lost identity as a country, been humiliated by loss of land, home, many of her people reduced to refugee status either within or outside the land. *I do not agree with vengeance but I can understand why it happens.*

The violence now escalates with the Yom Kippur War of 1973, fought by the coalition of Arab states led by Egypt and Syria against Israel from 6–25 October. It began when the coalition launched a surprise attack on Israeli positions in the Israeli-occupied territories on Yom Kippur, the holiest day in Judaism, which that year coincided with the Muslim holy month of Ramadan. Egyptian and Syrian forces crossed ceasefire lines to enter the Sinai Peninsula and Golan Heights, respectively – captured and occupied by Israel since the 1967 Six-Day War. Both the United States and the Soviet

Union gave massive supplies to their respective allies, leading to a near-confrontation between the two nuclear superpowers.

The Egyptians crossed the Suez Canal, advanced into the Sinai Peninsula, eventually halted by Israel. Within three days, however, Israeli forces had managed to push the Syrians back from the Golan Heights to pre-war ceasefire lines, launching a four-day counter-offensive deep into Syria. Within a week, Israeli artillery began to shell the outskirts of Damascus. Egyptian president Anwar Sadat believed that capturing two strategic passes located deeper in the Sinai would make his position stronger during the negotiations. He therefore ordered the Egyptians to go back on the offensive, but the attack was quickly repulsed. The Israelis then counterattacked, crossed the Suez Canal into Egypt and began slowly advancing southwards and westwards in over a week of heavy fighting which inflicted heavy casualties on both sides.

On 22 October a United Nations-brokered ceasefire failed to hold, each side blaming the other. By 24 October the Israelis had improved their positions considerably and completed their encirclement of Egypt's Third Army and the city of Suez. (This development led to tensions between the United States and the Soviet Union.) Now, a second ceasefire was imposed cooperatively on 25 October to end the war.

This war had far-reaching implications. The **Arab World** felt psychologically vindicated by early successes. But for Israel the war effectively ended its sense of invincibility following the Six-Day War. Casualties were very heavy: Israel suffered between 2,521 and 2,800 killed in action, with 7,500–8,800 soldiers being wounded. Arab casualties were higher, though accuracy is difficult: the lowest casualty estimate is 8,000 (5,000 Egyptian and 3,000 Syrian) killed and 18,000 wounded, the highest 18,500 (15,000 Egyptian and 3,500 Syrian) killed, 35,000 wounded (http://en/wikipedia.org/wiki/yom_kippur_war).

Whereas the outlook appeared gloomy, as my title indicated, there was still a chink of hope, and this was provided by President Sadat who opened up a constructive dialogue for peace. On 9 November 1977 Sadat stunned the world when he told parliament that he would be willing to visit Israel and address the Knesset. Shortly afterward, the Israeli government cordially invited him to address the Knesset. So in November of that year, Sadat became the first Arab leader to visit Israel, thus *implicitly recognizing Israel.*

The contemporary writer and researcher, Tony Klug, thinks that the Sadat initiative of November 1977 may have some important indicators for the current situation:

> President Sadat eventually achieved his purpose, primarily by appealing, not so much to Israeli Prime Minister Begin and his government but, more importantly, over their heads to the Israeli people, who were electrified by his visit. He took command of Israeli public opinion because they came to believe and trust him. He addressed them directly on their own soil, not as a future reward for peace but as a way of attaining it. Simultaneously, Egyptian spiritual leaders were urged to stress those portions of the Koran that call on Muslims to make friends with the Jews and downplay those parts that speak ill of the Jews. Sadat understood and played to the psychological need. He had a goal and went for it.
>
> (Klug 2013, p. 5)

What Klug does is to reinforce the need for psychological and spiritual understanding between all peoples involved – and the appeal to faith sources in the search for peace.

The Road to Peace

Dan Cohn-Sherbok

Your last exchange clarified a number of points of misunderstanding. I think we both agree that reconciliation requires an acknowledgement of the totality of evil – in this case the human atrocities committed by both the Israelis and the Palestinians. As the historical narrative unfolds, there will, I fear, be much to condemn on both sides. What I believe we are both trying to do in our dialogue is to uncover the truth about the Middle East crisis no matter how illusive.

You are right to highlight the significance of Sadat's initiative during the post Yom Kippur War period. Let me turn to the circumstances leading up to this event. Following the war, the United States attempted to achieve a separate peace between Israel and Egypt. As a consequence, the PLO was excluded from a comprehensive peace agreement. During this period Israel suffered severe economic difficulties. In the election of 17 May 1977 Menachem Begin and the Likud bloc were elected to power breaking Labour's hold on the Jewish state. Adopting a right-wing policy, Begin argued that Israel had the right to control Judaea and Samaria (the West Bank). In his view, although Resolution 242 obliged Israel to withdraw from occupied territories, the resolution did not specify that this should be done on all fronts. Hence, any withdrawal from the Sinai would fulfil this requirement. Undeterred, Sadat declared that he was prepared to go anywhere in search of peace. Following this initiative, Begin invited Sadat to visit Israel.

Prior to his journey, Sadat went to Syria to consult with Assad. Incensed by Sadat's initiative, Assad, the PLO and a number of Arab leaders claimed that Sadat's trip to Jerusalem would undermine a comprehensive solution to the Middle East conflict. Despite such objections, Sadat arrived at Ben-Gurion airport on 19 November. Crowds surrounded the airport, and the nation watched this event on television. The next morning Sadat prayed at the Al-Aqsa mosque, and later visited the Church of the Holy Sepulchre and Yad Vashem. In the afternoon he addressed the Knesset, stressing the importance of peace. He declared:

> It is fated that my trip to you, the trip of peace, should coincide with the Islam feast, the holy feast of Al-Adha, the feast of sacrifice, when Abraham, peace be unto him, the great-grandfather of the Arabs and Jews, submitted to God. I say when God Almighty ordered him, Abraham went, with dedicated sentiments, not out of weakness but through a giant spiritual force and a free will to sacrifice his very own son, prompted by a firm and unshakeable belief in ideals that lend life a profound significance.
> (Legum and Shaked (eds.) 1976–1977, *Middle East Contemporary Survey*, vol 2, pp. 134–142)

Sadat went on to point out that he had not come to Jerusalem to pursue a separate agreement between Egypt and Israel. What he hoped to achieve, instead, was a peaceful agreement which would end the Israeli occupation of the Arab territories occupied in 1967. His aim was to ensure the fundamental rights of the Palestinian people and their right to self-determination including their right to establish their own state. The Palestinian problem, he stressed, was the crux of the entire conflict. What was critical was a comprehensive solution to the Middle East conflict. In reply Begin emphasized that both he and other Israelis were pleased by Sadat's presence in the Holy Land. The flight time between Cairo and Jerusalem is short, he said, but the distance between Cairo and Jerusalem was previously endless.

On 26 November 1977 Sadat announced that the next step on the road to peace would be a preparatory conference in Geneva. In Washington Zbigniew Brzezinski introduced the theory of concentric circles of the peace process building on the Egyptian–Israeli accord, and then expanding outwards including Palestinians on the West Bank and Gaza and then moving on to a wider circle involving the Syrians and others. The PLO and Syria, however, denounced the US-supported peace process between Egypt and Israel. As a consequence, Assad, who had previously been a central figure in the peace process, became isolated. He formed a Front of Steadfastness and Opposition to Egypt.

At a meeting in Tripoli, only Algeria and Yemen participated along with Syria and the PLO as well as their host Colonel Qaddafi. The Saudis and Kuwaitis and Jordanians did not attend. Iraq was involved initially but walked out. Incensed, the Front denounced Sadat's betrayal of Arab interests and decided to freeze political and diplomatic relations with Egypt. In response Sadat broke off all relations with the participants plus Iraq. In addition, he declared that the PLO's participation in the Front annulled its right to represent the Palestinian people. It is a tragedy that Sadat's initiative was doomed to failure, and that his life would end with assassination by Egyptian fundamentalists several years later.

Chapter 13
The Palestinian Problem

Obstacles to Peace

Dan Cohn-Sherbok

From 14 to 22 December 1977 a pre-Geneva conference took place in Cairo: Sadat invited the United States, the Soviet Union, Israel, Syria, Lebanon, Jordan, the United Nations and the Palestine Liberation Organization (PLO). Only Israel, the United States and Israel attended. A week later Sadat and Begin met at Ismailia and agreed to set up military and political committees. In his concluding statement, Sadat made it clear that the position of Egypt was that a Palestinian State should be established. Israel's position was that Arabs in Judaea and Samaria (the West Bank and Jordan) and the Gaza Strip should enjoy self-rule.

Israel's view of Sadat's approach was explained by Ezer Weizman, Minister for Defense, to the Likud members of the Knesset. In his opinion, the Egyptians were proposing a separate agreement with Israel if a formula could be found which would delay the question of a comprehensive settlement. Begin proposed a plan for autonomy for the Palestinian Arabs of Judaea, Samaria and Gaza. Security and public order were to continue to be the responsibility of Israel. However, administrative autonomy and the selection of an administrative council were to be granted to the Palestinians. Residents would be free to choose either Israeli or Jordanian citizenship, and Israelis would be free to acquire land and settle in Judea and Samaria. Regarding sovereignty, Israel would claim sovereignty to Judaea, Samaria and Gaza. Yet it was recognized that other claims exist and the issue would be left open. Concerning Sinai there would eventually be complete withdrawal. In the Knesset Rabin criticized the Begin plan for providing too many concessions. Such a scheme, he stressed, would bring Israel back to the borders it had before the 1967 war. The Knesset, however, approved the scheme.

On 4 January 1978 Carter and Sadat met in Aswan. In a communique they agreed to recognize the legitimate rights of the Palestinian people and enable them to participate in the determination of their future. On 17 January 1978 the Political Committee established by the Ismailia Summit met in Jerusalem, but a day later Sadat withdrew his representatives. For Egypt, Israel's withdrawal from Sinai was crucial, yet it appeared that Israel was not prepared to make such an agreement. On 3 January, Israel secretly decided to bolster its settlements in Sinai and to create a further six settlements in eastern Sinai. When news of this plan was disclosed, Israel dropped the idea of six new settlements but continued with its intention of strengthening the existing settlements. Begin had initially promised that when an agreement was finally reached, there would be a complete Israeli withdrawal from Sinai; the existence of Israeli settlements in Sinai, however, indicated that this would not be so.

In Washington, Israel's intransigence over Sinai was deeply troubling. Editorials criticizing Begin's attitude appeared in the press. During this period the Peace Now movement emerged in Israel, protesting against the government's policies. Relations between Israel and the United States became even worse as a result of Israel's response to a Fedayeen raid on 11 March 1978. In retaliation Israel launched an offensive (Operation Litani) in Southern Lebanon.

Alarmed by these developments, the United States pressed for Security Council Resolution 425 which called upon Israel to cease its military action against Lebanese territorial integrity and withdraw its forces. The resolution also called for a United Nations force in southern Lebanon. In Israel, the American intervention was bitterly resented, particularly since it ignored the fact that Israel had been provoked by the Fedayeen attack. Nevertheless, by June 1978 Israel had withdrawn its forces from the area.

From 16 to 18 April talks took place between Moshe Dayan and Cyrus Vance, US Secretary of State. At these meetings Dayan proposed that the parties should agree on a framework for bringing about autonomy for the Arab inhabitants of the West Bank and Gaza. The Begin plan, he suggested, should provide a basis for discussion. Such a framework was designed to provide a formula that would enable Israel to postpone the question of a comprehensive settlement while concluding a separate agreement with Egypt. At the end of July President Carter sent Vance to the Middle East with invitations to Begin and Sadat to meet with him at Camp David.

The Camp David talks began on 5 September and continued for two weeks. The discussion focussed largely on the West Bank, Gaza and the Palestinians. Yet the real area of negotiation concerned Sinai. Although relations between the Israelis and Egyptians were strained during the meetings, Camp David adopted two frameworks: a Framework for Peace concerned with the West Bank and Gaza, and a Framework for a Peace Treaty between Egypt and Israel. Egypt, Israel, Jordan and the Palestinians were to participate in negotiations about the future of the West Bank and Gaza, and a five-year period of transitional autonomy was planned. The Frameworks were accompanied by letters; one from Begin to Carter which promised that the question of the removal of the settlers would be put before the Knesset, and a letter from Sadat to Carter declaring that if the settlers were not withdrawn from Sinai, there would be no peace treaty between Egypt and Israel. A further letter from Sadat to Carter reiterated the Arab position on Jerusalem. Once Begin returned to Israel, he was committed to the removal of the settlers and the conclusion of a peace treaty. Although the Camp David Accords were warmly welcomed in the United States, the reaction in the Arab world outside Egypt was hostile. At the ninth

Arab Summit in Baghdad on 1–5 November which was attended by every Arab State except Egypt which was not invited, the Camp David Accords were condemned. The Framework for Peace was bitterly denounced – this was not what was envisaged by a comprehensive solution to the Middle East conflict.

Camp David – A Failed Peace Initiative and Its Aftermath

Mary Grey

You end your last exchange with this statement:

> At the ninth Arab Summit in Baghdad on 1–5 November which was attended by every Arab State except Egypt which was not invited, the Camp David Accords were condemned. The Framework for Peace was bitterly denounced.

Your conclusion that the Arab States were responsible needs more discussion, especially given the later regret that if these Accords had been implemented further violence might have been prevented.

Initially the signs were so encouraging. The US President, Jimmy Carter, was – and is – a man of great integrity, determined to achieve a breakthrough and to find a way for the Palestinians to recover a land (Carter 2006, pp. 37–54; Carter 1982, pp. 319–403). He also had a very cordial relationship with President Sadat which was to endure after the event. But he was aware that with the succession of Menachem Begin as Prime Minister of Israel – his background was as a leader of the militant underground group, the Irgun – that a more hawkish mood was prevalent in the country. We need to appreciate the personal effort that Carter put into keeping the negotiations going. Neither Sadat nor Begin would negotiate with each other, so Carter went from one to the other to keep discussion alive – both threatened to leave several times. (Both Carter and Sadat received the Nobel Peace Prize simultaneously.)

It soon became clear that Begin was more interested in discussing Sinai than a future for the West Bank and Gaza. As Carter himself perceived, Israel was far keener to have a separate Peace treaty with Egypt than to do anything about the West Bank and Gaza.

However, as you wrote, agreement was reached and signed. So why did it ultimately fail?
According to Kenneth Stein

> The Accords were another interim agreement or step, but negotiations that flowed from the Accords slowed for several reasons. These included an inability to bring the Jordanians into the discussions; the controversy over settlements; the inconclusive nature of the subsequent autonomy talks; domestic opposition sustained by both Begin and Sadat and, in Sadat's case, ostracism and anger from the Arab world; the emergence of a what became a cold peace between Egypt and Israel; and changes in foreign policy priorities including discontinuity in personnel committed to sustaining the negotiating process.
> (Stein 1999, pp. 254–261)

Clearly, the fact that Sadat had not managed to bring the Arab States along with him was a crucial factor. When the Camp David accords were signed, Jordan's King Hussein saw it as a slap to the face: with a number of Arab States in growing opposition to Sadat, Jordan could not risk accepting the Accords, without the support from its powerful Arab neighbours, like Iraq, Saudi Arabia, and Syria. In fact, the Accords also prompted the disintegration of a united Arab front in opposition to Israel. Because of the vague language concerning the implementation of Resolution 242 (that required Israel's withdrawal from the Occupied Territories), the Palestinian problem now became the primary issue. Many of the Arab nations blamed Egypt for not putting enough pressure on Israel to deal with the Palestinian problem in a way that would be satisfactory to them. Syria also informed Egypt that it would not reconcile with the nation unless it abandoned the peace agreement with Israel (http://en.wikipedia.org/wiki/camp_David_Accords).

The Palestinians felt very let down. Carter – despite his personal political triumph – and Sadat had gained nothing substantial for them. As Morris notes,

> Begin was probably the most satisfied. He had successfully warded off all efforts to pin him down on the Palestinian

problem; and he had avoided a commitment to withdraw from any part of the West Bank or Gaza.

(Morris 1999, p. 486)

Indeed, he thinks, Begin had never seriously contemplated giving the West Bank and Gaza any substantial measure of self-rule (Morris 1999, p. 487).

Although most Israelis supported the Accords, the Israeli settler movement opposed them because Sadat would not agree to a treaty in which Israel had any presence in the Sinai Peninsula at all.

I think, for the reasons I cite, you should be more sensitive to the impact of the Accords on the Palestinians and the reason for the rejection of the Framework. Even the UN had problems with it:

> Because the agreements were concluded without the participation of UN and PLO and the UN General Assembly found that they did not comply with the Palestinian right of return, of self-determination and to national independence and sovereignty, and also condoned continued Israeli occupation, the *Framework for Peace in the Middle East* was rejected. In *Resolution 34/65 B* of 12 December 1979, that agreement and all similar ones were declared invalid.

In sum, even though I think the efforts of Carter and Sadat are not to be forgotten in this unfolding story, that it is wrong to lay the blame solely on the Arab States that the Accords ultimately were not successful: the Occupation remained untouched – the suffering continued.

The Death of the Camp David Accords

Dan Cohn-Sherbok

I do not think that historical facts will support your interpretation of both Prime Minister Begin's attitude toward Palestinian autonomy as well as your view of the Arab reaction to the Camp David Accords. As I mentioned, the Israeli government's perception of Sadat's approach to a comprehensive settlement (including the West Bank) was outlined in December 1977 by Ezer Weizman,

Minister for Defense. The Egyptians, he explained, would be willing to accept a separate agreement with Israel if a formula were found that would enable them to delay the question of the comprehensive settlement to a later date. In the quest for such a formula, Begin put forward his plan for autonomy for the Palestinian Arabs of Judea, Samaria and Gaza. The main principles of the Begin Plan were administrative autonomy and the selection of an administrative council; security and public order would continue to be the responsibility of the Israeli authorities: residents would be free to choose either Israeli or Jordanian citizenship; residents of Israel would be free to acquire land and settle in Judaea and Samaria (and vice versa). On sovereignty, Begin offered a delaying clause: 'Israel stands by its rights and its claim of sovereignty to Judaea, Samaria and the Gaza district. In the knowledge that other claims exist, it proposes for the sake of the agreement and the peace that the question of sovereignty in the areas be left open' (O'Brien 1988, *The Siege*, p. 581). In the Knesset Yitzhak Rabin attacked the Begin plan for conceding too much to the Arabs.

As I previously noted, at Camp David the Framework for Peace was concerned with a comprehensive ideal: it aimed to constitute a basis for peace not only between Egypt and Israel but also between Israel and each of its other neighbours. It referred to negotiations between Egypt, Israel, Jordan and the representatives of the Palestinian people about the future of the West Bank and Gaza. A five-year period of transitional autonomy was envisaged to ensure a peaceful and orderly transit of authority. The language was fully compatible – on Begin's interpretation of what he had agreed to – with the Begin Plan.

When Begin returned from Camp David, he strongly supported the Camp David Accords and sought to persuade the Cabinet to agree. As Moshe Dayan recalled:

> The Prime Minister was authoritative and single-minded in his defense of the agreement, emphasizing its positive qualities and mercilessly attacking those ministers who were doubtful or opposed. As a highly experienced parliamentarian, and every inch a political party man, he used skilful debating tactics and procedural techniques. He arranged for the Knesset debate to

be arranged the following day so there was no time to convene the parliamentary Foreign Affairs and Defense Committee. He also refused to hold discussions within his own party before the debate, customary when major policy decisions are to be taken.

(O'Brien 1988, *The Siege*, p. 502)

Despite the warm reception of the Camp David Accords in the United States, there was no sign of a peace process catching on, or rippling out, among the Arab states. Hussein coldly rejected the role of Sadat's successor in the peace process. On the day the news of Camp David broke with the envisaged role for Jordan, Hussein declared that Jordan was neither legally nor morally bound by anything agreed at Camp David.

The feature that most aroused the wrath of the assembled and united Arabs at Baghdad was that which was intended to placate them: The Framework for Peace, with autonomy and 'transit of authority'. At Baghdad the Arab world emphatically rejected any implementation of the autonomy provisions. The Arabs wanted autonomy scrapped altogether along with the rest of the Camp David Accords.

For a time after the treaty, the Carter Administration continued its efforts to widen the peace process. In particular, it aimed to bring the PLO into the negotiations. Previously the PLO had rejected UN Resolutions 242 because of its failure to recognize the legitimate rights of the Palestinians and its designation of them as refugees – for this reason the PLO had been excluded from the negotiating process. A suggestion that an amendment be added to Resolution 242 and 338 was proposed by Kuwait in the summer of 1979. The White House supported the idea, but Sadat complained that the resolution idea was misguided. Syria agreed. At first the PLO was enthusiastic, but in time they changed their view. In March 1980 a PLO spokesman stated that an addition or amendment to 242 would be unacceptable. What the PLO demanded instead was a new resolution, totally separate from 242. Arafat added that such a new resolution should not provide for secure and recognized frontiers for Israel. Such Palestinian and Arab opposition effectively killed off the Carter peace initiatives.

The Massacres of Sabra–Shatila

Mary Grey

You are never willing to concede that what you call 'Arab intransigence' may in fact be a justified and growing sense of grief at their loss of and country and continuing suffering. As I wrote (section 'Camp David – a Failed Peace Initiative and Its Aftermath'): *the Occupation remained untouched – the suffering continued.*

What can be said in truth at the end of the period we have been discussing – the Camp David Accords is that the peace between Egypt and Israel, despite some hiccups, did hold and became 'a beacon to the rest of the Arab world, attracting moderates and offering a viable alternative to continued endless hostilities' (Morris 1999, p. 493). Although we need to acknowledge that in the assassination of Sadat, Egypt had paid a bitter price.

But the unresolved problems with the Palestine returned to haunt Israel and we enter upon a very bitter episode. The PLO headquarters were now based in Beirut, Lebanon, from where they launched raids on Israel. On the 6 June 1982, 80,000 Israeli soldiers invaded Lebanon to try to establish a 20-mile security zone.

I want to focus on the most famous/infamous episode of this war. Because General Ariel Sharon was determined that all PLO should be expelled and was convinced that 2,000 were hiding in refugee camps, Phalangist troops[1] moved into the Sabra and Shatila Palestinian refugee camps west of Beirut.

This was one of the most cruel incidents in Israel's struggle against the Palestinians and the one which captured the world's attention, especially that of young people. I remember the posters on my 14-year-old son's bedroom wall at that time: *Sabra and Shatila – never forget!*

In the Sabra and Shatila massacre between 762 and 3,500 civilians were massacred, mostly Palestinian and Lebanese Shia, by the Lebanese Christian Phalangist militia in the camps in Beirut, from approximately 6:00 pm on 16 September to 8:00 am on 18 September 1982. This massacre was presented as retaliation

---

[1] The Phalangists – the Lebanese Christian political party based in East Beirut – were Israel's main Christian partner.

for the assassination of newly elected Lebanese president Bachir Gemayel, the leader of the Lebanese Kataeb Party. It was said that the Phalangists were obsessed with the idea of revenge: Israeli General Rafaeel Eitan said,

> They are thirsty for revenge. There could be torrents of blood.
> (Morris 1999, p. 543)

It was wrongly assumed that Palestinian militants had carried out the assassination, which is now generally attributed to native, pro-Syrian militants.

As I said, Israel had invaded Lebanon with the intention of rooting out the PLO. Under the supervision of the Multinational Force, the PLO withdrew from Lebanon following weeks of battles in West Beirut and shortly before the massacre took place. Various forces – Israeli, Phalangist and possibly also the South Lebanon Army (SLA) – were in the vicinity of the camps at the time of the slaughter, taking advantage of the fact that the multinational forces had removed barracks and mines that encircled Beirut's Muslim neighbourhoods and kept the Israelis at bay.

The Israeli advance over West Beirut in the wake of the PLO withdrawal, which enabled the Phalangist raid, was considered a violation of the ceasefire agreement between the various forces. The actual killers were the 'Young Men', a gang recruited by Elie Hobeika, the Lebanese Forces intelligence chief, from men who had been expelled from the Lebanese Forces for insubordination or criminal activities. The killings are widely believed to have taken place under Hobeika's direct orders. Hobeika's family and fiancée had been murdered by Palestinian militiamen, and their Lebanese allies, at the Damour massacre of 1976, itself a response to a previous massacre of Palestinians and Lebanese Muslims at the hands of Christian militants. Hobeika later became a long-serving Member of the Parliament of Lebanon and served in several ministerial roles (see http://en.wikipedia.org/wiki/sabra_and_shatila_massacre).

Hobeika's force moved from house to house, killing the inhabitants and meeting with very little resistance. The massacre went on uninterruptedly for 30 h. Even though reports of what's going on reaching Israel Defense Force (IDF) headquarters, nothing was done. I will spare you some of the horrifying accounts of the atrocities. The number of victims remains disputed.

The IDF surrounded the camps and at the Phalangists' request, fired illuminating flares at night. In 1982 a UN commission chaired by Sean MacBride concluded that Israel bore responsibility for the violence. In 1983 the Israeli Kahan Commission, appointed to investigate the incident, found that Israeli military personnel, aware that a massacre was in progress, had failed to take serious steps to stop it. Thus Israel was indirectly responsible, while Ariel Sharon, then Defense Minister, bore personal responsibility, forcing him to resign.

News of the atrocities dominated world headlines for days: for many Israelis the massacre came to symbolize the war itself.

What haunts me is that since 1948 there has been a steady process of de-sensitization with regard to the suffering of the Palestinians that allowed such an atrocity to take place: we will see this process of desensitization growing – even up to our own times.

Arabs and the Peace Initiative

Dan Cohn-Sherbok

In your last exchange you say that I never concede that Arab intransigence is justified. While I recognize the frustrations that Palestinians must have felt as refugees, I do not in any sense justify their actions as you seem to do. My major concern in our dialogue has been to highlight the faults of both Israelis and Palestinians in their conflict, and to see whether paths other than violence could have been followed. From the outset the indigenous Arab inhabitants of Palestine embarked on armed resistance, and this has been their hallmark. The Jews who settled in Palestine and established the State of Israel had hoped to live in peaceful coexistence with the Arabs. But this was not to be. The Palestinians and the surrounding Arab nations were intent on eradicating Israel from the map, and repeatedly they attempted to do so.

As we have seen, President Sadat courageously sought to find a peaceful solution to the struggle between the Zionists and the Palestinians. This was an essential aspect of his journey to Jerusalem, and the subsequent Camp David Accords. I do blame the Arabs for this failure. It was they, not the Israelis, who were intent on subverting what President Carter, Begin and Sadat had accomplished. I agree with the quotation you cited from Benny Morris: the Camp David Accords did offer a viable alternative to continued endless hostilities. It is a tragedy that this did not occur.

You are right about the terrible infamous episode of the onslaught against refugees in Sabra and Shatila. This was an act carried by the Lebanese Christian Phalangist militia. It was not the Israelis who were directly responsible, but they were implicated. They did facilitate this massacre. This is deplorable, and was rightly criticized by the Israeli Kahan Commission. As you noted, General Ariel Sharon, the Defense Minister bore his share of responsibility and was forced to resign. You are right to condemn Israel for its collusion with the Phelangists, but what I think you fail to recognize is the fact that Israel itself was intent on conducting an investigation into this incident. Unlike its surrounding neighbours, Israel is a democratic state which has invested power in its executive, legislative and judicial branches. Its citizens, even the highest military figures, are subject to the rule of law. It is simply inconceivable that neighbouring Arab states such as Saudi Arabia, Iraq, Syria, Egypt or Iran could have conducted a similar investigation into the conduct of its leaders. Egypt, for example, after having just embraced democracy has just undergone a military coup (rather than a legal process) to remove its democratically elected President.

I want to return to the period following the failure of the Camp David Accords. The Second Baghdad Conference which took place on 31 March 1979 condemned the treaty between Israel and Egypt just as the First Baghdad Conference condemned Camp David, and called for sanctions against Egypt. A later summit, at Tunis in November of the same year, reaffirmed these positions and maintained the isolation of Egypt. A feature of this period was an effort by conservative Arab leaders – Crown Prince Fahd and King Hussein – to mobilize the Muslim world for some kind of alleged jihad against Israel. A conference of Muslim Foreign Ministers adopted a resolution on this theme: 'The Islamic countries declare their commitment to the jihad because of what it embodies in its broad human dimensions on the ground that it constitutes steadfastness and confrontation against the Zionist enemy on all fronts: military, political, economic, informative and cultural' (O'Brien 1988, *The Siege*, p. 598). You say at the end of your last exchange that you are haunted by a steady process of desensitisation with regard to the suffering of the Palestinians. As a peace activist, I hope you are equally haunted by the spectre of the Palestinian and Arab desire to destroy Israel through armed war.

Admit the Picture Is More Ambiguous!

Mary Grey

You are always arguing that I should accept your version of the story: Arab intransigence and violence (especially the PLO) in contrast with law-abiding Israelis who respect democratic rule and want peace! The picture is not so simple. Nor do I accept your last remark:

> As a peace activist, I hope you are equally haunted by the spectre of the Palestinian and Arab desire to destroy Israel through armed warfare

because it is simply not the total picture! I explained how Jimmy Carter found Menachem Begin difficult, 'hawkish', in fact, and when he returned home, yes, Begin withdrew forces from Sinai (as agreed), but reneged on the agreements to stop expansion of the Settlements and show any compassion for the plight of the Palestinians. Was it law-abiding to refuse to stop the Settlement expansion? Was it law-abiding to refuse to honour UN Resolution 242 about the return of the Palestinian refugees?

It is simply not appropriate to invoke the current example of Egypt's attempt to remove and replace president Morsi[2]: we neither know the outcome yet, nor the total truth of the situation. When I was in Egypt last month – yes also in Tahrir Square! – I was conscious that the country was like a tinderbox: and now the spark has been ignited. It is easy for us both – in our comfortable contexts – to condemn violence, which I think we both do, but there have been times in

---

[2]This happened on 28 June 2013.

history when it appeared justified – as in the attempt to get rid of Hitler.

Again, was it legally justified for Israel, on 7 June 1981 to surprise the entire world by attacking and destroying the Iraqi nuclear plant at Osirak? This operation destroyed the nuclear reactor without losing a single fighter plane, and guaranteed the Likud Party a victory in the general election held 21 days later. The proximity of the operation to the Israeli election raised a howl of protest from the opposition, who described it as an election stunt. But the reality was more complicated, and is best described in terms of the Begin doctrine. In Begin's words, *anything that could or might pose an existential threat to Israel or of another Holocaust on the Jewish people must be defeated.* Whether Begin actually considered the Iraqi reactor a direct existential threat or was cynically trying to win another election is beside the point. Within the cabinet and in the face of opposition, Begin adhered to the doctrine bearing his name, insisting that the unfinished Iraqi nuclear reactor did pose an existential threat to Israel (Amit and Levit 2011, p. 99, citing Naor 1993, p. 220). This raid evoked massive international reaction. Sadat's comment was:

> Once again, we face the same Israel that is completely oblivious to what happens in the Arab world and to what the Arab world thinks of it.

In fact, there was a growing realization that Israel was blocking any hope for peace while building more settlements on Palestinian land, and a growing sense of anger and tension. And if Begin was hawkish – what about the late Ariel Sharon, his successor? As Shlaim (2009, p. 287) writes:

> The hallmarks of his career are mendacity, the most savage brutality towards the Arab civilians and a persistent preference for force over diplomacy to solve political problems. After making the transition from the army into politics, Sharon remained the champion of violent solutions.

And don't forget that Israel refused to talk to the PLO. I think a better comparison than Egypt would be Ireland during 'The

Troubles'. How many times did we hear that the British government refused to talk to the Irish Republican Army – for similar reasons: 'We don't talk to terrorists'? Yet the breakthrough to peace came precisely when they did exactly that. Another contemporary example would be 'Talking with the Taliban' – but the jury is out as to whether this will be successful.

But the last point I want to make today is that, in our search for peaceful solutions, it is a mistake to limit our judgments to government leaders and army commanders. There is plenty of evidence during this period – and later on – that many ordinary people, both Israelis and Palestinians wanted peace. For example, many Israelis were vocal in their opposition to the Lebanese war. In July 1982 nearly 100,000 Israelis marched through the streets of Tel Aviv demanding the withdrawal of troops from Lebanon (Ateek 1989, p. 44). In fact it was the brutal face of violence of the Lebanese War and the Sabra–Shatila massacres that activated thousands of international as well as Palestinian activists and Peace groups. As Mazin Qumsiyeh writes:

> The beginning of the decline of the fear of the might of Israel started precisely when the state showed its brutal face.
> (Qumsiyeh 2011, p. 128)

And as I hope to show, much of this resistance was non-violent.

Chapter 14
The Uprising

The Non-violent Intifada of 1987

Mary Grey

We enter on a period of intensifying conflict. As with all conflicts we have to distinguish between immediate causes and deep-seated ones and look at the wider picture. As the Palestinian suffering intensified, so did their resentment along with it. In fact the roots for an uprising had been sown as soon as the Israelis began to buy land in the West Bank and started slowly taking over the areas with the military occupation. The Settlements increased – they had been condemned by the UN Security Council Resolution 446. Remember that the word Palestine had been expelled from school text books and universities were closed for long periods. (I remember when in 1987 my College, St Mary's in Strawberry Hill, Twickenham invited a group of students from the West Bank University of Bir Zeit, their University was closed – and in fact the Intifada was about to begin. So our British students began to be closely aware of events in the West Bank.)

But there are more factors – like the number of the Palestinians in Israeli gaols – around 200,000 by 1987; like the fact that Israeli forces had murdered four young Palestinians at a Gaza checkpoint; and that an Israeli soldier opened fire on a group of peaceful Palestinian protesters that resulted in the killing of a 17–year-old boy. Incidents like this – especially in and around the refugee camps in Gaza became more frequent. As Dennis Ross – US envoy to the Middle East – wrote:

> The riots did not stop. Strikes and stone-throwing at Israeli soldiers and settlers became a daily reality, and the Palestinians soon gave this reality a name: The Intifada, the Uprising.
> (Ross 2004, pp. 41–42)

So, unlike the second Intifada, this first event was an expression of the Palestinian frustration: it was simple civil disobedience against Israeli rule. It was not even orchestrated by the PLO – and many of its methods were non-violent. It was an uprising of a whole people, women and men, young and old.

> It was a systematic mobilization of the Palestinian people that formed different small organizations to stand up for their rights. The first years of the movement involved not paying taxes, boycotting Israeli products and political graffiti etc. Even in the later years of the movement, it was the people standing up to the strongest military force by throwing little stones at them while they were being shot at.

The symbolism of David and Goliath comes to mind. These 'children of the stones' captured the imagination of the Arab intellectuals. Naim Ateek, writing of the non-violent character of the uprising, considers that the Intifada established the capability of the Palestinian people to resist non-violently the occupation of their country (Ateek 2008, p. 6).

It was a statement of defiance, says Ross, that they would not settle for occupation:

> Victimization has deep roots in the Palestinian mind. Whereas the preoccupation with security governs the Israeli approach to negotiations with all of its neighbours, the need to end victimization and to be accorded dignity, respect and genuine independence governed the Palestinians.
> (Ross 2004, p. 42)

Because the Palestinians felt themselves victims they found it impossible to be empathetic to Israeli needs. And you will be the first to point this out. They genuinely saw the Israelis as strong and themselves as weak. So, although this uprising lasted until 1993 it did not bring the longed for freedom for the Palestinians – but brought them to the attention of the world community. Global powers recognized the intensity of the situation and condemned the attack by Israeli forces. But what I find tragic is that this early inspiration in the non-violent character of the Palestinian resistance could not be held onto. Ateek writes:

> The Palestinians tried their best to keep the flames of the Intifada burning through non-violence resistance. The Israeli army, however, intensified its brutal practices, while the international community was ineffective in pressuring Israel to implement the UN resolutions.... The stamina of the Palestinian people ultimately wore down.
> (Ateek 2008, p. 105)

My question to you at this point, and I realize there are other dimensions to be discussed, given the length of time this conflict had been rumbling on, did the international community not bear some responsibility to try to end the Israeli occupation and bring some form of justice to the Palestinians? Should we not take some of the blame in this polarized situation?

An Alternative View

Dan Cohn-Sherbok

You have spoken forcefully about the Palestinian suffering. There is no question that resentment about their plight fuelled the first uprising. Yet – as you appear to do throughout our discussion – you concentrate solely on the anguish of the Palestinians. Previously and frequently you have quoted Benny Morris in support of your interpretation of events. I don't know whether you are aware that he has had a change of heart, and I want to quote at length what he has written more recently in an interview in *Ha'aretz* which gives a very different picture from your presentation. Referring to the War of Independence (or Nakba), he argues that the uprooting of the Palestinians was an essential step in the creation of Israel:

> A Jewish state would not have come into being without the uprooting of 700,000 Palestinians. Therefore it was necessary to uproot them. There was no choice but to expel that population. It was necessary to cleanse the hinterland and cleanse the border areas and cleanse the main roads. It was necessary to cleanse the villages from which our convoys and our settlements were fired on.

In response to the Palestinian rejection of President Carter's peace accords and the beginning of the Second Intifada (which we will discuss later), he explained:

> My turning point began after 2000. I wasn't a great optimist even before that. True. I always voted Labour or Meretz or Sheli and in 1988 I refused to serve in the territories and was jailed for it, but I always doubted the intentions of the Palestinians. The events of Camp David and what followed in their wake turned the doubt into certainty. When the Palestinians rejected the proposal of [prime minister Ehud] Barak in July 2000 and the Clinton proposal in December 2000, I understood that they are unwilling to accept the two-state solution. They want it all. Lod and Acre and Jaffa.

Regarding suicide bombings, he said: 'I don't see the suicide bombings as isolated acts. They express the deep will of the Palestinian people. That is what the majority of the Palestinians want.' On the subject of Israel's Arab citizens, he claimed:

> The Israel Arabs are a time bomb. Their slide into complete Palestinization has made them an emissary of the enemy that is among us. They are a potential fifth column. In both demographic and security terms they are liable to undermine the state. So that if Israel again finds itself in a situation of existential threat, as in 1948, it may be forced to act as it did then. If we are attacked by Egypt (after an Islamist revolution in Cairo) and by Syria, and

chemical and biological missiles slam into our cities, and at the same time Israeli Palestinians attack us from behind, I can see an expulsion solution. It could happen. If the threat to Israel is existential, expulsion will be justified.

In his view, the Israel–Palestinian conflict is a facet of a global clash of civilisations between Islamic fundamentalism and the Western world. 'Revenge,' he writes, 'plays a central part in the Arab tribal culture. Therefore, the people we are fighting and the society that sends them have no moral inhibitions.' Endorsing a Palestinian state, he believes that such a solution will reduce the urge for violence against Israelis:

> We have to try to heal the Palestinians. Maybe over the years the establishment of a Palestinian state will help in the healing process. But in the meantime, until the medicine is found, they have to be contained so that they will not succeed in murdering us. Something like a cage has to be built for them. I know that sounds terrible. It is really cruel. But there is no choice. There is a wild animal there that has to be locked up in one way or another.

For Morris, the Jews are the real victims in this conflict:

> That's so for the Jewish people, not the Palestinians. A people that suffered for 2,000 years, that went through the Holocaust, arrives at its patrimony but is thrust into a renewed round of bloodshed, that is perhaps the road to annihilation. In terms of cosmic justice, that's terrible. It is far more shocking than what happened in 1948 to a small part of the Arab nation that was then in Palestine . . . We are the greater victims of history and we are also the greater potential victim. Even though we are oppressing the Palestinians, we are the weaker side here. We are a small minority, in a large sea of hostile Arabs who want to eliminate us. So its possible that when their desire is realised, everyone will understand what I am saying to you now. Everyone will understand we are the true victims. But by then it will be too late.
>
> (en.m.wikipedia.org/wiki/Benny_Morris)

You stress in your last exchange the non-violent character of the Palestinian uprising. As you note, Naim Ateek argues that the Intifada established the capability of the Palestinian people to resist non-violently on the occupation of their country. Yet, this is not Benny Morris's view. According to Morris, violent action is more in accord with their true nature, as is evidenced by nearly a century of armed uprising against the Jews in their midst. Faced with the possibility of annihilation and extinction, it is the Jews, Morris believes, who are the true victims in this conflict.

Another Alternative – Palestinian Christian Non-violence

Mary Grey

Benny Morris's *volte-face* has been known for some time. What I always understood from the interview you cite is that initially, he had set out to discover what actually happened in 1948. (If you remember I mentioned Pappé's comment that he failed to use oral history and memory.) His change of view is more about exonerating Israel for its violent expulsion of the Palestinians than it is a denial of events. As you quoted, he now thinks Israel was perfectly justified because of 'security fears'. Well, Morris must live with his own conscience. What I seriously object to is this interpretation of the Israeli/Arab world. You write:

> In his view, the Israel–Palestinian conflict is a facet of a global clash of civilisations between Islamic fundamentalism and the Western world. 'Revenge', he writes, 'plays a central part in the Arab tribal culture.' Therefore, the people we are fighting *and the society that sends them have no moral inhibitions.* (my italics)

What Morris has chosen to ignore is that this is not simply an Israeli/Arab clash, but that there is a strong Christian presence in this society, which has been offering – since the 1960s – a non-violent alternative. (I do not know if Morris deliberately ignores Christians, but it is a frequent stereotype of the Arab presence in Palestine/Israel: all Arabs are Muslims and all Muslims are terrorists. This is untrue and a grossly offensive stereotype.)

The Christian presence in Israel/Palestine dates from the birth of the church at Pentecost (Acts of the Apostles, Chapter 2). Although seriously weakened since 1948 by emigration, it has steadily been pursuing a non-violent witness. For example, the Melkite Archbishop, Joseph Raya, took up the cause of two evacuated Christian villages, Iqrit and Kufu Bir'im, which the army illegally bulldozed on Christmas Eve 1951. Despite protests and sit-ins by both Arabs and Israelis, there was no permission for the villagers to return. In 1974 the Archbishop wrote to the Prime Minister, Golda Meir:

> There is not enough justice in this country. There is neither democracy nor liberty. . . . If you base security on the denial of justice, there is no accumulation of money which will guarantee that security; not even an army as strong as the Romans will ensure it.
> (Lilienthal 1978, p. 133, cited in Ateek 1989, p. 58)

Secondly, the United Christian Council in Israel – mostly Protestant denominations – has spoken out forcefully on behalf of the human rights of Christians in Israel. Some indigenous clergy – Greek Catholic, Roman Catholic, Maronite, Episcopalian, Baptist and so on – have expressed concern for justice and peace (Ateek 1989, p. 59). Undoubtedly the Palestinian Church has been let down by the global Church and by theologians, who have felt, or been made to feel, that to criticise Zionism, especially given the history of Christian anti-Judaism, is to continue to practise anti-Semitism.

But there has been a more visionary development in the founding in 1985 by Mubarak Awad, of the Palestinian Centre for Non-violence in Jerusalem:

> In the first year, the Centre engaged in education and outreach, including translation of works of and about Mahatma Gandhi, Martin Luther King Jr, Gene Sharp and Abdul Ghaffar Khan. Workshops such as 'How to Get your Rights without Firing a Single Shot' were held. Arabic pamphlets entitle 'Non-Violence in the Occupied Territories' were distributed in 1983.
> (Qumsiyeh 2011, pp. 131–132)

The Centre urged the Palestinians to revisit their ancestral homes and to explain to current residents – in sorrow and love, not heat and anger – the history of events. Other non-violent protests took place and Awad received both support and criticism. In the end the Israeli Government denied Awad a residence permit. He was arrested and kept in solitary confinement for 40 days, despite appeals by people like Coretta King, and a US Senator. Even the Secretary of State, George Schultz, spoke out against the deportation order. His actual deportation on 13 June 1988, elevated Awad's stature globally, writes Mazin Qumsiyeh and gave his ideas significant publicity (Qumsiyeh 2011, p. 131).

This kind of popular, non-violent resistance continued in the form of strikes, sit-ins and demonstrations. In fact these events multiplied from 933 incidents to 1,358 in 1985, to 2,887 in 1987 – and novel methods were introduced. Women were notably to the fore in such events. Qumsiyeh writes movingly about non-violent resistance as *sumud,* steadfastness:

> *We could write volumes about resistance by simply living, eating, breathing in a land that is coveted. We resist by going to school, by cultivating what remains of our lands, by working under harsh conditions and by falling in love, getting married and having children. Resistance includes hanging onto what remains of Palestine when it has been made crystal-clear in words and deeds that we are not welcome in our lands.* (my italics)
> (Qumsiyeh 2011, p. 235)

But, I hear you say, that is not how the Palestinians are perceived by Israel. I think the picture changes substantially – but not totally – with Saddam Hussein's invasion of Kuwait and the knock-on effect for the Arab world.

Palestinians and Armed Struggle

Dan Cohn-Sherbok

I applaud the non-violent approach of the Christians you cite (so very different from the Christian Phalangists who slaughtered innocent victims in the Sabra and Shatila refugee camps). They of course constitute a small minority of those living in the Holy Land. It is a pity they were unsuccessful in persuading Palestinian Muslims and the Arab nations themselves to follow such a policy. Instead, as Benny Morris notes, the vast majority of the Palestinians and those living in Arab lands who are Muslims sought to drive out the Israelis through armed struggle. Now, I want to return to the events of the period we are discussing. It is important to note that within Israel there was increasing sympathy for the plight of the Palestinians in the occupied territories. In 1989 a human rights organisation, B'Tselem, was created which criticized breaches of human rights by the Israeli forces. Another human rights organisation, Hotline: Centre for the Defense of the Individual was established to aid the Palestinians who had been denied the right to leave the country. In April 1989 the Israeli police reported that they had uncovered a network of illegal classes held by two West Bank universities at private schools in East Jerusalem, all schools in the University and the West Bank and the Gaza Strip having been closed by military order as a collective punishment because of resistance to the occupation. These meetings were closed down. In protest an expert on criminology, Professor Stanley Cohen of the Hebrew University, declared that such an action was an infringement of Jordanian law and a violation of the Geneva Convention and the Universal Declaration of Human Rights. During this period other figures lamented the defacement of Israel's humanistic ideals.

As the Intifada intensified, Yitzhak Rabin recommended that elections should take place in the West Bank and the Gaza Strip. On 14 May 1989 this scheme was presented by the National Unity government as one of several proposals: to strengthen peace between Egypt and Israel, to seek peace agreements with other Arab states, and to attempt to resolve the problem of Arab refugees in camps outside Israel. The peace initiative, however, was dependent on several conditions: Israel would negotiate only with the Palestinians not connected with the PLO who resided in the occupied territories; there would be no change in the status of occupied territories; Israel would not agree to an additional Palestinian state in the Gaza district and in the area between Israel and Jordan. Such conditions, however, were not acceptable to the PLO, and as a consequence the Intifada continued. On 20 May the leadership distributed a leaflet calling on Palestinians to kill a soldier or settler for every Palestinian killed in a conflict with Israeli troops. In the following months, the Palestinian schools were closed since they were perceived as focal points of insurrection leading to conflict between the Palestinian youth and Israeli troops.

In the view of Yitzhak Rabin, the Intifada represented the will of small groups who sought to discover their national identity and insist on its recognition. Such an acknowledgement was officially given by the American Secretary of State at the beginning of March 1990. Seeking to find a solution to the Palestinian problem, he asked the government of Israel whether they were ready to engage in negotiations with Palestinian representatives about the West Bank and the Gaza Strip. The Israeli Foreign Minister, Moshe Arens, was anxious for such discussion to occur, but Prime Minster Shamir objected. Angered by such intransigence, the Labour Party withdrew its support from the National Unity government. Shamir's government was then defeated on a vote of no confidence. During this period Arafat called on the Palestinians to renew violence against Jewish immigrants.

These events were interrupted by the Iraqi invasion of Kuwait in August 1990. Nearly a year later, on 18 October 1991 the Madrid Conference took place with President Bush and President Gorbachev as the main speakers. At the conference Israel was represented by Prime Minister Yitzhak Shamir and the Arab states were represented by their foreign ministers. Two months later in December 1991 another conference took place in Washington dealing with the procedures for future talks. Israel insisted it was not willing to discuss territorial concessions. Instead, it desired to focus on the Palestinian autonomy. The Palestinians, however, were not content with such limitation. After these talks, the Jews and Arabs met in a number of cities to explore various practical proposals. Such collaborative ventures were interrupted by the Israeli election in which Labour became the largest party. Seeking to extend the agenda beyond the subjects discussed at Madrid and Washington, Prime Minister Yitzhak Rabin stated that the Israeli government would propose a continuation of the talks based on the framework of the Madrid Conference. Aware of the Palestinian suffering during the previous decades, he proposed a form of the Palestinian self-government in the West Bank and the Gaza Strip. At the time he stated:

> As a first step toward a permanent solution we shall discuss the institution of autonomy in Judaea, Samaria, and the Gaza District. We do not intend to lose precious time. The Government's first directive to the negotiating teams will be to set up the talks and hold ongoing discussions between the sides. Within a short time we shall renew the talks in order to diminish the flame of enmity between the Palestinians and the State of Israel.
>
> (Gilbert 2008, *Israel*, p. 552)

The Enduring Spirit of the First Intifada

Mary Grey

I am very heartened when you write about Israeli peace efforts – the initiatives of Yitzhak Rabin – and the founding of Human Rights organizations like *Peace Now* and *B'Tselem*; these keep the spark of hope alive that, ultimately, the desire for peace will prevail.

I want to add two factors: the first is the effect of Saddam Hussein's invasion of Kuwait in 1990 (which you have mentioned). Initially the Palestinians were in admiration of his defiance with regard to the West. But Arafat made a huge mistake in throwing his lot in with Saddam Hussein, unlike most of the Arab States. The invasion had devastating consequences in that the Kuwaitis, Saudis and others expelled hundreds of thousands of Palestinians from the Gulf (Ross 2004, p. 48). In connection with this event, it needs to be pointed out that the other Arab States used the Palestinians like a political football! (You hinted at this in their treatment of the refugees, kept in camps under distressing conditions.) They continued to act out of self-interest.

Which is why the position of Arafat now became crucial – the second point. It was he who kept the Palestinian cause alive. Yet, based as he was at a distance (Tunisia), he had played no part in the Intifada – in fact he was shaken by the fact that a civilian population could act so effectively. This, says Avi Shlaim, 'accomplished more in its first few months than had decades of PLO military occupation' (Shlaim 2009, p. 33). It was at this moment that Arafat took the lead in the political process – but the peace efforts you describe only became possible when Likud – the Labour Party – came to power in Israel, given the previous refusal to talk to the PLO.

I want to end my contribution to this chapter by highlighting the significance of the First Intifada for the Palestinians. This on-going conflict does not represent a level playing field. The Palestinians have not regained their land or homes; the effects of the illegal occupation become ever severer and their economy is ruined: their very identity is threatened. Yet the Intifada, as well as evoking novel methods of resistance – as I described in my last letter – marked a revival of interest in everything Palestinian – flags, art, cooking, dance – in fact all aspects of culture: this could sometimes evoke a ludicrous reaction:

> Israeli officials were furious when Palestinians set to their clocks to a different time when Israeli time set the clock back one hour on 26 August 1990. On that day, Palestinians wearing watches with the unadjusted time were punished.
> (Qumsiyeh 2011, p. 152)

Yet, the cost in terms of loss of life or injury was immense:

> In the first two years of the uprising, Israeli forces and settlers killed 824 Palestinians, injured over 80,000 deported 58, arrested more than 70,000, imposed 6,163 days of curfew, uprooted 77,689 trees, and demolished 1,225 homes or sealed them off. (By contrast, 8 Israeli soldiers and 3 settlers were killed.) In total between 1987 and 1991, 1,100 Palestinian civilians were killed and thousands injured while engaging in non-violent resistance or not resisting it all (i.e. they were shot in their homes, in school etc.).
> (Qumsiyeh 2011, p. 153)

Someone who sums up the spirit of this first Intifada was Faisal Al Husseini, a non-violent activist. Born in Baghdad, he was active among the Palestinian students in Cairo, and joined the Palestinian army in 1967, but later became a key leader in the Palestinian non-violent resistance in Jerusalem. Most of his activities focused on this. After the Israeli occupation he became a member of Fatah, leading the political and nationalist struggle against the occupation. Sentenced to a year in prison in 1967, he would suffer many imprisonments and harassments. Following many professions, he set up the Arab Studies society and led the campaign to end the siege imposed by the Israeli forces on the Golan Heights.

One important achievement – among many – was to set up with an Israeli colleague, a number of ad hoc committees, which evolved into the 'Committee confronting the Iron Fist' (in the 1980s). This was one of the first Palestinian-led groups to involve Israelis, and implicitly accepted the idea of a two-state solution. (Such moderate ideas were considered a sell-out by others.) His key role in the Intifada we are discussing is considered his greatest achievement. I end with part of his poem written to capture the spirit of non-violent resistance in 1990:

> Oh God, the chest is replete with bitterness ... do not turn that into spite. Oh God, the heart is replete with pain, do not turn that into vengeance. Oh God, the soul is replete with fear, do not turn that into vengeance. Oh God, my body is weak, do not turn my weakness into despair. Oh God, I, your servant, am holding the embers ... so help me maintain my steadfastness. Oh God, faith is love ... Oh God, faith is forgiveness, ... Oh God, faith is conviction ...
>
> (Qumsiyeh 2011, p. 157)

The poem is much longer. It evokes the spirit of the Hebrew prophets or a St Francis of Assisi. Such a spirit offers abiding hope.

The Possibility of Peace

Dan Cohn-Sherbok

You have written extensively about both Muslim and Jewish peace movements. Their role in the Palestinian–Israeli conflict is important. But of even greater significance were the historical events which encouraged steps toward peace during the period we have been discussing. By the end of the First Gulf War in the spring of 1991, the circumstances for a peace deal between the Israelis and Palestinians were more favourable than before. A number of long-term factors were highly relevant:

- The majority of Palestinians accepted in reality, if not always in theory, the existence of the state of Israel.
- Despite the Intifada and other confrontations, the majority of Israelis and Palestinians came to see that it would be the best if they could find a peaceful solution to their conflict.
- The Yom Kippur War and the Lebanese invasion had persuaded a number of Israelis that it would be better not to rely on military force to contain the situation.
- The 1978 Camp David agreements set a precedent of a land-for-peace agreement.
- The collapse of Pan-Arabism lowered the external threat to Israel and encouraged the Palestinians to initiate a plan for settlement.
- After the exile from Lebanon where the PLO forces were driven in May 1991, the PLO became a homeless and impoverished organization (Ross 2007, *The Israeli-Palestinian Conflict*, p. 204).

There were also short-term factors which contributed to the desire for a peaceful solution:

- The disintegration of the USSR and the end of the Cold War deprived militant Palestinians of Soviet backing and also enabled the USA to pressurise Israel since it no longer had a key role as a political ally in the Middle East.
- In an emerging global economy Israel had to find a new economic role.
- The appearance of local leadership at the beginning of the Intifada threatened the PLO's position as the head of the Palestinian movement.
- The Gulf War had shown Israel in a new light; for the first time, it had become a dangerous liability. Hence, the US administration was determined that Israel should accept peace terms.
- The Gulf War had reversed the way Israelis and Palestinians were viewed. By siding with Saddam Hussein, Arafat had undermined

the credibility of the Palestinian cause. Simultaneously, by not attacking Iraq Israel had ceased to appear as a militaristic power in the Middle East.
- Radical Islam had emerged as a powerful force in Iran and Lebanon as well as Palestine itself. As a result the USA began to recognise that their real enemies were the Islamists who rejected many of the principles of democracy. In response to this threat, the West was determined to unite all those who prized western values (Ross 2007, *The Israeli-Palestinian Conflict*, pp. 204–205).

As I previously noted, following the liberation of Kuwait, US President Bush proposed a combined US–Russian peace conference, or series of conferences, to deal with the entire range of Middle East issues. Secretary of State James Baker drew up a plan embracing Syria and Jordan as well as Israel and the Palestinians. Initially the Palestinians were offered less than a state but more than autonomy. Yet, without the PLO being directly involved in the negotiations, Arafat refused to participate on these terms. Eventually, however, the PLO did attend the opening conference as part of the Jordanian delegation. On 30 October 1991 the conference opened in Madrid before a world-wide TV audience.

The talks dragged on throughout 1991 – progress was slow because various events in the Middle East disrupted the negotiations. In February 1992 for example, an Israeli helicopter gunship killed the Hezbollah leader Sheikh Abbas Mussawi in Lebanon with his wife and son. In October, a block of non-PLO Palestinian groups united under the banner of the National Democratic and Islamic Front to oppose the peace process. In November several Palestinian stone throwers were shot. A month later, when Hamas kidnapped an Israeli soldier, Israel deported 415 suspected Hamas militants to southern Lebanon which refused to accept them. This provoked an Arab-walk out from the talks in Washington. Nonetheless, the peace process continued.

Chapter 15
Arab–Israeli Negotiations

The Road to Peace

Dan Cohn-Sherbok

We have both been encouraged by steps taken during this period to establish peace in the Holy Land. The peace process at this point began on 19 July 1992 when James Baker arrived in the Middle East to seek a solution to the conflict between Israel and its neighbours. Two days later Yitzhak Rabin went to Cairo in order to renew negotiations for a peace settlement. The next month he travelled to the United States to meet President Bush. On 24 August, Israel cancelled the deportation orders for 11 Palestinians. The same day talks between Israel and the Palestinians were resumed in Washington. Several days later Israel released 8,000 Palestinians who had been kept in detention. Simultaneously, Peres, acting as Foreign Minister, engaged in renewed negotiations. In September he met Prime Minister John Major in London, who agreed to end the arms embargo as well as the ban on British companies selling North Sea oil to Israel. In addition, Major agreed to intercede to end the boycott on British and European companies doing business with Israel.

Despite these steps, tension mounted in the West Bank and Jerusalem during November and December. These efforts to renew the peace process inflamed members of Hamas and Islamic Jihad who were bitterly opposed to compromise. With the encouragement of Iran, Hamas condemned the Israeli occupation while improving the educational, welfare and health care of the Palestinian population. During this period Israeli soldiers were occasionally trapped by gangs of Palestinian youths and fired on them with live ammunition.

Despite numerous acts of violence on both sides, talks between Israel and the PLO began on 20 January 1993. At a villa outside Oslo, representatives met for three days. At the meeting several of the PLO submitted proposals involving the Israeli withdrawal from the Gaza Strip, a mini Marshall Plan for the West Bank and Gaza, and economic co-operation between Israel and the Palestinian authorities. On 9 February the Oslo talks reached a new stage. Meeting with Rabin, Shimon Peres argued that Israel should seek to induce Arafat to leave Tunis and return to the West Bank and Gaza. He then set out the advantages of the proposals that had been presented by the Arab delegates.

On 11 February the Oslo talks continued, and a draft declaration of principles was drawn up as well as a paper establishing guidelines for a regional Marshall Plan. Between 20 and 22 March secret meetings took place in Oslo in which it seemed that an accord between Israel and the PLO might emerge. This was followed by another meeting on 14 June in Oslo; two months later the Oslo Accords were approved by both the Israelis and the Palestinians. After the PLO had been required to renounce terrorism, a ceremony took place in Washington on 13 September 1993 with Yitzhak Rabin and Yasser Arafat as the main representatives. After the signing Rabin reluctantly shook hands with Yasser Arafat. In the following months Israel and the PLO engaged in active negotiations for an Israeli withdrawal from the West Bank and the Gaza Strip.

Despite these steps towards peace, Hamas and Islamic Jihad pressed for a more radical solution to the Middle East problem. In an attempt to stem further violence, Rabin felt that an approach should be made to Syria for an agreement concerning the Golan Heights. Peres, however, believed that Jordan should be consulted first about its desire that all the land should be returned, that Israel should cease taking water from the River Jordan, and that Palestinian refugees should be allowed to return to their former homes.

The Oslo Accords served as the framework for the peace process and a basis for Israeli-Arab co-operation. The form of self-government authorized at Oslo and the withdrawal plans provided a basis for eventual Palestinian statehood. In Arafat's view, such self-governing institutions were vital to the future of Palestine as a nation state. However, just as in 1947, the Palestinian Arabs were being encouraged by more radical groups to oppose a two-state solution. Israeli extremists were also set to sabotage the Oslo Accords. On 25 February 1994 an Israeli gunman, Baruch Goldstein, opened fire on Palestinian Arabs inside the main mosque in Hebron, killing 25 people. In response to this massacre, Arafat broke off negotiations with Israel, yet after several weeks of pressure the talks were resumed. Discontented Palestinians, however, actively sought to undermine the peace process. On 6 April 1994 a member of Hamas blew himself up with a bomb in Afula killing eight Israelis. According to Hamas, this was to be the first in a serious of terrorist attacks in retaliation for the murders of Hebron. A week later another member of Hamas detonated a bomb, killing himself and six other people in a bus in Hadera. Determined to continue with the negotiations, Rabin warned that such acts of terrorism would not deter the Israeli government from seeking an agreement with the PLO. On 3 May, Rabin and Arafat met in Cairo to finalize a peace agreement. Just after midnight Arafat added a number of territorial alterations to the maps that had previously been agreed upon. Once Rabin had accepted these changes, a signing ceremony took place on 4 May. Under the Cairo agreement, a Palestinian authority headed by Arafat was given legislative, executive and judicial powers as well as responsibility for security, education, health and welfare. Israel would retain control of foreign affairs and defense.

Obstacles to Peace

Mary Grey

Thank you for outlining events that led to the Oslo Peace Agreement. What a significant event and what enormous efforts so many people put into it – it is narrated in detail by Dennis Ross, intimately involved with every detail as policy Advisor to George Bush, then Vice President of the United States, in his book, *The Missing Peace* (Ross 2004). Ross describes himself telling Shimon Peres, then Israel's foreign minister, at a small reception celebrating a breakthrough in negotiations, 'Ben-Gurion would be proud' (Ross 2004, p. 118).

That these efforts and eventual agreements met with such resistance is another of those tragic moments we regularly encounter in the telling of this story. The extreme actions on both sides conceal the fact that the majority of both populations – Israelis and Arabs – are actually longing for peace. One of the factors that would undermine peace efforts is that one of its planks was the emphasis on the recognition of the PLO as representing the Palestinians. Admittedly the PLO now recognized Israel and in theory would reject violence. But this meant that the non-violent movement I have been describing in the last chapter was given neither proper recognition nor encouragement.

The second obstacle to the success of Oslo was the Hebron massacre you alluded to in 1994. Not only did the Jewish settler, Dr Baruch Goldstein, murder 29 Muslim worshippers and wound dozens more, but in the riots that followed, the Israeli Defense Force killed many more Palestinians. Goldstein became a hero for the Jewish Right – his grave a place of pilgrimage for Israelis to this day (Lerner 2003, p. 104).

A third obstacle to the success of the Oslo Accords is that, according to Sara Roy, the unchanged imperatives of Israeli control remained in place. These were: to restrict and delimit the development of a Palestinian economy and create a template for continued dependency, weakness and control; and to preclude the creation of a sovereign Palestinian state and dismember the Palestinian people and weaken if not destroy their national and cultural character – and their impact on an already weakened society, which struggles to remain whole and humane (Roy 2007, p. 5).

There is witness to this by many people. Ateek (2008, p. 23) writes that the Oslo Accords, instead of ending the occupation, rather consolidated the occupation of Palestinian land, and entrenched the injustice. Israeli settlements expanded tremendously and many new ones came into being; the West Bank and the Gaza strip were fragmented by hundreds of checkpoints; more Palestinian land was confiscated for the building of roads and highways to the settlements; and most significantly, an elaborate systems of laws and regulations were established by Israel to control and oppress the Palestinians.

But the biggest obstacle to lasting peace – and here, you may agree with me – was what happened to Israeli Prime minister Yitzhak Rabin. Rabbi Michael Lerner, in his search for key people and movements able to transcend adversarial attitudes, identifies Rabin as giving an important lead (Lerner 2003, pp. 105–106). Rabin was deep into the next step called Oslo II, which was to involve the withdrawal of Israeli troops from the West Bank and Gaza.

At this point he encountered opposition from the Israeli Right who accused him of turning Israel over to the terrorists. This in its turn resulted in Rabin arguing more passionately with a more accommodating attitude to Arafat and the Palestinians, acting, as Lerner says, as if he really believed in peace. The Right in its turn stepped up its campaign against Rabin, calling him an enemy of the Jewish State and comparing him to Hitler. This kind of rhetoric reached its climax in the assassination of Rabin by a young Orthodox Jew, Yigal Amir, after Rabin had given a talk at an Israeli Peace Rally – 4 November 1995.

Dennis Ross described his utter devastation (Ross 2004, pp. 210–211) and used the occasion of Rabin's funeral to state that the pursuit of peace would not be stopped by a murderer. President Clinton's speech, with the added idea that giving in to 'the hatred of our enemies would sow hatred among ourselves', struck an emotional chord in Israel. As you know, all would depend on Rabin's successor. And that is where things began to go badly wrong.

In my own way I felt the impact of this crisis moment. I was leading seminars on 'Religion and Ecology' at the University of Southampton, La Sainte Union College, when one Jewish student, wanted to give her paper on 'Jewish Roots of Ecology' in memory of Yitzhak Rabin. It was the day after the assassination. The event took on a completely different character.

Undermining the Peace Process

Dan Cohn-Sherbok

You are right that The Oslo Accords offered Israelis and Palestinians the possibility of a hopeful resolution to years of bitter conflict. Of course there were difficulties with the initial proposals. Palestinians were not offered statehood; rather they were to be given a limited form of autonomy on the West Bank and Gaza. From their point of view this was not an ideal solution. Yet it might have proved to be the first step towards the eventual creation of a Palestinian state. The tragedy was that these promising negotiations were undermined by political extremists who sought to subvert the peace process.

You correctly highlight the actions of Baruch Goldstein who opened fire on Palestinian Arabs inside the main mosque in Hebron, killing 25 people. This was a moral outrage. Similarly a week after Rabin was denounced as a traitor to the Jewish state at a rally in Jerusalem (on 28 October 1995), Rabin was assassinated by an Orthodox Jew, Yigal Amir. This act of terrorism was denounced throughout the world by Jews and Arabs alike. At a memorial meeting in Tel Aviv, King Hussein declared:

> I never thought the moment would come like this, when I would grieve the loss of a brother, a colleague, and a friend, a man, a soldier who met us on the opposite side of the divide, whom we respected as he respected us.
>
> (Cohn-Sherbok 2012, *Introduction to Zionism and Israel*, p. 209)

Nonetheless you overstate your case by focusing solely on the actions of extremists within the Zionist camp. In your denunciation of Israel, you omit to mention that it was Palestinian extremists as well who sought to subvert the peace process. I have already referred to Hamas' unwillingness to accept what was agreed at Oslo. Let me remind you of Hamas' history and philosophy. Created in 1987 early during the First Intifada, this organisation was a Palestinian offshoot of the Sunni Muslim Brotherhood. In its covenant drawn up the next year it renounced all compromise in its holy mission. From 1993 it added suicide bombings to its armoury, sometimes employing women and children on these missions. You must not forget the steps taken by such Arab extremists to subvert the Oslo Accords. For example, several days after the signing of the Israel–Jordan treaty at Wadi Araba in October 1994, 29 Israeli soldiers and a civilian were killed at Beit Lid on 22 January 1995 by a suicide bomber.

Hence, it is important to see that both Jewish and Arab religious opponents are to blame for subverting these historic steps towards a peaceful resolution to the Palestinian–Israeli conflict. Yet, having said this, there is no doubt that a shift in political opinion in Israel profoundly affected the peace negotiations. After Rabin's assassination, Shimon Peres was elected as Prime Minister. In the face of renewed attacks on Israel, the Oslo agreement came under increasing pressure. Although both Rabin and Peres were adamant that terrorism would not be allowed to undermine the peace process, the Israeli opposition parties unleashed a frenzied campaign against the Oslo Accords. In the election campaign, Yeshiva students and young members of Likud roamed the streets denouncing Peres. Following the election, Labour had the largest number of seats in the Knesset; however, in the vote for Prime Minister, Benjamin Netanyahu narrowly won the election. Together with parties opposed to the Oslo peace process, as well as the religious bloc, a new Russian immigrant party and the centrist Third Way Party, Netanyahu was able to form a coalition government. This set the stage for a different orientation towards the Palestinian problem. Unable to achieve the type of co-operation attained by Rabin and Peres with the Palestinian authorities, Netanyahu exacerbated relations with the Palestinians by opening the exit of an ancient tunnel that ran under the Old City next to the Temple Mount. In response, Palestinians engaged in acts of violence that resulted in the death of 15 Israeli soldiers and around eighty Palestinians. Such violence set the stage for the collapse of the peace process begun with such hope by leaders of both Israel and the Palestinians.

Were the Oslo Accords Just?

Mary Grey

Whereas I totally agree that Hamas extremism also must take some blame for the undermining of the Oslo Accords, I think that once again, you are unable to see the severe limitations of these from a Palestinian perspective.

I think I've hinted previously that the fact that these were Agreements between two very unequal actors one possessing great power and the other possessing virtually none at all. As Sara Roy pointed out (Roy 2007, p. 216):

> Although the PA was assigned responsibility for various sectors of activity under Oslo, ultimate authority over the territories – and the power to impose it – remained entirely with Israel. Further, by agreeing to official Israeli control over the West Bank and Gaza Strip, the PA, ipso facto, accepted both the existence and legitimacy of Israeli occupation.

Secondly, as she points out, a 'land for peace' formula left the amount of land returned unclear. Israel made no commitment to return to the 4 June 1967 borders, that is, to withdraw from the entire West Bank and Gaza Strip. In truth, negotiations came down to a question of how much land Israel, backed by the U.S., was willing to give up.

Furthermore, even if it is true that that although the absolute area under full or partial Palestinian control had increased during the Oslo Accords, these areas were non-contiguous and remained isolated cantons separated by areas under the control of Israel, allowing the occupation to remain unchanged – and in a powerful form. This is the cry I hear always in the West Bank – *end the Occupation!*

But it was the policy of separation that worsened the Palestinian position:

> not only did Israel seek to insure the demographic and political separation of Palestinians and Israelis, but also sought to separate and isolate Palestinians from each other and from their land, thereby containing (as opposed to expelling) the Palestinian demographic threat.
>
> (Roy 2007, p. 217)

Even more serious was the way that the Oslo discussion's ignored key issues core issues such as borders, refugees, Jerusalem and settlements to a later (end) phase of negotiations, that is, the Camp David summit. In the interim, Israel established key facts on the ground, which severely compromised negotiations, for example, the expropriation [with the Palestinian Authority (PA)'s approval] of at least 70,000 acres of Palestinian land, the doubling of the settler population, the construction and expansion of settlements and a vast network – 250 miles – of bypass roads that not only connected Israeli settlements to each other but to Israel as well.

Hence, despite dramatic changes in the Israeli position at Camp David in July 2000, Prime Minister Barak's offer to the Palestinians was anything but generous. At best, it would have left Palestinians with an edifice of autonomy in geographic non-contiguous areas and little more, a reality they could not accept.

As you are aware, Shimon Peres succeeded Rabin. He was very different person with no great love for the Palestinians. At this key moment, Peres chose not to pursue the peace initiatives of his predecessor but to take vengeance on Palestinian terrorist leaders. You have already alluded to the threat posed by Hamas and I have highlighted the difficulties caused by identifying Hamas with the PLO. This situation was worsened by Yasir Arafat's failure to condemn Hamas's violence – which in turn exacerbated the mood of the Israeli Right. The disunity among Palestinian leaders has to be taken as a serious obstacle in the search for peace. The mood of despair at this moment would be heightened when Benjamin Netanyahu succeeded Perez as Prime Minister. He refused to end some of the key agreements of Oslo.

The Oslo Agreements now seemed as good as dead.

The Danger of Intransigence

Dan Cohn-Sherbok

I think your analysis of Oslo illustrates the danger of adopting an inflexible attitude to negotiation. This has been the hallmark of both Palestinian and Israeli approaches to possible peace agreements from Oslo I to the present. Both sides seek a just and lasting peace:

they see co-existence as vital to the region. Yet, despite this vision of reconciliation, the key political figures involved in discussions have repeatedly adopted positions which have made it impossible to reach agreement. I want to stress this has been as much a failure of the Israeli government as the Palestinian leadership.

Let me focus on what you have just written as an example of the kind of intransigence that has crippled the possibility of a constructive solution to the Middle East crisis. You begin by quoting Sara Roy. She argues that negotiations between the Palestinians and the PLO were (as you said) between unequal powers. Given such imbalance, she states, it was envisaged that Israel would have ultimate authority over the occupied territories. By implication, she asserts, the PA accepted the legitimacy of Israeli occupation. Yet, even if an unequal balance of power existed between Israel and the Palestinians, this should not have been perceived as an overwhelming stumbling bloc to agreement. No doubt Oslo's acceptance of Israel's role in the occupied territories was not ideal from a Palestinian perspective. But what Oslo proposed was a beginning, the first stumbling steps towards ultimate statehood.

The same point applies to Roy's observation concerning Israel's lack of commitment to return to the 1967 borders. I agree: for the Palestinians this was not ideal. But to adopt an uncompromising position, as Roy does, makes negotiation impossible. The same point applies to the assertion that the Declaration of Principles and later interim agreements do not acknowledge Israeli occupation and Palestinian national rights. Even if this is true, the key point is that Oslo would have been a breakthrough on the road to peace. What is critical, despite various limitations of the Oslo Accords, is that Palestinian control over previously occupied territories could have been institutionalized.

It is true that other critical issues were not dealt with at Oslo such as the right of return of refugees, and the end of settlements. These issues were to be explored at the Camp David Summit in 2000. But the fact that not all issues were discussed does not mean that Oslo was fatally flawed (as the authors you cite seem to suggest). On the contrary, Oslo could have been a turning point rather than a dead end.

My central contention in reviewing various authors you have quoted is to warn against adopting a position that demands the full and total fulfilment of either side's list of demands. If a solution can ultimately be found to the stalemate that currently exists, then genuine and painful compromise must take place. I have spoken so far of what appears to me as Palestinian intransigence based on a Palestinian narrative of events. But I want to stress that there is similar Zionist inflexibility which stands in the way of a peaceful solution. It is equally absolutist. Here is an example taken from an article published today by Victor Sharpe: 'Two State Solution It's Very Expression Echoes the Euphemisms of Nazi Germany':

> The suicidal euphemism to mask Israel's destruction is the 'Two State Solution'. This abomination, along with the equally damning phrase 'land for peace' has permitted a delusional belief that two states can live side by side in peace with each other. One state is Israel, a democratic state. The other state would be Palestine an artificial creation and a terrorist entity supported by Iran that would live and breathe in relentless and genocidal aggression towards its neighbour Israel.
> (israeladvocate@israeladvocate.net)

Such rhetoric (which can be matched from Palestinian sources) and the absolutist assumptions about the Holy Land that lie behind such statements pose serious obstacles on the path to peace.

This Elusive Peace – Another Significant Dimension

Mary Grey

While we have been having this Chapter's exchange (mid-July 2013), the likelihood of yet another Peace Process beginning is very high. Yet we are both already reading negative predictions about its possible success. In fact there have been 13 major initiatives between the First Intifada (1987) and 2003. There have to be some serious obstacles to peace – some of which I outlined (quoting Sara Roy) – and causing this repeated failure. At the end of this Chapter further analysis is called for.

It is not only intransigence that is the cause. And I find it curious that you say I am citing solely Palestinian sources to support my arguments. Sara Roy, for starters is Jewish American! She went to Gaza for research purposes, saw the desperation on the ground – which we have not really discussed – and based the analysis I cited from her own experience. I also cite Rabbi Michael Lerner frequently, because I really believe his call for a missing mutuality and empathy between the conflicting sides is a sine qua non for reconciliation. Many spiritual writers from both our traditions involved in conflict resolution what could be called 'crossing the road' to encounter people and to understand the view from the other side (Nouwen 1996, p. 228).

Such a stance involves a strong leadership who really desire peace with justice. As we are both observing, both sides lacked leaders with such wisdom. Both Netanyahu and Barak showed few signs of Israel being willing to relinquish land/settlements, and little conscience for the fact that they continued to act illegally with regard to UN legislation. Arafat in his turn lacked the same wisdom: he returned from the Camp David summit II to acclaim from the Palestinians but little concrete gain for them.

And here I want to invoke the role played by the Americans – which in the end was ambiguous. How could one doubt the sincerity of both President Carter and Clinton in being brokers of peace? An ex-Arab League ambassador told me recently of the huge effort put in by Carter to keep both sides talking. Dennis Ross (US envoy to the Middle East, 1988–2000) worked tirelessly during the Oslo period with genuine sympathy and great diplomatic skills. Yet the very initiative of America both highlights the fact that this conflict is now an international concern, but also that American support for Israel loads the dice still further against the Palestinians in an unequal power play.

Many believe that Israel has not given up its dream of a new Middle East and still want to force as any Palestinians as possible out of the country allowing a docile remnant to accept its place to serve its Israeli masters. As Naim Ateek has written:

> For its own public image in the world, Israel cannot openly say 'no' to peace initiatives, especially when the United States is

involved ... when the initiative comes from the United States, Israel complies, usually after sending its reservations (as it did with the road map).

(Ateek 2008, p. 26)

Israel still adheres to its long-term objectives and attempts to avoid conflict resolution on the basis of international law. Moreover, if things do not go well for Israel, it can have recourse to its influence through the American-Israel Public Affairs Committee (AIPAC). Due to the power of the Israel lobby in the American government, says a well-documented report of 2006, it is difficult to accept that the United States can have a genuine role as 'honest broker' in the Peace Process (Ateek 2008, p. 27). This is one reason for the negativity with regard to the Peace Process with which I began this letter.

But I want to conclude on a more positive note with the concluding reflections of Dennis Ross after the Oslo Accords and their eventual failure (Ross 2004, p. 772). Ross is firm that no imposed solution will work:

> Ultimately the United States may make its greatest contribution to peace by standing against efforts to impose solutions and standing for the principle that regional leaders must finally exercise their responsibilities to confront history and mythology. Only when they are prepared to do that will the peace agreements endure. Only then will agreements be seen for what they are – authentic and legitimate reflections of what Israeli, Palestinians and Arabs have decided. We can help them make these decisions, but we cannot substitute our will for theirs.

I wonder if you agree?

Chapter 16

Before and after September 11 – The Second Intifada 2000 and the Attack on the Twin Towers

A New Wave of Violence – Sharon Lights the Match!

Mary Grey

Our last chapter was on the whole hopeful – as so much goodwill went into the Oslo Accords. But as a result of these, the Palestinians were left with mounting frustration that any settlement with even a modicum of justice would be reached: the Israelis were both disenchanted with the Palestinians and disillusioned with results of Oslo (Shlaim 2009, p. 207).

The apparent spark for the wave of violence was the visit of Ariel Sharon, the leader of the Israeli opposition Likud party, to the Temple Mount, to the Al-Aqsa Mosque, reverenced as a sacred site, the third holiest site for Muslims. This was on 28 September 2000. To complicate matters, it is also the holiest site in Jerusalem for Judaism – the site of the original Temple – and was under the (illegal) Israeli authority since 1980. Sharon was only permitted to enter the compound after the Israeli Interior Minister had received assurances from the Palestinian Authority's security chief that no problems would arise if he made the visit. The stated purpose for Sharon's visit of the compound was to assert the right of all Israelis to visit the Temple Mount. However, according to the Likud spokesman Ofir Akunis, the purpose was actually to 'show that under a Likud government [the Temple Mount] will remain under Israeli sovereignty'. Shortly after Sharon left the site, angry demonstrations by Palestinian Jerusalemites outside erupted into rioting. Israeli police responded with tear gas and rubber bullets, while protesters hurled stones and other missiles, injuring 25 policemen, of whom one was seriously injured and had to be taken to hospital. At least three Palestinians were wounded by rubber bullets.

There is also dispute as to whether the Intifada was actually planned by Yasser Arafat beforehand because of the perceived failure of the Oslo Accords after the Camp David Summit (II). Be this true or not, Sharon's visit certainly ignited the violence that derailed the Peace Process. The Palestinians condemned Sharon's visit to the Temple Mount as a provocation and an incursion, as were his armed bodyguards that arrived on the scene with him. Critics claim that Sharon knew that the visit could trigger violence, and that the purpose of his visit was political (http://en.wikipedia.org/wiki/Second_Intifada).

The complex causes of this second Palestinian uprising were, first of all, resistance to the continuing, progressively more severe, indefinite military occupation of the West Bank and Gaza Strip, accompanied by policies of colonial-type land and resource expropriation within those Israeli-occupied territories, as well against the continued denial of basic civil and political rights to Palestinians. For example, there were now over 600 checkpoints set up to control lives of Palestinians, together with a network of roads and highways to further isolate Palestinian villages and communities from each other.

As contrasted with the First Intifada, which as I argued, was largely non-violent, the Second was characterized by a prolonged period of intensified popular resistance on the part of the

Palestinians to Israeli means of control, through methods ranging from the Palestinian traditional *sumud,* and non-violent demonstrations, to a far greater level of organized armed resistance and suicide bomber attacks. This was a tragedy, wrote Naim Ateek, that Palestinian extremists, in the face of mounting level of Israeli violence

> made matters much worse by collaborating with Israel, either consciously or unconsciously, providing Israel with justification for its actions. Instead of recognizing Israel's ability to manipulate, they have fallen into a trap. Palestine's grievous slide into a morass of suicide bombings represents a tragic deterioration of the Palestinian community.
>
> (Ateek 2008, p. 46)

The Second Intifada was also distinguished by the particularly pronounced brutality of this Israeli response to provocation. The death toll, including both military and civilian, is estimated to be about 3,000 Palestinians and 1,000 Israelis, as well as 64 foreigners. B'Tselem's figures show that up till 30 April 2008, 35.2 per cent of the Palestinians who were killed directly took part in the hostilities, 46.4 per cent 'did not take part in the hostilities' and 18.5 per cent where it was not known whether they were taking part in hostilities. Of the Israeli casualties, B'Tselem reports that 31.7 per cent were security force personnel and 68.3 per cent were civilians. A 2005 study conducted by Israel's International Institute for Counter-Terrorism (ICT) concluded that Palestinian fatalities have consisted of more combatants than noncombatants. Up to 2005, the ICT put Israeli combatant casualties at 22 per cent and civilian at 78 per cent.

It was during this period in particular that the Palestinians acquired internationally the reputation of being terrorists. Yet it is often (conveniently) forgotten that Israel has developed 'one of the most comprehensive and lethal systems of control and suppression the world has ever seen' (Ateek 2008, p. 46):

> Israel has been successful in using propaganda against the Palestinians. It paints the Palestinians as violent and savage in order to justify its actions against them ... Israel's strong allies

in Washington cover up Israel's violations and heap blame on the Palestinians.

(Ateek 2008, p. 46)

We are both against violence – but now the humiliation and desperation of the Palestinians could no longer be contained. The world had ignored the First Intifada: it could not ignore the Second.

Reviving the Peace Process
Dan Cohn-Sherbok

At the end of the last chapter you pointed out that some of the writers that you quoted and whom I have criticized (such as Sara Roy) are in fact Jewish. I think you have misunderstood my point. My criticism is that these authors – regardless of whether they are Jewish, Palestinian or Christian – have in my view uncritically embraced the Palestinian narrative of events. Instead of perceiving the complexity of the Middle East conflict, they have simplified the struggle between Israelis and Arabs and have focused exclusively on the plight of the Palestinians. To my mind they are victims of Palestinian propaganda in just the same way that the writer whom I quoted at the end of the last chapter is blinded by the Zionist interpretation of the Jewish struggle against the Palestinians.

Perhaps it might be useful to review the events leading up to Ariel Sharon's provocative visit to the Temple Mount.

As we both have noted, Prime Minister Netanyahu was not sympathetic to aims of the Oslo Accords. On 7 November 1996 Peres in a speech to the Knesset, Peres warned of the dangers of allowing the peace process to collapse. You have criticized the participation of the United States in these negotiations because of its bias toward Israel, yet, it seems to me it has played a vital role in the quest for peace in the region. In October 1998 Prime Minster Netanyahu and Yasser Arafat met in Washington to discuss the peace process. After prolonged argument, Israel and the Palestinians agreed to embark on a new stage of cooperation. According to the Wye Agreement, Israel would effect a further West Bank redeployment, involving 27.2 per cent of the occupied territory. Thirteen per cent of this area would pass from Israeli occupation to Palestinian civil control. The remaining 14.2 per cent, which was previously under joint Israel–Palestinian Authority control, would come under Palestinian rule. In addition, the Israelis and Palestinian would together establish a committee to consider the third phase redeployment that was mandated by the 1995 interim agreement.

At this meeting with Prime Minister Netanyahu, Yasser Arafat agreed that the Palestinian authorities would take all measures necessary to prevent acts of terrorism, crime and hostilities. This would include a Palestinian security plan, shared with the United States, to ensure systematic and effective combat of terrorist organisations and infrastructure. To ensure peace in the region, bilateral Israeli–Palestinian security co-ordination would be restored, and a US–Palestinian committee would be created to monitor militant groups. The Palestinians further agreed to apprehend, investigate and prosecute specific individuals suspected of violence.

Conflict between Israel and its Arab neighbours had thus not been overcome through the settlement initiated by Rabin and Peres; the peace process had been thwarted by intransigent attitudes on both sides. Yet, after the election of Ehud Barak in the summer of 1999, the notion of separation between Israel and the Palestinians became official Israeli policy. In his election campaign, Barak promoted the idea of a physical separation as an integral feature of a two-state solution, a concept which became the West Bank barrier (Separation Fence), electrified and surrounded with trenches, razor wire, electronic surveillance and control towers approximately 350 km long. Concerning this barrier, Barak stated:

> (The fence) is essential to Israel in order to guarantee Jewish identity ... and it is (equally) essential to the Palestinian nation in order to foster its national identity ... without being dependent on the state of Israel.
>
> (Sachar 2007 in *A History of Israel from the Rise of Zionism to Our Time*, p. 160)

The events of September and October 2000 regrettably undermined attempts to create peace in the Middle East. On 28 September Israel's hardline leader, Ariel Sharon, angered Palestinians by visiting a Jerusalem shrine sacred to Jews and Muslims. Dozens of police and several Palestinians were injured in the riots that followed. The next day six Palestinians were killed and close to 200 were wounded in clashes at the shrine. Subsequently, clashes erupted in the West Bank and the Gaza Strip. On 4 October Ehud Barak and Yasser Arafat flew to France to meet the US Secretary of State Madeleine Albright and French President Jacques Chirac. Despite this political activity, fighting between the two sides continued. On 6 October Israel sealed the West Bank and the Gaza Strip, and the next day demonstrations stormed Joseph's Tomb in Nablus. Fighting in Jerusalem, Nazareth and Hebron continued through the Jewish holy day of Yom Kippur, and in the following weeks the violence continued amidst a flurry of diplomatic activity.

As hostility between Israelis and Palestinians intensified, Barak called for an election to take place later in the year resulting in the election of Ariel Sharon as Prime Minister. Negotiations for a final settlement resulted in a deadlock in July 2000. Palestinians insisted that refugees should have the right to return to their former homeland – this would have led to a Palestinian majority in the country. Israel insisted on annexing key portions of the Palestinian area, leaving most settlements intact, and offered only a limited form of Palestinian statehood. On 28 September 2000 violence erupted when Ariel Sharon made a visit to the Temple Mount in Jerusalem. Nonetheless, in January 2001 peace talks were held at Taba, an Egyptian resort town. Although the Oslo Accords had faded into history, these talks held out the possibility for a final resolution to the ongoing conflict.

The Horrific Impact of 'The Wall'

Mary Grey

I have admitted the truth of the violence on both sides, as well as the regret of Naim Ateek that Palestinian extremists had abandoned the way of non-violence in the Second Intifada. Yet you ignore my point about the imbalance of power, and the fact that increasing desperation of the Palestinians had driven some of them to this violence. You also do not seem to admit that the possibility of Jewish peace activists recognizing the injustices heaped upon the Palestinians could have changed their world-view and that this was not merely a blind response to propaganda. So I repudiate your last statement:

> To my mind they are victims of Palestinian propaganda in just the same way that the writer whom I quoted at the end of the last chapter is blinded by the Zionist interpretation of the Jewish struggle against the Palestinians.

I ask you if you really consider if the efforts for healing Israel/Palestine of Rabbi Michael Lerner, a faithful Jewish Rabbi, frequent visitor to Israel, are due to his being a victim of propaganda. As I have said, I am looking for people of reconciliation who look beyond polarized positions and recognize what is true justice and what is its opposite.

Secondly, you narrate the construction of the 'separation barrier' – known internationally as 'The Wall' – as part of Barak's proposal for a two-state settlement. But you give no reaction as to the effect on this for the people of the West Bank. As you know, the very word conjures up South African Apartheid, the dividing wall in Belfast and the wall that used to divide East and West Germany. The total length of this Wall is planned to be 700 km. You are also aware that Israel argues that the barrier is necessary to protect Israeli civilians from Palestinian terrorism, including the suicide bombing attacks that increased significantly during the Second Intifada. That there have been a reduced number of incidents of suicide bombings since the construction of the barrier is used by them as a measure of its success and continues to act as a preventative measure. But its opponents argue that the barrier is an illegal attempt to annex Palestinian land under the guise of security, that it violates international law, has the effect of undermining negotiations (by establishing new borders), and severely restricts Palestinians who live nearby, particularly their ability to travel freely within the West Bank, including to and from the lands on which their subsistence depends, and to access work in Israel. In a 2004 advisory opinion resulting from a Palestinian-initiated UN resolution, the International Court of Justice considered that 'Israel cannot rely on a right of self-defense or on a state of necessity in order to preclude the wrongfulness of the construction of the wall.' The Court asserted that 'the construction of the wall, and its associated régime, are contrary to international law' (en.wikipedia.org/wiki/israeli_west_bank_barrier).

I think our readers deserve to know the human impact of this barrier. In fact, it is the single feature of the Occupation that most opens the eyes of pilgrims and tourists as to what is actually happening in the West Bank. Take Bethlehem, for instance. At Christmas, when most Christians in Britain sing carols about 'the Little Town of Bethlehem' as the (believed) site of Jesus's birth, with its words 'How still we see thee lie' and its 'deep and dreamless sleep', the actual residents are living in a walled prison in their own land. If, early in the morning, you have been through the check-point that controls entry to Bethlehem – as I have – you see a long line of Palestinian men going to work in Jerusalem being routinely humiliated by young Israeli soldiers, facing searches – even strip searches. And these are the lucky ones – who have been given permits to travel. I know people who have given up trying to go to Jerusalem because of this humiliation. And this is particularly painful on festival days – for both Muslims and Christians. Graffiti on the wall painted by peace activists and celebrity visitors paint a picture of a spirit that refuses to be destroyed, but the reality becomes steadily grimmer.

I do not defend suicide bombing at all, but understand to what lengths continuous and worsening suffering can drive people. And this is before we factor in the effects on the conflict of the attacks on the Twin Towers in New York that killed more than 3,000 people.

The Separation Barrier

Dan Cohn-Sherbok

I have every respect for you and others who sympathize with the suffering of Palestinians; the terrible situation of hundreds of thousands of refugees in the camps is a cause for deep concern. Yet, you have repeatedly evaded my questioning about this tragedy which I have posed numerous times in our discussion. The surrounding Arab nations did not rescue their Palestinian brothers and sisters who have endured great hardship in these camps. There is no doubt that we Jews would have acted differently. We would not have abandoned Jewish refugees in the same way. Indeed, the creation of the state of Israel was a response to such depravation in Eastern Europe and elsewhere. Surely this calls for condemnation on your part instead of silence.

I do believe that there is Palestinian propaganda just as there is Jewish propaganda. And yes, I do think that many of the writers you cite have been susceptible to it. Dare I say you have too. It is understandable that sensitive individuals (like you) will incline to side with those who are perceived as underdogs in a conflict. I admire their compassion. But such sympathy can blind one to the complexities of political and social conflict as well the suffering of those on the other side of an armed struggle.

You have denounced the Israeli government for creating a security fence. I too am concerned that it is an ugly, defacing scar on the landscape and it has made Palestinian life increasingly difficult. It would have been better if it had never been needed. However, in castigating the Israeli government, you have, I believe intentionally ignored the dilemmas facing the Jewish state. It is undeniable that the separation barrier (or Wall) was created as a response to Palestinian terrorism. Its aim has been to protect Israeli civilians from terrorist attacks including the suicide bombing that increased significantly during the Second Intifada.

You will remember that the idea of creating a physical barrier between the Israeli and Palestinian populations was first proposed in 1992 by the then prime minister Yitzhak Rabin, following the murder of an Israeli teenager in Jerusalem. Rabin said that Israel must 'take Gaza out of Tel Aviv,' in order to minimize friction between the two peoples. Following an outbreak of violent incidents in Gaza in October 1994 Rabin announced his stance that Jews have to decide on separation as a philosophy.

The first section of the wall (as slabs of concrete contiguous for miles) that stood as a barrier was constructed during the Oslo Accords. Rabin stated:

This path must lead to a separation, though not according to the borders prior to 1967. We want to reach a separation between us and them. We do not want a majority of the Jewish Jewish residents of the state of Israel, 98 per cent of whom live within the borders of sovereign Israel, including a united Jerusalem, to be subject to terrorism.

Following a Palestine violence outbreak in 2002 Israel began construction of a barrier that would separate most of the West Bank from areas inside Israel. The Israeli Supreme Court made reference to the conditions and history that led to the building of the barrier in the September 2005 decision. It described the history of violence against Israeli citizens since the breakout of the Second Intifada and the loss of life that ensued on the Israeli side. The court ruling also cited the attempts Israel had made to defend its citizens, including military operations carried out against terrorist attacks. It stated that these actions did not provide a sufficient answer to the immediate need to stop the severe acts of terrorism. Despite all these measures, the terror did not end. The attacks did not cease. Innocent people paid with life and limb. This is the background behind the decision to construct the separation fence. In 2012 it was reported that Israeli negotiators had proposed to Palestinians that the barrier would become a border between Israel and the State of Palestine.

As a result of the construction of the separation fence, there is no doubt that there has been a significant reduction in the number of incidents of suicide bombings. According to statistics published by the Israeli government between 2000 and July 2003, when the first continuous segment of the barrier was built, 73 Palestinian suicide bombings were carried out from the West Bank, killing 293 Israelis and injuring over 1,900. However, from August 2003 and the end of 2006 only 12 attacks were carried out, killing 64 Israelis and wounding 445. What your attack on Israeli policy overlooks is the fact that the creation of the separation barrier was a response to Palestinian terrorism and suicide bombing. It was a response to Palestinian violence, and as such it is the Palestinians who are ultimately to blame for its creation.

The Imperative of Truth

Mary Grey

I had fully expected you would retort by giving me the statistics on the reduced number of suicide bombings. But I had never expected that you would stick so one-sidedly to the Israeli pretext for the Wall and ignore my personal account of the humiliation imposed on the Palestinians. Nor did I expect that you would again taunt me with disregarding your question as to Palestinian refugees in other lands. I had answered you earlier that the issue for Palestinians in Lebanese or Syrian refugee camps was precisely that their Palestinian identity was the crucial factor: to be absorbed into the country of their host was to endanger the right or return, which, as you know perfectly well, remains as important today as it ever was.

Secondly, yes, I recognize that there is propaganda on both sides. But there is also the question of truth and justice – and that is what I strive for. I have repeatedly told you that I seek to cite people able to look beyond the rhetoric who offer empathy, forgiveness and reconciliation. I agree that the issues are complex and I do admit that the suicide bombings have caused terror and sufferings and I completely disagree with these violent actions. You write:

> Its aim has been to protect Israeli civilians from terrorist attacks including the suicide bombing that increased significantly during the Second Intifada.

That is not the whole story. The wall is not being built on Israel's border but rather well within Occupied Palestinian Territory, thereby de facto annexing Palestinian land and ensuring that Israel's colonies remain. It is estimated that approximately 43 per cent of the Occupied West Bank (containing approximately 94 per cent of the illegal Israeli settlers) will be de facto annexed by Israel. As I have said, the wall is being built in such a way as to divide Palestinian population centres from their adjacent agricultural land and water resources. Israel has effectively isolated Palestinian population centres from one another, and restricted not only freedom of movement of individuals but also of goods and services, thus worsening an already crippled Palestinian economy.

The wall takes many forms. In some areas, for example, around the Palestinian town of Qalqilya, the wall is an 8-m high wall of solid concrete (twice the height of the Berlin Wall) with armed watch towers positioned every 200 m. In other areas, the wall is a barrier comprised of trenches (up to 4 m deep), electrified fences, razor wire and military roads. There is also a 30–100 m wide 'buffer zone' east of the wall with electric fences, trenches, sensors and military patrol roads.

Nor are you right in claiming that this is a 'Security Wall'. The wall is not protecting Israeli citizens inside Israel – *rather it is protecting Israel's occupation, illegal colonies and on-going colonization of Palestinian land*. If Israel were truly interested in its security it would (1) abide by international law and withdraw completely from the territories it occupied in 1967 – the Wall has already been condemned by an International court in 2004 – and/or (2) build the wall on its 1967 pre-occupation border, rather than in the Occupied Palestinian Territories. Too long has Israel used the pretence of 'security' for the continued annexation and colonization of Palestinian land, and the notion of a 'security' wall fits into Israel's long-term goal of annexing as much Palestinian land as possible together with as few Palestinians as possible.

It appears that Israel's ultimate goal is to make life so difficult for Palestinians – through the loss of land, loss of water resources, demolition of homes and markets, restrictions on movement and access to health and education – that the Palestinians will eventually leave. Once complete, the wall will leave less than 13 per cent of historic Palestine for the indigenous Palestinian population.

In addition to disobeying the International Accord, breaking the Oslo Accords, the Wall breaks the fourth Geneva convention. In a report on the wall, former UN Secretary-General, Kofi Annan, stated that Israel has repeatedly stated that the Barrier is a temporary measure. However, the scope of construction and the amount of occupied West Bank land that is either being requisitioned for its route or that will end up between the Barrier and the Green Line are of serious concern and have implications for the future. Moreover, placing of most of the structure on occupied Palestinian land could impair future negotiations.

Furthermore, the damage that is being caused by the wall cannot be reversed: Palestinian farmers have already lost their crops, their land and their primary source of livelihood; and Palestinian homes and businesses have been demolished for the wall's construction.

Despite the wall's presence, Israel continues to carry out 'security' related attacks in the Gaza Strip including military invasions, aerial bombings, killing of Palestinian civilians (including children); (iv) land confiscations; (v) home demolitions and (vi) assassinations of 'ticking time bombs' *even though there has never been a suicide bomber entering Israel from the Gaza Strip* (http://www.nsu-pal.org).

Finally, I want to cite former US President Jimmy Carter who, a good friend of Israel has strived faithfully for peace for years. In his *Peace not Apartheid*, he describes the wall as a prison, not a security fence (Carter 2006, p. 196). He brings many voices as witnesses to the unjust sufferings inflicted. He also – significantly – says that Palestinians will now have insufficient territory with which to establish a viable state and, this being so, Israel will be constantly troubled by a dispossessed people fighting for their rights.

As we enter this new period for peace-making – (August 2013 – initiated by US Secretary of State, John Kerry) I cannot see how Israel can realistically continue to refuse to confront the truth of its actions: to do so will lose all credibility in the eyes of the world.

The Security Fence (or Wall)

Dan Cohn-Sherbok

It is true that you have pointed out that it is vital that Palestinian refugees should not lose their identities through absorption into the societies in which they live. But it did not occur to me that you intended for this to be a justification for continuing to keep these refugees in terrible conditions in the camps. To have done so for this reason is utterly inhumane. Yet, if you are right, this has been the intention of surrounding Arab nations. Rather than ensuring that their Palestinian brothers and sisters are free from such suffering and misery, the governments of these countries in which the camps are located simply allow refugees to endure considerable hardship and deprivation. Are you truly content with such a policy? I am not. As a Jew, I grieve for them and believe they should have been rescued from such conditions long ago.

Regarding the security fence (or Wall), it is absurd to pretend that it was constructed with the fundamental intention of annexing Palestinian land. Rather, it was (as the Israeli leadership has stressed from the beginning) designed to protect Israeli citizens from terrorist attack and suicide bombings. As I noted, after scores of suicide bombings and daily terrorist attacks which killed more than 850 people and wounded thousands more since September 2000, Israel's unity government decided to construct a security fence between Israel and the West Bank to prevent Palestinian terrorists from infiltrating into Israeli population centres.

As you will remember, the Palestinians committed themselves to the Oslo Accords, and in the road map they agreed to dismantle terrorist networks and confiscate illegal weapons. Yet, after more than 10 years of negotiations and a mounting toll of Israeli civilian casualties, it became obvious that the Palestinian Authority made a strategic choice to use terror to achieve its aims. Before the construction of the fence, terrorists simply needed only to walk across an invisible line to pass from the West Bank into Israel: no barrier of any kind existed. About 75 per cent of the suicide bombers who attacked targets inside Israel came across the border in this way.

However, during the 34 months from the beginning of the violence in September 2000 until the construction of the first continuous segment of the security fence at the end of July 2003, Samaria-based terrorists carried out 73 attacks in which 293 Israelis were killed and 1950 wounded. In the 12 months between the erection of the first segment at the beginning of August 2003 and the end of June 2004, only three terrorist attacks were successful, and all three occurred in the first half of 2003.

Since the construction of the fence commenced, the number of attacks has declined by more than 90 per cent. The number of Israelis murdered and wounded has decreased by more than 70 per cent, and 85 per cent, respectively since the erection of the fence. In other words, the security fence did its work.

You have sought to portray the security fence as a kind of Berlin Wall. Yet it should be noted that unlike the Berlin Wall, the fence does not separate one people and deny freedom to those on the other side. Israel's security fence separates two peoples – Israelis and Palestinians, and offers freedom and security for both. Further, while many Israelis are prepared to live with Palestinians, it is the Palestinians who maintain that they do not want to live with any Jews and call for the West Bank to be *judenrein*. Moreover, the fence was not constructed to prevent those who live in one state from escaping – on the contrary, its aim is to prevent terrorists from entering Israel. Finally, it should be noted that of the total length of the barrier, less than 3 per cent is actually a 30 feet high concrete wall. Most of the barrier consists of a chain-link type fence combined with underground and long-range sensors, unmanned ariel vehicles, trenches and guard paths. Manned checkpoints constitute the only way to travel back and forth through the fence. In most places the barrier is about 160 feet wide.

You have expressed horror that Israel has constructed this security barrier: yet you must be aware that similar security measures have been taken by other countries: the United States is building a fence to keep out illegal Mexican immigrants; Spain built a fence with European Union funding to separate its enclaves of Centa and Metlilla from Morocco to prevent poor people from sub-Saharn Africa from entering Europe; India constructed a 460 mile barrier in Kashmir to halt infiltrations supported by Pakistan; Saudi Arabia built a 60 mile barrier along an undefined border zone with Yemen to halt arms smuggling of weaponry and announced plans in 2006 to build a 500 mile fence along its border with Iraq; Turkey built a barrier in the southern province of Alexandria which was formerly in Syria and is an area that Syria claims as its own; in Cyprus the UN sponsored a security fence reinforcing the island's de facto partition (www.jewishvirtuallibrary.org/source/peacefence). As I said, it would have been much better if the security fence had not been needed. Yet, I reiterate the point that it is the Palestinian determination to terrorize Israel through attack and suicide bombings which is to blame for its erection.

Chapter 17
Continuing Conflict

Towards Peace

Dan Cohn-Sherbok

I want to return to the peace process following the events of 2001. Determined to press ahead, the United States sought to persuade Palestinians and Israelis that a negotiated settlement was vital to security in the Middle East. In April 2001 the Mitchell report was published which made a series of wide-ranging recommendations. The report concluded that it was essential that the government of Israel and the Palestinian Authority act swiftly and decisively to halt violence. The immediate objective of this report was to rebuild confidence and resume negotiations. The report explained that during the committee's mission their aim had been to fulfil the mandate agreed at Sharm al-Sheikh. The report stated:

> We value the support given our work by the participants at the summit and we commend the parties for their co-operation. Our principle recommendation is that they recommit themselves to the Sharm al-Sheikh spirit and that they implement the decisions made there in 1999 and 2000. We believe that the

summit participants will support bold action by the parties to achieve these objectives.

The restoration of trust is essential, and the parties should take affirmative steps to this end. Given the high level of hostility and mistrust, the timing and sequence of these steps are obviously crucial . . . We urge them to begin the process of decision immediately.

Accordingly we recommend that steps be taken to:

End the violence

*The GOI (Government of Israel) and PA (Palestinian Authority) should reaffirm their commitment to existing agreements and undertakings and should immediately implement an unconditional cessation of violence.

*The GOI and PA should immediately resume security co-operation.

Rebuild Confidence

*The PA and GOI should work together to establish a meaningful 'cooling off period' and implement confidence-building measures, some of which were detailed in the October 2000 Sharm al-Sheikh Statement and some of which were offered by the United States on 7 January 2001 in Cairo.

*The PA and GOI should resume their efforts to identify, condemn and discourage incitement in all its forms.

*The PA should make clear through concrete action to Palestinians and Israelis alike that terrorism is reprehensible and unacceptable, and that the PA will make a 100 per cent effort to prevent terrorist organizations and to punish perpetrators. This effort should include immediate steps to apprehend and incarcerate terrorists operation within the PA's jurisdiction.

*The GOI should freeze all settlement activity, including the 'natural growth' of existing settlements.

*The GOI should ensure that the Israel Defense Force (IDF) adopt and enforce policies and procedures encouraging non-lethal responses to unarmed demonstrations, with a view to minimizing casualties and friction between the two communities.

*The PA should prevent gunmen from using Palestinian populated areas to fire upon Israeli populated areas and IDF positions. This tactic places civilians on both sides at unnecessary risk.

*The GOI should lift closures, transfer to the PA all tax revenues owed, and permit Palestinians who had been employed in Israel to return to their jobs, and should ensure that security forces and settlers refrain from the destruction of human homes and roads, as well as trees and other agricultural property in Palestine areas. We acknowledge the GOI's position that actions of this nature have been taken for security reasons. Nevertheless, the economic effects will persist for years.

*The PA should renew co-operation with Israeli security agencies to ensure to the maximum extent possible, that Palestinian workers employed within Israel are fully vetted and free of connections to organizations and individuals connected to terrorism.

*The PA and GOI should consider a joint undertaking to preserve and protect holy places sacred to the traditions of Jews, Muslims, and Christians.

*The GOI and PA should endorse and support the work of Palestinian and Israeli non-governmental organizations involved in cross-community initiatives linking the two peoples.

(Cohn-Sherbok, *Introduction to Zionism and Israel*, pp. 215–217)

Regrettably violence continued into 2001 and 2002 despite attempts by the Mitchell commission and others to restore peace. On 11 September 2001 al-Qaeda terrorists hijacked airliners and flew them into the World Trade Centre in New York and the Pentagon outside Washington. A fourth hijacked plane, apparently heading for the White House, crashed into a field in Pennsylvania after passengers attacked the terrorists to prevent them from carrying out their mission. This event disrupted the Middle East peace process and refocused attention on the threat posed by al-Qaeda to the West.

Operation Defensive Shield

Mary Grey

I am saddened by your persistent lack of sympathy for the Palestinians living under Occupation and being semi-imprisoned by the Wall, despite the evidence I have produced to show that it – the Wall – has been condemned by so many international figures with sympathies on both sides and who genuinely want peace and reconciliation (for example Jimmy Carter). My plea to recognize the whole truth of the situation (Chapter 16, section 'The Imperative of Truth') I consider to be extremely important if we are to get anywhere in proposing pathways to peace. I do fully accept that there was violence on the Palestinian side, and small groups of terrorists, but I object you on considering all Palestinians as terrorists. Remember how Naim Ateek had lamented the fact that a small group had become radicalized, and how much he regretted it, but that this was not the position of the whole people (see sections 'A New Wave of Violence – Sharon Lights the Match!' and 'The Horrific Impact of "The Wall"' of Chapter 16).

Secondly, my plea for truth and for trust to be restored between the two peoples was a proposal of the Mitchell report. Initially this showed promising signs both because Senator Mitchell had played a key role in the Peace Process of Northern Ireland – and in addition he had some Lebanese American background (although this may have counted against him in some circles). But, Mitchell never succeeded in getting the backing of Congress for his proposals he made concerning Hamas (that they be brought in out of the cold), and concerning a settlement freeze. According to Rashid Khalidi:

> This was not the first, nor was it to be the last time, that leading members of Congress sided with an Israeli government against an American administration ...
>
> (Khalidi 2013, p. 98)

Mitchell was told that his proposals were in direct violation of the US laws. But, Khalidi continues, these were laws put in place by the efforts of the Israeli lobby – and I have already emphasized the influence of the American-Israel Public Affairs Committee (AIPAC) on the US policy.

As the conflict continued, the Israelis now embarked on a new offensive, which would damage their international reputation. This was **Operation *Defensive Shield***, a large-scale military operation conducted by the Israel Defense Forces in 2002, as the Second Intifada rumbled on. This, the largest military operation in the West Bank since the 1967 Six-Day War, was, reputedly, an attempt by the Israeli army to stop the increasing deaths from terrorist attacks, especially in suicide bombings. In fact it was sparked off by a suicide bombing, when, on 27 March 2002, at a hotel in the Israeli resort city of Netanya, a Palestinian suicide bomber detonated himself amongst a crowd during the Passover Seder at the Park Hotel. Thirty people were killed – mostly elderly people on holiday. The attack became known as the Passover massacre (see http://en.wikipedia.org/wiki/operation_defensive_shield).

Operation Defensive Shield began on 29 March 2002, with an incursion into Ramallah. Yasser Arafat was placed under siege in his Ramallah compound. It was then followed by incursions into the six largest cities in the West Bank, and their surrounding areas. The Israel Defense Forces invaded Tulkarem and Qalqilya on 1 April Bethlehem the next day, Jenin and Nablus the next. From 3 to 21 April the period was characterized by strict curfews on civilian populations and restrictions of movement of international personnel, including at times prohibition of entry to humanitarian and medical personnel as well as human rights monitors and journalists.

The UN report on the subject says, 'Combatants on both sides conducted themselves in ways that, at times, placed civilians in harm's way. Much of the fighting during Operation Defensive Shield occurred in areas heavily populated by civilians and in many cases heavy weaponry was used.' To give an idea of the violence I want to cite the massacre at Jenin.

Jenin – built on the ruins of an ancient Canaanite city – is in the north of the West Bank, overlooking the Jordan valley. The Jenin Massacre (1–11 April) took place in the Jenin refugee camp in the West Bank. The Israel Defense Forces entered the camp, and other areas under the administration of the Palestinian Authority, during the Second Intifada, as part of Operation Defensive Shield. The Jenin camp was targeted after Israel alleged that it had served as a launch site for the camp, and other areas under numerous terrorist attacks against both Israeli civilians and Israeli towns and villages in the area (http://en.wikipedia.org/wiki/jenin_massacre). The IDF employed infantry, commando forces and assault helicopters. Palestinian militants had prepared for a fight, booby trapping the camp and after an Israeli column walked into an ambush, the army began to rely more heavily on the use of armored bulldozers to clear out booby traps laid inside the camp. On 11 April Palestinian militants began to surrender and Israeli troops began withdrawing from the camp on 18 April.

Jenin remained sealed throughout the invasion and claims of a massacre were circulated in the mass media by Palestinian officials. Stories of hundreds of civilians being killed in their homes as they were demolished spread throughout international media. Although subsequent investigations found no evidence to substantiate claims of a massacre, and official totals from Palestinian and Israeli sources confirmed between 52 and 54 Palestinians, mostly gunmen, killed, and 23 IDF soldiers as having been killed in the fighting, yet disturbing reports still circulated about civilians being targeted especially within the refugee camp. A large area of this was demolished (Finkelstein 2003, p. xxlv). The IDF was accused by Amnesty International and Human Rights Watch of war crimes: for example, a 37-year-old, paralyzed man was killed by his home being bulldozed: his relatives were refused permission to bring him out to safety.

I could go on – but this is enough. Was Israel's reputation irrevocably harmed?

Defensive Shield

Dan Cohn-Sherbok

It truly grieves me that the Palestinians have consistently opposed the creation of a Jewish homeland in Palestine, and that for nearly 100 years have sought to drive out the Zionists by armed struggle. You pretend that it is only a small minority of Palestinians who have adopted terrorist tactics. You cite Naim Ateek as evidence of a non-violent approach. Yet you know that the Palestinians have always embraced violence. Indeed, in a democratic election the population chose Hamas as their leadership, an organisation that explicitly encourages warfare against Israel. The creation of the security fence (or Wall) was deliberately designed as a means of protecting the Israeli population from repeated onslaught including suicide bombings. I deeply regret it was needed. But I understand its rationale.

The same applies to Operation Defensive Shield which commenced on 28 March 2002. You portray it as a form of vengeful attack on innocent victims. Yet its real goal was to dismantle the terrorist infra-structure developed by PA, or allowed to operate in territory under the PA control. The operation consisted of moving Israeli forces into the West Bank and Gaza for the purpose of arresting terrorists, finding and confiscating weapons and destroying facilities for the manufacture of explosives. Do you truly deny that this was so?

According to Ariel Sharon, the aim of this was to counter the terrorist threat:

> IDF soldiers and officers have been given clear orders: to enter cities and villages which have become havens for terrorists, to catch and arrest terrorists and primarily, their dispatchers and those who finance and support them; to confiscate weapons intended to be used against Israeli citizens, to expose and destroy terrorist facilities and explosives, laboratories, weapons

production factories and secret installations. The orders are clear: target and paralyse anyone who takes up weapons and tries to oppose our troops, resists them or endangers them.
(www.palestinefacts.org/defensiveshield)

You must not overlook the historical background to these events. For nearly a year and a half before Israel commenced Operation Defensive Shield, Palestinian terrorists from the West Bank and the Gaza Strip had become an almost daily scourge on Israeli society. Instigated by their own leaders, Palestinians initiated the Second Intifada in September 2000 and quickly started using the lethal tactics of terror. From September 2000 through the end of February 2002, nearly 300 Israelis were killed by Palestinian terrorists, many in suicide bombings. The events of March 2002 changed the Israel defense establishment's philosophy on counter-terrorism. In what became known as 'Black March', Palestinians unleashed 15 suicide bombing attacks against Israel, nearly one every other day. With the streets literally stained in blood, the Israel public demanded action from their government to stop these atrocities.

In his address to the nation on March 31, Sharon highlighted that his government had made every effort to reach a ceasefire, but had now been forced to take action:

> Israel is in a war, a war against terror... This is a war that was forced on us. It is not a war that we decided to embark upon. This is a war for our home... We must wage an uncompromising fight against this terror, uproot these weeds, and smash their infra-structure because there is no compromise with terror.
> (www.jewishvirtuallibrary.org/source/history/defensiveshield.html)

You concede that there is no evidence for the so-called massacre of Jenin. But you are clearly determined to believe the propaganda. Operation Defensive Shield began in response to a Palestinian suicide bombing on innocent, elderly Israeli citizens in Netanya. Subsequently the Israelis received intelligence (which proved to be completely true) that the Jenin camp was full of weapons which the Palestinians had no hesitation in using to launch attacks against Israel. Then when the Palestinians finally surrendered, they said they had suffered a massacre at the hands of the Israelis. This reminds me of the fictional youth who murdered his parents, and then demanded the clemency of the court on the grounds he was an orphan.

The Need for a Reconciling Stance

Mary Grey

I appeal to you to stop taking such a polarized view of the Palestinians as violent – 'Yet you know that the Palestinians have always embraced violence' (section 'Defensive Shield'). I do not 'pretend' anything. I fully realize the horror of suicide bombings and have consistently condemned them. I also accept the need that Israel feels for security, being surrounded by Arab States. But I am convinced that if we are to say anything helpful about peace we have to try to rise above deeply polarizing views.

This is what I find so impressive about Kofi Annan, the former UN Secretary General. He took a determined initiative for peace between Israelis and Palestinians throughout his term of office. He firmly supported Israel – being present at the opening of a new wing of the Yad Vashem Holocaust Museum and in his speech acknowledging Israel's uniquely tragic history, and long experience of anti-Semitism. Yet he also sympathized with Palestinian suffering and its causes. When Prime Minister Ariel Sharon joked with him on the building of the Wall, 'Good fences make good neighbours', Annan's reply was 'but only if the fence is not built through your neighbours' land' (Annan 2012, p. 253).

He took a similarly objective view of Operation Defensive Shield. He strongly condemned Hamas's 'Passover' bombing, calling President Arafat four times that night urging him to condemn it. He was also appalled by the atrocities that the Palestinians committed, but then realized that the scale of killing that the Israelis were inflicting was far worse, with nearly 500 Palestinians dead and 1,500 wounded.

He was also extremely perturbed at what happened at Jenin – which you seem to want to dismiss as justified. Requesting Israel to send an immediate search-and-rescue mission – which was refused – he sent his envoy, Roed-Larsen to Jenin with the United Nations Work and Relief Agency (UNWRA) Commissioner General, Peter Hansen. This is what he reported:

> What he saw was horrific beyond belief. It is totally destroyed. It looks like an earthquake has hit it. I am watching 2 brothers pull their father from the ruins, the stench of death is horrible. We are seeing a 12 year old boy dug out, totally burned.
> (Annan 2012, p. 280)

But when Kofi Annan asked for a multinational peacekeeping force in Palestinian territory, Israel refused.

There was a similar violent attack and siege on the Church of the Nativity in Bethlehem (3 April to 10 May 2002). As you know, this is a cherished Christian site, second in importance only to the Church of the Holy Sepulchre in Jerusalem. The attack took place because of Palestinian militants hiding in the Church:

> When the force arrived, the wanted persons were already there. Dozens of militants, Fatah, Hamas, Palestinian Islamic Jihad and Palestinian Security Forces fled into the church . . . along with some 200 monks and other Palestinians who arrived at the site for different reasons, and were held as hostages by the gunmen.
> (http://en.wikipedia.org/wiki/Siege_of_the_Church_of_the_Nativity)

The soldiers were instructed to fire at anyone spotted inside the church. Throughout the siege, Israeli Army snipers killed seven fighters inside the church from their rooftop position and an Armenian monk was also injured. A major gun battle broke out, causing a fire. The IDF said that the Palestinians had opened fire from a bell tower, wounding two Israel Border Police gendarmes. The Israeli troops returned fire, and threw a smoke grenade, starting a blaze on the second-floor: another Palestinian was killed.

Of course there was huge reaction. Michel Sabbah, former Latin patriarch of Jerusalem said the gunmen had been given sanctuary, and that 'the basilica is a place of refuge for everybody, even fighters, as long as they lay down their arms. We have an obligation to give refuge to Palestinians and Israelis alike.'

On 7 April Vatican City warned Israel to respect religious sites in line with its international obligations: the Vatican was following events 'with extreme apprehension'. A spokesman for Catholic monks in the Holy Land accused the Israelis of 'indescribable acts of barbarity'. Pope John Paul II urged people to pray for peace in the Middle East and described the violence as having reached 'unimaginable and intolerable' levels. Prime Minister, Ariel Sharon, said that troops would remain in place until the militants inside were captured. British Foreign Office Minister, Ben Bradshaw, described Israeli actions in the area as 'totally unacceptable'.

On 20 April the Greek Orthodox Church of Jerusalem called upon Christians worldwide to make the upcoming Sunday a 'solidarity day' for the people in the church and the church itself, and called for immediate intervention to stop what it referred to as the 'inhuman measures against the people and the stone of the church'. It also asked Christians, Muslims and Jews to gather at the main entrance to Bethlehem and march to the Church.

On 23 April negotiations to end the siege began, mediated by the Archbishop of Canterbury's representative, Canon Andrew White. After two days of negotiations, the Palestinians were willing to discuss a possible deportation of the militants to what a senior official called a 'friendly foreign country'. But negotiations were protracted and complicated it was not until 10 May that the siege was finally over and 13 men left the church, laid down their arms and were exiled.

I tell this story – all too briefly – to illustrate the complexity of the issues we deal with, and to plead with you to respect people like Kofi Annan – and others – who long for peace so much that they try to empathize with the needs of both peoples in this conflict.

Palestinians and Violence

Dan Cohn-Sherbok

In your last response you criticized me for taking a polarized view of the Palestinians as violent. You have also stressed that it is vital that the whole truth of the situation is acknowledged. For the sake of truth, it must be admitted that the Palestinians have officially and consistently embraced violence as a solution to the Middle East crisis. This is undeniable, and it is a distortion to pretend that it has not been the case. I appreciate your quest to find a peaceful solution to the conflict between the Palestinians and the Israelis, but this does not justify a misrepresentation of history. Let me quote from three major documents to illustrate the Palestinian strategy. The first is from the Fatah Constitution which deals with method:

Article (17) Armed public revolution is the inevitable method to liberating Palestine.

Article (18) Entire dependence on the Palestinian people which is the pedestal forefront and on the Arab Nation as a partner in the fight, and realizing actual interaction between the Arab Nation and the Palestinian people by involving the Arab people in the fight through a united Arab front.

Article (19): Armed struggle is a strategy and not a tactic, and the Palestinian Arab People's armed revolution is a decisive factor in the liberation fight and in uprooting the Zionist existence, and this struggle will not cease unless the Zionist state is demolished and Palestine completely liberated.

Article (20) Achieving mutual understanding with all the national forces participating in the armed struggle to attain the national unity.

The second document is the PLO Charter again dealing with method:

Article (9) Armed struggle is the only way to liberate Palestine. This is the overall strategy, not merely a tactical phase. The Palestinian Arab people assert their absolute determination and firm resolution to continue their armed struggle and to work for an armed popular revolution for the liberation of their country and their return to it. They also assert their right to self-determination and sovereignty over it.

Article (10) Commando action constitutes the nucleus of the Palestinian popular liberation war. This requires its escalation, comprehensiveness and the mobilisation of all the Palestinian popular and educational efforts and their organisation and involvement in the armed Palestinian revolution. It also requires the achieving of unity for the national (watani) struggle among the different groupings of the Palestinian people and the Arab masses, so as to secure the continuation of the revolution, its escalation and victory.

The third document is the Hamas Charter, which again calls for armed struggle:

Hamas regards Nationalism (Wataniyya) as part and parcel of the religious faith. Nothing is loftier or deeper in Nationalism than waging Jihad against the enemy and confronting him when he sets foot on the land of the Muslims. And this becomes an individual duty binding on every Muslim man and woman . . .

(Peace) initiatives, the so-called peaceful solutions, and the international conferences to resolve the Palestinian problem, are all contrary to the beliefs of the Islamic Resistance Movement. For renouncing any part of Palestine means renouncing part of the religion; the nationalism of the Islamic Resistance Movement is part of its faith, the movement educates its members to adhere to its principles and to raise the banner of Allah over their homeland as they fight their Jihad . . .

There is no solution to the Palestinian problem except by Jihad. The initiatives, proposals and International Conferences are but a waste of time, an exercise in futility . . . (www.mythsandfacts.org/conflict/statute-treaties/all.htm).

These are the official pronouncements of the main Palestinian organisations. So much for your contention that the Palestinians are lovers of peace.

The Many Types of Violence and the Many Faces of Resistance

Mary Grey

I see nothing will stop you from persistently calling *all* the Palestinians violent. You clearly want to identify an entire people by the violent actions of certain violent groups while ignoring other elements of the same society. Would you dismiss the entire British people as violent because we went to war in Iraq and Afghanistan and ignore the thousands of people who opposed the war and continue to think it was a tragic mistake, unleashing further currents of violence in those countries, and tensions which still rumble on?

Was it right that justice should be done for the Jewish people at the expense of taking away the land from the indigenous people, the Palestinians – when even the Balfour Declaration had called for the need to respect their rights – as I have argued earlier? Doesn't a wronged people have the right to protest and resist what has been done to them? (Of course I know that the question is, *what kind of resistance is allowable.*) Why do you ignore the efforts of some Palestinians to work peacefully for a settlement? For example, the late President of Palestine, Yasser Arafat, although guilty of many violent actions in his early career (and also possibly guilty of corruption), later worked earnestly towards a peaceful settlement encouraged by Presidents Carter and Clinton, for which he was awarded the Nobel Peace Prize (together with Yitzhak Rabin and Shimon Peres in 1994). I am aware that some will say that the problem in many ways did begin with Arafat, who promised to pursue Palestinian statehood only through non-violent means. Mahmoud Abbas, his successor, has remained faithful to the commitment to non-violence, but this has gained the Palestinian people absolutely nothing so far! Israel has continued to build settlements, withhold monies owed to Palestine, imprison Palestinians without trial – including children, demolish many homes, and so on . . . Yet when Hamas fires rockets from Gaza, they seem to achieve results! (Such is the common perception.)

Why do you persist in ignoring the efforts of Palestinians – and Israelis – who work together for peace and specifically oppose the culture of military violence? For example, the 'Combatants for Peace' movement was started jointly by Palestinians and Israelis, who have taken an active part in the cycle of violence; Israelis as soldiers in the Israeli army (IDF) and Palestinians as part of the violent struggle for Palestinian freedom. After wielding weapons violently for many years, and having seen one another only through this guise, they decided to put down their guns and to fight for peace.

They believe that only by joining forces, will they be able to end the cycle of violence, the bloodshed and the occupation and oppression of the Palestinian people. They no longer believe that it is possible to resolve the conflict through violent means.

I could cite more examples: you must have heard of Miko Peled, the grandson of Dr Avraham Katsnelson who was a Zionist leader and signer of Israel's Declaration of Independence in 1948. His father was Matti Peled, an officer in the 1948 war, and a general in the war of 1967 when Israel conquered the west Bank, Gaza, the Golan Heights and Sinai. When his 13-year-old niece Smadar was killed in a suicide bomb attack, this tragedy led him not to revenge, but into exploring the stories and pain of the Palestinian people and becoming a peacemaker (Peled 2012).

But I will end with the story of Jean Zaru, a Quaker activist from Ramallah, whose husband was the Principal of the Friends school in Ramallah for 18 years – and whom I know personally. In her book, *Occupied with non-violence*, she tells not only of her personal painful experiences and the efforts to put into practice non-violent methods while teaching Muslim Christians together; but also of the spirituality of *sumud* – steadfastness – that I have mentioned earlier (Zaru 2008, 72–73). Story after story is told of hundreds of unarmed villagers facing courageously Israeli tear gas, in protesting the uprooting of thousands of olive trees to make way for the Wall. Nonviolence, she says, is not new but the growing movement of non-violent resistance is a new development – and I have already cited Mazin Qumsiyeh on this. In 2005 a national conference was held in Ramallah with hundreds of community leaders asking to be trained in non-violent methods – even entire villages! Sadly, she says, the media do not often report this: 'they do not create the kind of news that the media sees'.

Maybe you also do not 'see' this – or want to? Are you content to remain in your narrative of Palestinian violence or will you look further. The possibility of peace may depend on us changing our perceptions.

Chapter 18
Gaza and Beyond

Gaza – A Crucible of Suffering

Mary Grey

For some reason in this exchange we have barely mentioned Gaza. And yet, Gaza is seldom far from my thoughts, both as a place of intense suffering as well as being blamed for the ongoing conflict. The Israeli journalist Amira Hass relates that being told to 'Go and drink the sea in Gaza' is the equivalent of being told to 'Go to Hell' (Hass 1996, p. 10).

So what has been going on? First, a little history. When we speak of Gaza there is both Gaza city and the Gaza Strip under discussion. Gaza city is of ancient biblical or even pre-biblical origins. Gaza is Muslim with a small Christian minority. 75 per cent of the population is under 25. Usually we are speaking of the Gaza Strip which was captured by British forces during the First World War, becoming a part of the British Mandate of Palestine. After the 1948 Arab–Israeli War, Egypt administered the newly formed Gaza Strip territory and several improvements were undertaken in the city. Then Gaza was captured by Israel in the Six-Day War in 1967, but in 1993, the city was transferred to the Palestinian National Authority. In the months following the 2006 election, an armed conflict broke out between the Palestinian political factions of Fatah and Hamas: this resulted in the Hamas taking power in Gaza. As a result Egypt and Israel imposed a blockade on the Gaza Strip. Israel eased the blockade allowing consumer goods in June 2010, and Egypt reopened the Rafah border crossing in 2011 to pedestrians (paraphrased from http://en.wikipedia.org/wiki/Gaza).

Although the primary economic activities of Gaza were small-scale industries, agriculture and labour, the economy has been devastated by the blockade and recurring conflicts. The Gaza Strip has been separated from Israel by the Israeli Gaza Strip barrier since 1996, which has helped reduce infiltration into Israel. Since the beginning of the Second Intifada, Gazans are no longer permitted to enter Israel for work purposes. Special permits to enter Israel for medical purposes have also been greatly reduced, which has made travel for Palestinians almost impossible.

The nub of the unfolding tragedy in Gaza is that Hamas, now the ruling party in Gaza, does not accept the existence of the state of Israel and uses violent tactics to oppose it. Palestinian tactics have ranged from carrying out mass protests and general strikes, as in the First Intifada, to mounting suicide bombing attacks and firing Qassam rockets into east southern Israeli residential areas. Israeli tactics range from conducting mass arrests and locking up Palestinians in administrative detention to setting up checkpoints and building the Israeli Gaza Strip barrier and West Bank barrier, to carrying out assassinations targeting militants and leaders of Palestinian organizations.

The 2004 Israel–Gaza conflict refers to the series of battles between Palestinian militants and the Israel Defense Forces (IDF). Several Qassam rocket attacks on Israel (Sderot and the Negev) led the IDF to retaliate with airstrikes and land incursions. The fighting included two IDF operations, Operation Rainbow and Operation Days of Penitence. Operation Rainbow was a military operation from 18 May 2004 to 23 May 2004 in Rafah to clear terrorist infrastructure, find smuggling tunnels connecting the Gaza Strip to Egypt and kill militants after the deaths of 13 Israeli soldiers in guerrilla attacks. Israel said the operation was also aimed at preventing a shipment of Strela-2 (SA-7 Grail) anti-aircraft missiles,

AT-3 Sagger anti-tank guided missiles and other long-range rockets which are stored on the Egyptian side of the border from being smuggled through tunnels into the Gaza Strip.

Operation Days of Penitence was an IDF operation in the northern Gaza Strip, conducted between 30 September 2004 and 15 October 2004 focused on Beit Hanoun, Beit Lahia and Jabalia refugee camp, which were used as launching sites of Qassam rockets on Sderot and Israeli settlements in the Gaza Strip, and in response to the death of two children in Sderot. The operation resulted in the deaths of between 104 and 133 Palestinians, and five people on the Israeli side.

The Palestinian death toll since 2000 reached over 4,600 people. In fact, more than 1,000 have been killed and about 5,000 injured in the 2008–2009 Israeli offensive against Gaza alone. This offensive started on Saturday 27 December in 2008, with massive air strikes on all Palestinian government buildings. In June 2007 internal fighting broke out between Hamas and Fatah and Hamas fully consolidated its power by staging an armed coup d'état and taking control of the Gaza Strip. Following the fighting that occurred between 7 and 15 June 2007, also known as the Battle of Gaza 2007 in which 118 Palestinians were killed and over 550 were wounded, the entire Gaza Strip came under full control of a Hamas government. It is the sheer scale of Palestinian deaths that has made the Gazan situation an international concern.

As a response to the Hamas takeover, Israel sharply restricted the flow of people and goods into and out of Gaza. About 70 per cent of Gaza's workforce has become unemployed or without pay, and about 80 per cent of its residents live in poverty. This gives some clue as to why Amira Hass, cited above, referred to 'Go drink the sea at Gaza' to mean 'Go to Hell!'.

So outraged have internationals activists become over the poverty and death trap that Gaza has become, that several 'mercy' boats have set off for Gaza with humanitarian relief and well-known international activists on board. As you know, they have been prevented from reaching Gaza by the Israeli army, which even boarded a Turkish ship and killed some activists, causing a hostile reaction from Turkey.

I wonder if you have any sympathy for the Gazan people . . . ?

Continuing Violence

Dan Cohn-Sherbok

You have outlined the unfolding tragedy of Gaza, but before turning to the events leading up to the Gaza conflict, I want to comment on some observations you made in the last chapter. At the end of the chapter you castigated me for failing to recognize that there are Palestinians who have adopted a policy of non-violence. You wrote:

> You clearly want to identify an entire people by the violent actions of certain violent groups while ignoring other elements of the same society.

You go on to cite various proponents of a non-violent approach including someone you know personally, Jean Zaru, a Quaker activist from Ramallah.

I do not deny that among the Palestinians there are peace activists. But the vast majority of Palestinians from the nineteenth century until the present day have advocated violent struggle against the Zionists. As I noted, this has been a strategy embraced by the central Palestinian organisations: the PLO, Fatah and Hamas in their official charters. Possibly a tiny minority of the Palestinian population reject this policy, but there is no question that the overwhelming majority of Palestinians have adopted this tactic to rid Palestine of a Jewish homeland. As you know, the wars against Israel beginning with the War of Independence in 1948 have been motivated by this objective.

You also make the curious reference to Yitzhak Rabin and Yasser Arafat as examples of peace advocates. In our discussion of the Oslo Accords, I stressed the importance of this initiative in which they had a central role. But, from the beginning and throughout his career, Yasser Arafat insisted on the importance of armed struggle. Similarly Yitzhak Rabin was a central figure in the Israeli military. Both of these figures played a key role in the quest for a peaceful solution to the Palestine–Israel conflict, but throughout their lives they advocated the use of violence to achieve political ends. Shimon Peres too, whom you mention, has always been a staunch advocate of armed defense. On both sides of this struggle, Palestinian and Jewish leaders have embraced violence as the overriding means to advance their cause. Arafat, Rabin and Peres were given the Nobel Peace Prize, not because they were non-violent peace activists like Gandhi, but because the Nobel Committee recognized that after nearly a century of armed conflict, these leaders sought to resolve their differences through a negotiated agreement.

You have discussed Gaza at some length. But I want to turn to the events leading up to Israel's response to rocket attacks. Following the Operation Defensive Shield, Yasser Arafat signed into law the Basic Law or constitution of the Palestinian transitional state. This law guaranteed basic rights, but stated that Palestinian legislation would be based on the principles of Sharia law. In June 2002 following a wave of Palestinian suicide attacks, Israeli forces reoccupied the West Bank. At this stage President Bush made a speech concerning the Middle East in which he outlined plans for a Palestinian state following democratic reforms. It was untenable, he stated, for Israeli citizens to live in terror. Further, it was unreasonable for Palestinians to live in squalor and occupation. Bush went on to challenge Israel to support the emergence of a Palestinian state, to withdraw from the Occupied Territories, and to stop building settlements.

In August and September 2002 attempts were made to bring about Palestinian ceasefire initiatives but these were opposed by extremist groups. In addition, the killing of Saleh Shehadeh, head of the military wing of Hamas, curtailed negotiations. During this period there was a respite from major suicide attacks, facilitating an Israeli–Palestinian plan to return full Palestinian authority in Gaza and Bethlehem. This period of relative calm ended with suicide bombings in Umm el-Fahm and on a Tel Aviv bus. In retaliation the Israelis proceeded to attack Gaza, excluding entry into Gaza city and besieging Yasser Arafat and about 200 others in the Muqata's compound in Ramallah. At this point the USA exerted pressure on Israel to stop destroying buildings and withdraw; despite a UN resolution, Israel continued the siege.

Following an Israeli election in which Ariel Sharon was re-elected Prime Minister, the Palestinian–Israeli conflict was eclipsed when the United States and Great Britain attacked Iraq in March 2003 overthrowing the regime of Saddam Hussein. In the first part of

2003 the United States expressed its refusal to negotiate with Yasser Arafat, and Mahmoud Abbas began to emerge as a more acceptable figure. Initially Arafat sought to undermine the post of Prime Minister, but he was later forced to grant him a degree of power. In October 2003 Abbas resigned as Prime Minister, citing a lack of support from Israel and the United States as well as internal incitement against his government. Responding to terrorist attacks, Israel launched Operation Rainbow in the Gaza Strip in May 2004; Operation Days of Penitence was launched in September and October 2004. In November 2004 Yasser Arafat died, and Mahmoud Abbas was elected President in January 2005. During this period, Israel's unilateral disengagement plan was adopted by the government. The aim was to remove the permanent Israeli presence in the Gaza Strip as well as four settlements in the northern West Bank. Civilians were evacuated, and residential buildings demolished. By 12 September 2005 Israel had completed its disengagement and fully withdrew from the Gaza Strip.

Amongst the Palestinians there was an increasing support for Hamas which had created various institutions and social services aimed at improving the life of Palestinians. In opposition to the Palestinian Authority (PA), Hamas stated that it did not recognize Israel's right to exist, nor did it accept the Oslo process or any other peace process with Israel. It openly stated that it encouraged terrorist attacks. In January 2006 elections Fatah and Hamas candidates competed for seats in the Palestinian Legislative Council. Due to widespread dissatisfaction with Fatah, Hamas won a majority of seats and was able to appoint a Prime Minister as well as a number of cabinet posts. Alarmed by these developments, the West branded Hamas a terrorist organisation and cut off aid to the Palestinian government. During November 2006 there were efforts by Mahmoud Abbas to form a unity government with Hamas, but this produced no tangible results. In January 2007, fighting continued between Hamas and Fatah. Eventually President Abbas and Palestinian Prime Minister Haniyeh met in Saudi Arabia. It was agreed that Hamas would dissolve the existing government and form a unity coalition with Fatah. Yet, by May 2007 a deal between Hamas and Fatah appeared to be fading and new fighting broke out. Eventually in response to the rocket fire from the Gaza Strip, Israel launched air strikes against various targets. In June 2007 full-scale fighting broke out between factions in several communities, and Hamas won control of the entire Gaza Strip, establishing a separate Gaza Strip government. Throughout this period the Palestinians in Gaza fired over 2,700 rockets into Israel – this was the background to the Gaza conflict which you have described. You continually attack Israel for this action – yet it must be remembered it took place against a background of ongoing hostility from Hamas which had consistently refused to accept Israel's existence and was determined to destroy the Jewish state. I do have sympathy for the Palestinians caught up in this conflict. But do you similarly have sympathy for the Israelis who have had to endure terrifying rocket assaults?

Who Started It?

Mary Grey

Of course I have sympathy with Israelis citizens who have suffered death and injuries from Hamas-propelled rockets. Of course I am grieved for the deaths and injuries that have resulted, but also for the people of Sderot who live in fear, as well as for the children who suffer post-traumatic stress disorder. I have consistently criticized this violence.

But what I also criticize is your reluctance – or refusal – to go beyond the rhetoric of, 'Hamas fired the Qassam rockets, so Israel is justified in retaliation.' If you remember the Just War theory – originating with Sts Augustine and Thomas Aquinas in the Middle Ages – on of the key criteria is 'proportionate response'. But what has been and is happening in Gaza is beyond all proportionate response. Here is what Noam Chomsky wrote after a visit to Gaza in November 2012, where he characterizes Gaza as the world's largest open-air prison:

> Even a single night in jail is enough to give a taste of what it means to be under the total control of some external force.
>
> And it hardly takes more than a day in Gaza to appreciate what it must be like to try to survive in the world's largest open-air prison, where some 1.5 million people on a roughly

140-square-mile strip of land are subject to random terror and arbitrary punishment, with no purpose other than to humiliate and degrade.

Such cruelty is to ensure that Palestinian hopes for a decent future will be crushed, and that the overwhelming global support for a diplomatic settlement granting basic human rights will be nullified. The Israeli political leadership has dramatically illustrated this commitment in the past few days, warning that they will 'go crazy' if Palestinian rights are given even limited recognition by the UN.

This threat to 'go crazy' ('nishtagea') – that is, launch a tough response – is deeply rooted, stretching back to the Labor governments of the 1950s, along with the related 'Samson Complex': If crossed, we will bring down the Temple walls around us.

Thirty years ago, Israeli political leaders, including some noted hawks, submitted to Prime Minister Menachem Begin a shocking report on how settlers on the West Bank regularly committed 'terrorist acts' against Arabs there, with total impunity.

Disgusted, the prominent military-political analyst Yoram Peri wrote that the Israeli army's task, it seemed, was not to defend the state, but 'to demolish the rights of innocent people just because they are Araboushim (a harsh racial epithet) living in territories that God promised to us'.

Gazans have been singled out for particularly cruel punishment. Thirty years ago, in his memoir 'The Third Way', Raja Shehadeh, a lawyer, described the hopeless task of trying to protect fundamental human rights within a legal system designed to ensure failure, and his personal experience as a Samid, 'a steadfast one', who watched his home turned into a prison by brutal occupiers and could do nothing but somehow 'endure'.
       (http://truth-out.org/opinion/item/12635-noam-chomsky-my-visit-to-gaza-the-worlds-largest-open-air-prison)

Since then, as he has written, the situation has become much worse. The Oslo Accords made Gaza and the West Bank are a single territorial entity. But by that time, the U.S. and Israel had already initiated their program to separate Gaza and the West Bank, so as to block a diplomatic settlement and punish inhabitants in both territories, a punishment that became severe for the Gazans in 2006, when they elected Hamas as their government. That provoked a brutal siege, as you know. Because the Gazans blocked a coup attempt, this led to a sharp escalation of the siege and attacks, culminating, in winter 2008–2009, with Operation Cast Lead, one of the most vicious exercises of military force in recent memory: A defenseless civilian population, trapped, was subjected to relentless attack by one of the world's most advanced military systems, reliant on U.S. arms and protected by U.S. diplomacy.

Of course, as you are continually arguing, there had to be Israeli pretexts. The usual one, as I wrote at the beginning of this letter, is 'security': in this case, against homemade rockets from Gaza. Gideon Levy, journalist with Ha'Arets in Jerusalem, points out the emptiness of this claim:

> Israel is causing electricity blackouts; laying sieges; bombing and shelling; assassinating and imprisoning; killing and wounding civilians, including children and babies, in horrifying numbers – but 'they started it'.
>
> (Levy 2010, p. 19)

Levy points out that Israel's disengagement from Gaza in 2005 did nothing to change the living conditions of the people living there and the reality of its being vast prison. Our readers need to know that Israel controls Gaza's water supply, electricity and means of communication. In fact the life and death of its people – who are prevented from seeking urgent medical aid in Egypt – or indeed anywhere.

Levy asks, if Hamas had not fired rockets, would Israel have lifted the economic siege? Nonsense! he says! (Levy 2010, p. 20) and admits that Israel started it through the Occupation – and there is no violence worse than the violence of an occupier. Even the question, 'Who started it?' is an evasion distorting the whole picture. I appeal to you to look at this whole picture and to the barbaric cruelty that Israel inflicts on Gaza.

Gaza

Dan Cohn-Sherbok

I believe you do me an injustice. Throughout our discussion I have sought to offer a balanced critique of both the Palestinian determination to curtail the Zionist quest to create a Jewish state in the Holy Land and unwarranted actions undertaken by the Israeli government. I am not anxious to defend Israel right or wrong. At some risk to myself I wrote the following article for the *Western Mail* (the main newspaper in Wales) after the Israeli attack on Gaza. I do not believe you have offered a similar evaluation of Palestinian inspired terrorism including suicide bombing. Instead you continually and unrelentingly offer an apology for the Palestinians with only a grudging criticism of their capacity for merciless violence:

> Over the Christmas vacation my wife and I were staying in Kensington in London near the Israeli Embassy. Every day I went for a walk in Kensington Gardens. All last week the Embassy was surrounded by police and metal barriers. In the background were mounted riot police. In the late afternoons a crowd of Palestinians gathered behind the barricades and shouted slogans in support of the Palestinian cause. Interspersed among the crowd were placards denouncing Israeli policy as well as children waving Palestinian flags.
>
> This past Saturday tens of thousands of protesters against the war marched from Hyde Park down Kensington Church Street.
>
> We were having lunch in a cafe on their route and watched from our table near the window. The throng was composed of young Arabs as well as the elderly wearing badges and holding flags. Many of those in the crowd were ordinary British citizens sympathetic to the cause.

After lunch we made our way across the street and were caught up in a flood of protestors. One took a multicoloured badge from his coat and handed it to me. 'Join us', he said as he marched off into the distance. My wife pinned it on my lapel and we followed the crowd as they descended in the direction of the embassy. I must have been the only rabbi caught up in the march. Yet despite my Jewish credentials, I had no hesitation in joining the protestors even if this happened by accident.

Every day as I watched television and read the newspapers, I was sickened by the horror of this onslaught. I could not help but be reminded of Jews in the Warsaw Ghetto during the Second World War. who fought against the Germans. Few in number, these brave fighters engaged in a hopeless struggle against insuperable odds. Eventually they were killed and the Warsaw Ghetto set alight.

Paradoxically, the Jewish community seems blind to the obvious parallels. Supporters of Israel are anxious to point out that Hamas has officially refused to recognize the existence of the Jewish state in the Middle East. For this reason suicide bombers are willing to give their lives in the struggle to free the Holy Land from what are perceived as foreign invaders and usurpers. Hamas is intent on driving the Jewish population into the sea.

Such an argument is persuasive. But in my view this assault against Gaza will not destroy Israel's enemies. On the contrary, it will harden the hearts of those Palestinians who watch helpless as Gaza is bombed and destroyed. Arab nations will support their brothers and sisters who are massacred. And beyond the Arab world, sympathetic supporters of the Palestinians will turn against the Jewish state as well as Jews in the diaspora. Already we are hearing the cry for Jewish children to be killed wherever they live.

As I have noted previously, the Gaza conflict was caused not by Israeli aggression but by the merciless and unjustified policy of

Hamas. It was a mistake for Israel to carry out a massive attack as a result, and as you can see I criticized Israel for this assault. But over the last 100 years there have been innumerable instances of Palestinian brutality as bad or worse than this attack. I wait for a similar forthright and fulsome condemnation from you of these Palestinian atrocities.

Goldstone Report

Mary Grey

Your accusation is equally unjustified: I have continually – not grudgingly – criticized Palestinian violence: indeed I began my last exchange condemning Hamas' rockets. I welcome your – accidental – participation in the London protest, but cannot accept your statement that 'The Gaza conflict was not caused by Israeli aggression.' (See my citation of Gideon Levy in section 'Who started it?') Indeed, your insistence on a sense of 'balance' in the conflict – that is, equal aggression on both sides – is a distortion of the truth. Gaza's residents were driven out of their homes by Israelis, and, as I have been relating, have been enduring an escalating narrative of desperation. Their existence has been called the equivalent of concentration camp existence. At this stage of our discussion, I call on you to move away from this insistence on 'balance' in the conflict and to focus on justice.

To do this I want to invoke the Report of Senator Goldstone. On 3 January 2009, in response to the Gaza War, the Organisation of the Islamic Conference's executive committee asked the United Nations Human Rights Council (UNHRC) to send a fact-finding mission to Gaza. On 12 January, the council adopted Resolution S-9/1, deciding to dispatch an urgent, independent international fact-finding mission, to be appointed by the President of the Council, to investigate all violations of international human rights law and international humanitarian law by the occupying Power, Israel, against the Palestinian people throughout the Occupied Palestinian Territory, particularly in the occupied Gaza Strip, due to the current aggression, and calls upon Israel not to obstruct the process of investigation and to fully cooperate with the mission (http://www.en.wikipedia.org/wiki/Goldstone_report).

There was initial objection to the one-sidedness of the Report's Mandate by both Mary Robinson and Richard Goldstone, initially refusing the appointment for the same reason. But this bias was corrected when the Mandate was widened to investigate all violations of international human rights law and international humanitarian law that might have been committed at any time in the context of the military operations that were conducted in Gaza during the period from 27 December 2008 and 18 January 2009.

However, Israel refused to cooperate with the investigation, citing anti-Israel bias in the UNHRC and the mission's one-sided founding resolution and the team was denied access to military sources, and entrance to Gaza via Israel. The report was released on the 15 September 2009 and concluded that **both** the Israel Defense Force (IDF) and Palestinian militant groups had committed war crimes and possibly crimes against humanity. While the report condemned violations by both sides, I want to emphasize *that it differentiated between the moral and legal severity of the violations of the Israeli forces compared to those of Hamas and other Palestinian armed groups.*

Goldstone stated that the mission 'wasn't an investigation, it was a fact-finding mission' and that the conclusion that war crimes had been committed 'was always intended as conditional'. He described the allegations as 'a useful road map' for independent investigations by Israel and the Palestinians.

Mindful of what you said in your last letter, I want to stress that the report disputes Israel's claim that the Gaza war would have been conducted as a response to rockets fired from the Gaza Strip, saying that at least in part the war was targeted against the 'people of Gaza as a whole'. Intimidation against the population was seen as an aim of the war. The report also says that Israel's military assault on Gaza was designed to humiliate and terrorize a civilian population, radically diminish its local economic capacity both to work and to provide for itself, and to force upon it an ever increasing sense of dependency and vulnerability.

The report focused on 36 cases that it said constituted a representative sample. In 11 of these episodes, it said the Israeli military carried out direct attacks against civilians, including some in which civilians were shot 'while they were trying to leave their homes to walk to a safer place, waving white flags'. These 36 incidents had been chosen as representing the highest death toll, where there seemed to be little or no military justification for what happened. According to the report, another alleged war crime committed by IDF include 'wanton' destruction of food production, water and sewerage facilities; the report also asserts that some attacks, which were supposedly aimed to kill small number of combatants amidst significant numbers of civilians, were disproportionate.

As you are aware, Israel refused to recognize the report. Goldstone suffered personal rejection as a result of the report's statement that Israel's violence was on a more brutal scale. You are also aware that Rabbi Michael Lerner, Editor of the Journal *tikkun*, who offered support to Goldstone by inviting his family to celebrate his grandson's Bar Mitzvah in his Synagogue in San Francisco, suffered attacks to his family home. Subsequently, Goldstone withdrew this statement. But the incident draws attention to the fact that the Government of Israel publically refuses to accept criticism.

So I end this letter to you with an appeal and a story. An appeal to look to a wider truth in the interests of peace. And a story of someone who does this. On the 16 January 2009 three Palestinian sisters were killed when an Israeli tank fired two shells into their bedroom. They were the daughters of Dr Izzeldin Abuelish, a Gazan gynaecologist who held a consultant post in an Israeli Hospital. Minutes after the attack, Dr Abuelish telephoned a friend, the Israeli Channel 10 News journalist, Shlomi Eldar, to ask for help:

> By chance, Eldar was live on air. There followed what was surely what was one of the most distressing interviews ever broadcast. We watch the face of the Israeli anchorman slowly collapse, as the news of the disaster is relayed to him by his Palestinian friend. Eldar holds out his mobile, switched to speaker phone, as Abuelish's screams of despair ring out.
> (Abuelish 2011, pp. 101, 179, 197)

But what followed is more amazing. Abuelish, convinced that violence begets violence, refusing to give way to hatred, Abuelish learned Hebrew to be able to communicate with all his patients.

He believes that the most important disease to cure is the disease of hatred. He is indeed an inspiration.

The Return of the Exiles

Dan Cohn-Sherbok

You continually stress the importance of truth: this is repeated at numerous points in our discussion. Yet at the same time you are determined to put a Palestinian spin on the entire history of the region. What you seek above all is to vindicate the Palestinians and condemn the Israelis. Throughout our discussion you blame the Zionists for whatever suffering the Palestinians have endured. While it is true that you have criticized Palestinian terrorist tactics such as suicide bombing, you stress that terror must be understood against the background of Israeli aggression. While you do not seek to vindicate terrorism, you emphasize the desperation of those who sacrifice themselves in this way.

In your last exchange you have sought to demonstrate the iniquity of Israel's assault on Gaza. I agree with your criticism: this attack was disproportionate. That is why I joined the protestors in London and wrote my article for the Western Mail. I am troubled that you reject my assertion about a balanced view of the Palestinian–Israeli conflict. You say you are a peace activist when in fact it appears that you are a pro-Palestinian activist. What you seek is not reconciliation but a confession from the Jewish people that they were wrong in seeking a homeland in Palestine and an apology for their oppression of the Palestinian people. This is a constant thread that runs through our book, beginning with the Balfour Declaration. For 18 chapters you have unrelentingly pressed the case against Zionism. Whenever I have tried to explain the motivation for creating and sustaining Israel, you have responded by condemning the Jews, highlighting their iniquity and emphasizing how the Palestinians have suffered at their hands.

As you know, the peace process has just commenced. This is excellent news. Yet I fear for the outcome if the Palestinian negotiators adopt a stance similar to yours. If they seek to demonstrate how the Jewish people stole Palestinian land, unleashed a campaign of oppression against the Palestinians for nearly a century, crushed their aspirations and seek to annex their land, these negotiations will fail. The quest to find a solution to the Palestine–Israeli conflict will degenerate into a forum for vituperative denunciation.

I cannot but wonder if – unlike the Palestinian officials who are now in discussion with the Israeli negotiators – you reject the notion of a two-state solution. When Mahmoud Abbas appeared before the United Nations over a year ago, he pleaded for official recognition of Palestinian statehood. Yet I have met Palestinians who vehemently dismiss such a notion. Instead they are determined that there should be only one state in the Holy Land. They repudiate the concept of a Jewish state alongside a Palestinian state. What they seek instead is the integration of both Jews and Palestinians into a single entity. Why, they ask, should Palestinians allow Jewish usurpers of their land to occupy it when it should be returned to its rightful owners. Theirs is a cry for justice in the name of truth.

Do you join them? Are you on the side of those who call for the return of Palestinian land to those who were forced to leave their homes. You have described Palestinians who retain the keys of the houses their families once occupied, who dream of the lands that were tilled by their ancestors. Languishing in refugee camps, they live in the hope that they and their descendants will return to their mother land where they can plant olive trees and fear no more. Do you join them in seeking the right of return for those in exile? Do you wish to see the Jewish state disappear in the quest to return the land to its rightful owners?

Chapter 19
Beyond the Gaza War

Faltering Steps toward Peace

Dan Cohn-Sherbok

I want to continue with the events that took place after the Gaza conflict. On 20 January 2009 Barack Obama became the President of the United States. Soon thereafter he appointed George Mitchell as special envoy to the Middle East and instructed him to visit Israel, the West Bank, Jordan, Turkey and Saudi Arabia for peace talks. Obama stated that this was part of his campaign promise to listen to both sides of the conflict and work towards a Middle East policy. In March 2009 the US Secretary of State Hillary Rodham Clinton went to Israel. At this time she stated that Israel settlements and the demolition of Arab homes in East Jerusalem hindered the peace process. She also voiced her support for the creation of a Palestinian state. On 4 June 2009 President Obama delivered an address in Cairo which supported a Two-State solution.

In response to Obama, on 14 June the Israeli Prime Minister Netanyahu gave a speech at Bar Ilan University in which he endorsed a demilitarized Palestinian state. In his speech, he declared that the United Jerusalem is the capital of the Jewish people and the State of Israel. Israeli sovereignty was non-negotiable. He went on to state that if such a state were to be established, the Palestinians should have no military and they would also have to abandon their demand for the right of return. He also claimed that there should be natural growth of the existing settlements in the West Bank, while their permanent status should be subject to further negotiation.

The following month, on 12 July 2009, Mahmoud Abbas told Egyptian media that he would not abandon any part of the West Bank to Israel, that he would demand territorial contiguity between the West Bank and the Gaza Strip, and that he would never waive the Palestinian right of return. In a letter to President Obama he maintained that any peace deal should be based on the 1967 borders. The Palestinian negotiator, Saeb Erekat, rejected any middle-ground solution, stating that the Palestinians would reject any deal between the United States and Israel that would allow construction to continue in Israeli settlements.

On 23 August 2009 Netanyahu announced in his weekly cabinet meeting that negotiations between Israel and the Palestinians would begin the following month and would be officially launched during his forthcoming visit to New York after he accepted an invitation from President Barack Obama for a summit there. On the same day Mahmoud Abbas stated that there would be no negotiations as long as Israel continued its settlement construction. On 20 September 2009 the White House announced that it would host a three-way meeting among President Obama, Prime Minister Netanyahu and Palestinian Authority (PA) President Mahmoud Abbas within the framework of the United Nations General Assembly to establish a basis for renewed negotiations for a peaceful settlement of the Middle East conflict.

Two months later, on 25 November 2009 Israel imposed a 10-month construction freeze on all settlements in the West Bank. However, it continued its construction of 3,000 pre-approved housing units in the West Bank and did not extend the freeze to East Jerusalem. The Palestinian Authority, however, rejected the partial freeze and refused to enter negotiations. Nearly a year later, on 31 May 2010 relations between Israel and the Palestinians became further strained when Israel carried out the Gaza flotilla raid. The flotilla was organized by the Free Gaza Movement and the Turkish Foundation for Human Rights and Freedoms and Humanitarian

Relief. Its aim was to bring about humanitarian aid and construction materials with the intention of breaking the Israeli–Egyptian blockade of the Gaza Strip. Israeli naval commandos boarded the ships from speedboats and helicopters. The raid drew widespread criticism internationally.

Despite these setbacks, direct negotiations began between Israel and the Palestinian Authority in Washington DC on 2 September 2010. Nearly two weeks later a second round of Middle East talks concluded in Sharm el-Sheikh, Egypt. According to Mahmoud Abbas, during the meetings the Palestinian Authority and Israel agreed on the principle of land swap; Israel was to exchange small parts of its territory for border settlement blocs. The issue of the ratio of land Israel would hand over to the Palestinians in exchange for border settlement blocs was problematic – the Palestinians demanded that the ration be 1:1, but Israel offered less.

During the meetings, Hamas and Hezbollah were determined to threaten the peace talks if both sides reached a firm agreement. As the 10-month freeze on settlement construction was nearing its end on 16 September, Mahmoud Abbas declared that he would abandon the negotiations if settlement construction were renewed. Israel, he stated, had a moratorium for months, and it should be extended to three to four months more to give peace a chance. The Palestinian Authority leadership regarded Israel's construction of settlements as a violation of international law. On 25 September – a day before the expiration of the freeze – Abbas maintained in the United Nations General Assembly that Israeli settlements constituted a central Issue. Israel, he said, must choose between peace and the continuation of such constriction. The Israeli Foreign Minister refuted the view that the renewal of West Bank settlement construction was intended to undermine the peace process; in his view the Palestinians had failed to accept the gesture of a moratorium for nine months. Instead, they were attempting to pressurize Israel to continue the freeze. Israel, he said, was willing to continue peace talks, but without preconditions.

Israel's determination not to extend the moratorium was widely criticized. Mahmoud Abbas stated that Prime Minister Netanyahu could not be trusted as a genuine negotiator. On 2 October 2010 he said that peace negotiations would not continue until Israel imposed a new freeze on the construction of settlements in the West Bank. On 11 October Prime Minister Netanyahu offered a settlement freeze if the Palestinian Authority would declare its recognition of Israel as the homeland of the Jewish people. This suggestion was rejected by the Palestinian Authority. According to Mahmoud Abbas, the Palestinians would never sign an agreement recognizing Israel as a Jewish state. Speaking on behalf of the Palestinian Authority, chief negotiator Saeb Erekat declared that the PA rejects what he regarded as the racist demands of the Israelis. As the Palestinian negotiators explained, recognition of Israel as a Jewish state would undermine the rights of Israeli Arabs and eliminate the right of return for millions of Palestinian refugees.

What can we make of these events? In my view, both the Israelis and the Palestinians failed to make sufficient compromises so that the peace process could continue. It is profoundly disturbing that Israel was not prepared to extend the moratorium on settlement building. Already there had been a moratorium of 10 months – what could have been lost by extending the freeze? Similarly, the PA's intransigence about recognizing Israel as a Jewish state was utterly misguided. Indeed, during this period Yasser Abed Rabbo, the Secretary General of the Palestinian Liberation Organisation (PLO), declared in a press statement that the PLO would recognize Israel as a Jewish state in exchange for a sovereign Palestinian state within the 1967 borders including East Jerusalem. Although Rabbo's statement was immediately disowned by various Palestinians factions, his willingness to find a path to peace represents the kind of spirit of accommodation which is necessary on both sides if a Two-State solution is to be found.

The Complexities of the One- or Two-State Solutions

Mary Grey

I must begin by refuting your accusation in a previous exchange (Chapter 18, section 'The Return of the Exiles'). You tell me that I don't seek a 'reconciliation but a confession from the Jewish people that they were wrong in seeking a homeland in Palestine and an apology for their oppression of the Palestinian people' and that this is a constant thread throughout the book. Sometimes I wonder if you have read what I have actually said!

I have consistently maintained that once the State of Israel came into existence, I respect its legitimacy. But I tried to recall you to the promise of the Balfour Declaration which made the proviso that the land was given to the Jewish people on the understanding that 'the rights of the existing non-Jewish people were respected'. My constant argument is that this has never been respected: the Palestinian people were driven from their land, and since 1967 have been subjected to an increasingly humiliating Occupation. Was this justice? I have also never condemned the Jewish people as such: I have highlighted the activism for peace of many individuals, condemned the rockets of Hamas and sought to encourage all initiatives for peace where Israelis and Palestinians have cooperated. It is the policies and obduracy of the Zionist government that are the major obstacle.

Whereas I do not see how any peace solution can be acceptable if the land seizure is not tackled satisfactorily, I wonder if you understand the complexities of this and why many people feel in despair about the talks – particularly about the Two-State solution. People feel this unworkable, given the sheer amount of land seizures and growing number of settlements. Many say it is dead. The image of the pizza has been used: *the Israelis are eating the pizza and leaving only the tough crust for the Palestinians!*

Yet there are also problems with the One-State alternative. Uri Avnery, Israeli writer and founder of the Gush Shalom Peace Movement, writing in the Journal *Tikkun* in May 2013, says this, in countering the statement 'the Two-State solution is dead!' which he says has become a mantra (Avnery 2013). He even says that

> To advocate the two-state solution means that you are ancient, old-fashioned, stale, stodgy, a fossil from a bygone era. Hoisting the flag of the 'one-state solution' means that you are young, forward-looking, 'cool'.

Avnery points out that the idea of a 'bi-national state' was in vogue in the 1930s, advocated by such intellectuals as Judah Leon Magnes and Martin Buber, yet an idea which never gained any traction. Bi-nationalism was built on the principle of parity between the two populations in Palestine – 50 per cent Jews, 50 per cent Arabs. But since the Jews at that time were much less than half the population, Arab suspicions were reasonable. On the Jewish side, the idea looked ridiculous. The very essence of Zionism was to have a state where Jews would be masters of their fate, preferably in all of Palestine.

But, the renewed 'One-State solution' has not been generated by goodwill between two people but born of the despair following Occupation: the Occupation, he says, has already created a de facto One State – an evil state of oppression and brutality, in which half the population (or slightly less than half) deprives the other half of almost all rights – human rights, economic rights and political rights. The Jewish settlements proliferate, and every day brings new stories of woe (Avnery 2013).

Even if the spread of the settlements is cited as the sign of death, Avnery refutes its irreversibility. History is a hothouse of reversibility, he says – and offers many ways in which this problem could be resolved, if there is a will. Whereas those in favour of One State compare Israel with Palestine and oppose what they say would be an apartheid state, Avnery thinks the comparison is weak, citing Ben-Gurion who advised partition as the solution to S. Africa's problems.

What is interesting is that Avnery thinks that eventually Jewish Israelis and Palestinian Arabs will become sister nations, living side by side in harmony: but before that happens there should be a period of living in adjoining states with open borders. But to come to that point, there must be a period of living peacefully in two adjoining states, hopefully with open borders.

He ends with the challenge that if Israel now refuses to bow to world opinion and enable the Palestinians to have their own state in 28 per cent of historical Palestine, why would Israel now bow to world opinion in the future and dismantle Israel altogether? He also cites other examples of people who have found it impossible to live together in one state – the Soviet Union, Yugoslavia, Serbia, Czechoslovakia, Cyprus and Sudan – and ends by asserting that the Two-State solution is not dead: it is the only solution there is.

I had always believed the assertion that the Two-State solution is dead, but I do admit the complexities on a One-State solution. Everything revolves around the just settlement of the land question.

The Two-State Solution

Dan Cohn-Sherbok

Your discussion of the Two-State/One-State solution is of critical importance at the present moment; Palestinian and Israeli negotiators are currently engaged in discussion about the future of the Holy Land. From what you have just said, it is clear that you have serious doubts about the viability of a Palestinian state alongside a Jewish state given the current circumstances. But what are the alternatives? It seems to me that there are four possible scenarios; the first two involve massive ethnic cleansing:

(1) A Palestinian State: From the beginning of the Zionist movement, the indigenous Arab population was intent on driving out the Jewish inhabitants and curtailing any plans for a Jewish state in their midst. From the outside, the Arabs mounted an armed struggle, and this later materialized into a series of wars. The aim was to liberate Palestine from what were perceived as Jewish colonialists. Today Hamas continues to press for such a solution, and officially rejects the idea of a Jewish state. From its inception, it has opposed any form of peace agreement which involves the continued existence of Israel.

(2) A Jewish State: Throughout the history of Israel, there has never been a quest to drive all Palestinian Arabs from Israel. Instead, Arab inhabitants have been absorbed into the state and are regarded as full citizens. Due to the Arab–Israeli conflict, these citizens are subject to a number of restrictions that do not apply to Jewish citizens. Yet almost without exception there has been no attempt to drive all Arabs and any other non-Jews from the Jewish state. You have at various points claimed that Israel seeks to annex land in the Occupied Territories. If a policy of ethnic cleansing involving the annexation of the West Bank and the Gaza were to take place, then there could be a mirror image of the first scenario with an exclusively Jewish population. But no one appears to endorse such a plan.

(3) A United Palestine–Israel: As you noted, some early Zionists endorsed such a scheme, but this was a small minority. This is the third form of a One-State solution. There is very little

enthusiasm today for such an idea in Jewish circles for fear that Israel would be overwhelmed by Palestinian refugees and others. For most Jews, such an idea is completely unacceptable since it would undermine the idea of a Jewish state which was the original intention of the early Jewish settlers. Given the potential influx of Palestinians and the attendant logistic problems of absorption, such a notion would be anathema to most Jews in Israel and the diaspora.

(4) Two States. Despite critics who maintain that the notion of a Two-State solution is dead, this seems the most viable option today, and it is being actively pursued by the Palestinian Authority. As you know, in 2011, Mahmoud Abbas submitted an application for the admission of Palestine to the United Nations on the basis of the 4 June 1967 borders. In his speech to the General Assembly on 23 September 2011 he applied for his people to be given the right to be called citizens of their own state. Referring to the most recent negotiations with Israel, Abbas stated that the Palestinians did not cease in their efforts for initiatives and contacts. Over the past year, he said, the Palestinian negotiators did not leave a door to be knocked or a channel to be tested, or a path to be taken. Nor did they ignore any formal or informal party of influence and stature to be addressed. They positively considered the various ideas and proposals and initiatives presented from many countries and parties. Yet, in his view, the Israeli government dashed the hopes raised by the launch of negotiations. The core issue was the Israeli government's refusal to commit to terms of reference for the negotiations that were based on international law and the United Nations resolutions. Further, it frantically continued to intensify building settlements on the territory of the State of Palestine.

In the light of this state of affairs, the President on behalf of the PLO – the sole representative of the Palestinian people – stated the following:

(1) The goal of the Palestinian people is the realisation of their inalienable national rights in their independent State of

Palestine, with East Jerusalem as its capital, on all of the land of the West Bank, including East Jerusalem and the Gaza Strip.

(2) The PLO and the Palestinian people adhere to the renouncement of violence and rejection and condemning of terrorism in all its forms, especially state terrorism, and adhere to all agreements signed between the PLO and Israel.

(3) The Palestinian people adhere to the option of negotiating a lasting solution to the conflict in accordance with resolutions of national legitimacy and the PLO is ready to return immediately to the negotiation table on the basis of the adopted terms of reference based on international legitimacy and a complete cessation of settlement activities.

(4) The Palestinian people will continue peaceful resistance to Israeli occupation and its settlement policies and its construction of the annexation Wall.

(5) The Palestinian people rely on the political and diplomatic option and confirm that they do not seek to take unilateral steps.

In conclusion he stated:

> The time has come for our men, women and children to live normal lives, for them to be able to sleep without waiting for the worst that the next day will bring: for mothers to be assured that their children will return home without fear of suffering, killing, arrest or humiliation; for students to be able to go to their schools and universities without checkpoints obstructing them. The time has come for sick people to be able to reach hospitals normally, and for our farmers to be able to take care of their good land, without fear of the occupation seizing the land and its water, which the wall prevents access to, or fear of the settlers, for whom settlements are being built on our land and who are uprooting and burning the olive trees that have existed for hundreds of years. The time has come for the thousands of prisoners to be released from the prisons to return to their families and their children to become part of building their homeland, for the freedom of which they have settled.
>
> (www.haaretz.com, 29 December 2011)

From the beginning of the Zionist movement, the Arab opponents of Israel have advocated a One-State solution to the Middle East problem which I referred to above as scenario 1. In their view Jewish settlers in Palestine were colonialist invaders. For this reason there was no support for early partition plans. Yet, more recently there has been growing Palestinian acceptance of a Two-State solution as outlined above by Mahmoud Abbas. No longer is the PLO determined to eliminate the Jewish state and create in its stead an Arab polity comprising the territory of Israel and the currently occupied West Bank and Gaza Strip. In my view, we should embrace this first step towards solving what has been unsolvable in the past. We can only hope that in this way swords be turned into ploughshares before it is too late.

What Solution is Viable?

Mary Grey

It was very helpful to have the four scenarios outlined as you did. I heartily concur with your last sentence: 'We can only hope that in this way swords be turned into ploughshares before it is too late.'

Turning to your four possible solutions – I agree with you in rejecting the first two. But I also keep before my mind that it is the people on the ground – Israelis and Palestinians – who will make the crucial decisions: – the views of outsiders are of less importance. But we can lay before our readers honestly the positives and negatives of each option. The third option – the shared bi-national state to me is the ideal solution, but impractical for reasons at the moment both of us have set out. So we fall back on the fourth option – the Two-State solution.

But it is also important not to forget key components of what any solution must embrace, namely:

- Borders and division of the land;
- Strong emotions relating to the conflict on both sides;
- Palestinian concerns over continuing Israeli settlements and expansion in the West Bank;

- Palestinian concerns over water resources;
- The status of Jerusalem – considered sacred to all three faiths;
- Israeli security concerns over terrorism, safe borders, incitements, violence;
- The Right of return of Palestinian refugees living in the Palestinian diaspora.

This last factor has been a festering sore for six decades. Remember that Israel has been acting illegally all this time in ignoring the UN Resolution 194 which resolves that the refugees wishing to return to their homes and live at peace with their neighbours should be permitted to do so at the earliest practicable date, and that compensation should be paid for the property of those choosing not to return and for loss of or damage to property which, under principles of international law or in equity, should be made good by the Governments or authorities responsible.

In fact, at the 2000 Camp David summit, Israel did offer to set up an international fund for the compensation for the property which had lost by the 1948 Palestinian refugees, to which Israel would contribute. Israel offered to allow 100,000 refugees to return on the basis of humanitarian considerations or family reunification. All other refugees would be resettled in their present places of residents, the Palestinian state, or in third-party countries, with Israel contributing $30 billion to fund their resettlement. During this time, most of the original refugees had died without any compensation. Israel demanded that in exchange, Arafat forever abandon the right of return, and Arafat's refusal has been cited as one of the leading causes of the summit's failure.

Then in 2003 during the Road map for peace, Israeli Foreign Minister Silvan Shalom stated that the establishment of a Palestinian state was conditional upon waiving the right of return. Prime Minister Ariel Sharon said that the Palestinian Authority must also drop its demand for the right of return, calling it 'a recipe for Israel's destruction' (http://en.wikipedia.org/wiki/Palestinian_right_of_return).

So, even the Two-State solution must take this seemingly intractable issue into account. Naim Ateek, Founder and Director of Sabeel, Jerusalem, has always maintained a One-State option as the ideal, but now sees a Two-State solution as more realistic and practical. But he will not accept this at any price (Ateek 2008, pp. 169–170). The basis on which the Two-State solution should be founded is Israel's complete withdrawal from the West Bank and Gaza so that the Palestinians will have the West Bank and Gaza as a contiguous entity, with no interference from Israel.

He insists that lasting peace can only be based on justice and enunciates six essential principles that must be applied to each major issue:

(1) God who is worthy to be adored is one who loves and cares for all peoples.
(2) Under international law, the Palestinians have the right to exist in peace within internationally recognized borders.
(3) There is no perfect or ideal solution to the conflict but the international law and UN resolutions provide a compromise that satisfies basic demand of peace and justice.
(4) The conflict will never be resolved through military power or armed resistance.
(5) This vision takes into consideration the basic human and political rights of both Israelis and Palestinians.
(6) Injustice must not be rewarded. Where it is possible, what is unjust must be undone.

In addition he affirms the foundation in international law for the Two-State solution: the State of Israel will live in peace and security on no more than 78 per cent of the land beside a Palestinian State that is living in peace and security on no less than 22 per cent of the land. Both States will be sovereign and independent (Ateek 2008, p. 171).

Will the people and government of Israel accept these principles? How deep is their desire for peace? I write today as our own (British) government debates the possibility of armed intervention in Syria, because of the use of chemical weapons by the government against its citizens. This adds to the urgency of a peaceful resolution to the conflict in Israel–Palestine.

The Right of Return

Dan Cohn-Sherbok

I am glad we both agree that the way forward is the Two-State solution. In a recent book, *The Palestinian State: A Jewish Justification*, I stressed that the creation of a Palestinian state is now a matter of the utmost importance. Jews today, I wrote, need to draw from their religious heritage those ethical elements which can help the Jewish community solve the seemingly insoluble problem of the Middle East:

> What is now required is for Jews to empower the powerless: after more than a century of bloody conflict, the Palestinian people must have a state of their own. Drawing inspiration from the Exodus narrative and the quest to bring about God's Kingdom on earth, we Jews must wholeheartedly support the peace process. On the threshold of a new century, painful compromises must be made by Jews – as well as Palestinians – in an effort to find a way forward.
>
> (Cohn-Sherbok 2012, *The Palestinian State*, p. 6)

What I did not do in this book, however, is to wrestle with the issues you outline in your last exchange. Perhaps the most pressing is the right of return. As you note, this problem has dogged all negotiations between Israelis and Palestinians. I agree with you that the UN Resolution 194 is of pivotal consequence. The UN has decreed in this resolution that refugees wishing to return to their homes and live at peace should be allowed to do so, and that compensation should be paid for property of those choosing not to return. At the Camp David summit, Israel was prepared to set up a fund for compensation of property and allow 100,000 refugees to return. In exchange the Palestinians were to abandon the right of return. In 2003 during the Road Map for Peace, the Israeli Foreign Minister stated that the creation of a Palestinian State was conditional upon waving the right of return. This was echoed by a statement from Prime Minister Ariel Sharon.

A Two-State solution must grapple with this issue. What is possible? If the right of return is to be extended to Palestinians, who should have such a right, and where should returning refugees be allowed to settle? We will need to return to the issue of borders that Naim Ateek discusses. But assuming a Palestinian State were established in the West Bank and Gaza Strip, what should be done about the refugees? I want to return to the summit at Camp David. As you mentioned, the Palestinians insisted that the right of return be implemented. So as not to fundamentally alter Israeli life, the Palestinian negotiators promised that the right to return would be implemented by a formula agreed by both sides, which would channel a large number of refugees away from the option of returning to their ancestral home. Nonetheless each refugee would have the right to return to Israel. It was envisaged that the Palestinians who chose to return to Israel could do so gradually with Israel absorbing 150,000 refugees a year. The Israeli negotiators, concerned that such an influx would undermine the character of the Jewish state, therefore proposed that a maximum of 100,000 refugees should be allowed entry. All other Palestinian refugees should be settled in their current place of residence (either other countries or a Palestinian state), and Israel would help fund their absorption. In this regard an international fund of $30 billion would be created to which Israel would contribute in order to provide compensation for property lost by Palestinian refugees.

As you noted, there was no agreement at Camp David about this issue. Yet, it seems to me that the positions outlined by both the Palestinians and the Israeli negotiators could serve as a framework for a negotiated resolution of this problem. The limit suggested by the Israelis was too small; and the number of refugees proposed by the Palestinians too large. But there is scope here for compromise on both sides. The Palestinian negotiators were aware of the difficulties of massive immigration to Israel, and this is a positive step. What is needed is for a realistic figure to be accepted by both sides. This would enable UN Resolution 194 to become operative with a recognition of the logistic and financial obstacles involved. While the Palestinian dream of resettlement would only be partially fulfilled, a Palestinian state would have been established while at the same time the right of return could be implemented for a large number of descendants of those who had been displaced nearly a century ago. It is not ideal as a solution, but it could serve the needs of both sides.

Dan

What to Do about Settlements?

Mary Grey

As we end this chapter I am inspired by your quotation and heartily agree with your sentiment:

> On the threshold of a new century, painful compromises must be made by Jews – as well as Palestinians – in an effort to find a way forward.

Such painful compromises will involve real understanding as to how much this matters to Palestinians in the global diaspora who lost their homes in 1948 and 1967, as well as realistic compensation. But you are on the right track of a just solution. It could be that the international community has to commit to helping Israel to honour the need for just compensation and to admit to the complexity that justice will require.

In this respect, as we move forward to our last chapter, emotional considerations on all sides and authentic commitment to a just peace will become an overriding pre-requisite to any solution.

But as important as the 'Right of Return' is the vexed question of Israeli Settlements in the Occupied territories. These are Jewish civilian communities built on lands occupied by Israel during the 1967 Six-Day War and now exist in the West Bank, East Jerusalem and the Golan Heights. Settlements also existed in the Sinai and Gaza Strip until Israel evacuated the Sinai settlements in 2005. But Israel continues both to expand its settlements and settle new areas in the West Bank in spite of the Oslo Accords, which specified in article 31 that neither side would take any step that would change the status of the West Bank and the Gaza Strip pending the outcome of the permanent status negotiations. Israeli settlement expansion has continued unabated (see http://en.wikipedia.org/wiki/israeli_settlements).

Such expansion is a major obstacle to peace. The United Nations has repeatedly upheld the view that Israel's construction of settlements constitutes violation of the Fourth Geneva Convention. The International Court of Justice also says these settlements are illegal, and no foreign governments support Israel's settlements. In April 2012 UN secretary general Ban Ki-Moon, in response to moves by Israel to legalize Israeli outposts, reiterated that all settlement activity is illegal, running contrary to Israel's obligations under the Road Map and repeated Quartet calls for the parties to refrain from provocations. Similar criticism was advanced by the EU and the United States. Israel disputes the position of the international community and the legal arguments that were used to declare the settlements illegal.

But the fact that the international community considers the settlements in occupied territory to be illegal has not impeded Israel. But now even President Obama has ceased to call on a halt to settlement expansion as a pre-condition of peace.

So what numbers of settlers are we talking about? In July 2012 according to the Israeli interior ministry, 350,150 Jewish settlers live in the 121 officially recognized settlements in the West Bank, 300,000 Israelis live in settlements in East Jerusalem and over 20,000 live in settlements in the Golan Heights.

The aggravation and injustice of the Settlements does not only consist of the illegality of the land confiscation: to enter into a settlement – as I have done – is like entering a different world. Excellent access roads – prohibited to Palestinians – are available: good housing, shopping and leisure facilities, education, health clinics, waste disposal – all are available to settlers. Some long-established settlements – like Ma'ale Adumim – have acquired the status of cities. (The NGO Peace Now claimed that 86.4 per cent of Ma'ale Adumim was built on privately owned Palestinian land.)

Another huge obstacle to peace presented by settlers are acts of violence committed against Palestinians and Israeli security forces, predominantly in the West Bank. A good example of this is the settlement in an outlying district of Hebron, Kiryat Arba. Hebron itself is a conflicted city – being the site of the Tombs of the patriarchs, yet on Palestinian land – much of which is confiscated: even the main street is a no-go area for Palestinians. Because of the violence of settlers in Kiryat Arba, school children are accompanied daily to school by the Israeli army, by Christian Peacemaker teams and by the Ecumenical Accompaniment Programme in Palestine and Israel (EAPPI) – all of whom have carefully documented the violence of the settlers. (This is not only directed against children but ordinary civilians and shepherds on the hillsides, who are regularly shot at.)

Even if most West Bank settlers are 'law abiding' the vast majority are non-violent, there has been a rise in violent acts by fringe extremists against Palestinians and Israel Police and IDF troops. In 2007 Israeli prosecutors determined that of 515 criminal suits relating to violent activity committed by Israeli settlers against Palestinians and Israeli security forces, 502 related to right wing Jewish settlers in the Occupied Territories. In 2008 the senior Israeli commander in the West Bank said that a hard core of a few hundred activists were involved in violence against the Palestinians and Israeli soldiers. An EU heads of mission report found that settler violence had more than tripled in the three years up to 2011.

So, even if the majority of Israelis would like peace, there remains this hard core of settler violence that needs to be solved. How can such violence be explained? Much can be explained by ignorance. Many settlers have come from impoverished countries around the word – including Eastern Europe, promised a new way of life and a new start. They know nothing about the history Israel/Palestine and can only see the Palestinians as a hostile threat to their existence.

This is of course exacerbated by the way they are kept from all interaction with Palestinians – a fact which haunts all progress to understanding. But I will end this letter and this chapter by a small story which highlights a way to such understanding, offering hope of a way forward.

The *Tent of Nations* is a farm near Hebron, owned by the Nassar family. Israel is doing its best to evict the family and seize the land – which has been owned by this family since the Ottoman Empire. But Dawoud Nassar is determined not to give way to revenge and hate. He invites groups to come and discuss peace and forgiveness. One day a woman from the nearby settlement participated. She was amazed to see the poverty in which Dawoud and his family lived. 'We have swimming pools and you do not even have water', she cried. It was the beginning of a new understanding – and as such, a sign of hope as to the way to peace.

Chapter 20
The Future

What Chance for Peace?

Mary Grey

As we enter our last chapter I know we are both concerned to highlight realistic pointers to peace and reconciliation. Yet we do this at a fraught moment in time. As you are aware, international tensions run high over the response to the alleged use of chemical weapons in Syria as well as the unsettled aftermath of the violence in Egypt. All this has implications for Israel's fears for security, especially given the increasing strength of Iran, which harbours hostile feelings towards Israel.

In what can we base our hopes for peace, given this conflict that surrounds Israel/Palestine? Given the obdurate stance of the Israeli government? Two initial factors are that there has been less violence from Palestinians towards Israel recently and that there is a majority of Israeli citizens who want peace. Let us add to that the increasing influence of groups such as 'Combatants for peace' which brings together both Israelis and Palestinians who have suffered violence and who want peace. I have seen witnesses from this group recently,[1] but Uri Avnery also describes their influence

---
[1] Greenbelt 2013, UK.

as part of his argument that peace needs to include an emotional component:

> An Arab villager spoke quietly of his daughter, killed by a soldier on her to school. A Jewish mother spoke of her soldier son, killed in one of the wars. All in a subdued voice. Without pathos. Some spoke Hebrew, some Arabic.
>
> They spoke of their first reaction after their loss, the feelings of, the thirst for revenge. And then the slow change of heart. The understanding that the parents on the other side, the Enemy, felt exactly like them, that their loss, their mourning, their bereavement was exactly as their own.
>
> For years now, bereaved parents of both sides have been meeting to find solace in each other's company. Among all the peace groups acting in the Israeli–Palestinian conflict, they are, perhaps, the most heart-lifting.
>
> (Avnery 2013)

Given this appeal to an emotional underpinning to be taken seriously, I want to add a principled Gandhian stance. Mark Jürgensmeyer offers 10 rules for this (Jürgensmeyer 2005, pp. 63–64).[2]

The first is not to avoid confrontation, but to welcome an encounter between positions and the clarity it brings. The second is to stay open to communication and self-criticism. The third – find a resolution and stick to it – but once a harmonious alternative appears seize it and base your strategy on it. The next is to regard the opponent as a possible ally and to nothing to harm or alienate him or her. Fifth – make tactics consistent with the goal. For Gandhians this means nonviolent tactics – ensuring that the emerging state will be a non-violent society. Other principles include flexibility, being discerning as to which issues are crucial, being disciplined and knowing when to quit if an issue is deadlocked.

But I am convinced that peace and reconciliation require more than these tactical strategies, important though they are. I think that the urgency of the task calls both Jews and Christian to the heart

---

[2] Also cited in Ateek (2008, pp. 181–182).

of our faith. For Jews – as you know well – the ethics of prophetic justice are vital, and concern for the stranger is at the core of this. And, as the Psalm says: Justice and peace shall meet (Psalm 85.10) Christianity adds the idea of revolutionary forgiveness. An immense cry for revolutionary forgiveness on both sides is necessary. And the notion that this will recall both Jews and Christian to a lost soul has been articulated by many. I will lend with the reaction of Robert Cohen to the launch of Kairos UK at Greenbelt, 25 May 2013 – 'A Response to Palestinian suffering'. He articulates eloquently what I have been saying about the need for prophetic justice:

> A Jewish Kairos moment will begin on the margins of the Jewish community as more and more Jews begin to recognize that our relationship with the Palestinians will define our present and determine our future as much as it will theirs. It will come from Jews who begin to understand that the Occupation of the West Bank, the blockade of Gaza, the ethnic cleansing of East Jerusalem and the institutional discrimination of Israeli Palestinians is doing untold damage to the Jewish soul and to Judaism itself. The Jewish Kairos moment will come when we rediscover our Hebrew prophetic theology of justice and choose to take it seriously. Isaiah, Jeremiah, Amos and Micah were talking to us . . . and they still are.
>
> The Jewish Kairos will only come when we see the Zionist understanding of Jewish history and the nationalist solution to Jewish salvation as an aberration rather than a continuum of Jewish values. It will be a painful moment and require a new construction of the Jewish narrative, one that can incorporate the Palestinian narrative too. Palestinians will need to understand our pain and our trauma, as well as their own, if open hearted dialogue is to be possible. But this is not a conflict of equals. We hold the power. We have the superpower backing. The onus is on us.
> (http://www.micahparadigmshift.blogspot.co.uk/
> 2013/09/when-will-there-be-jewish-kairos-moment.html)

I do not underestimate the enormity of this task.

The Settlements

Dan Cohn-Sherbok

In *The Palestinian State: A Jewish Justification*, I expressed my conviction that the Palestinian people should have a homeland of their own. Urgent negotiations are needed to deal with the difficult issues facing both peoples. You are right to highlight the significance of Jewish settlements in the West Bank. You will remember that on 18 February 2011 the United States vetoed a United Nations Security Resolution condemning Israeli settlement activity. The purpose of this veto was to demonstrate that the Obama administration saw direct negotiation as the only way forward. Israel expressed appreciation for the United States action, whereas the Palestinian Authority condemned what they regarded as American bias. The next month Prime Minister Netanyahu considered a temporary peace deal that envisaged a Palestinian state created with provisional borders, and future borders to be negotiated at a later date. On 3 March, the Palestinians rejected this plan, stating that its position was unaltered. Due to this impasse, the Palestinian Authority declared that unless a deal was reacted by September 2011, it would unilaterally declare independence, seek recognition by the United Nations and apply for membership. According to Mahmoud Abbas, this new state would be ready to negotiate all the core issues and find a just solution for Palestinian refugees in accordance with United Nations General Assembly Resolution 194.

This is the recent historical background to our discussion of settlement building. What is to be done? I am troubled by the remarks you quoted from Robert Cohen. He is highly critical of what he refers to as the 'nationalist solution to Jewish salvation'. In his view this is an aberration of Jewish values. He goes on to denounce the Occupation of the West Bank, the blockade of Gaza and what he refers to as the 'ethnic cleansing' of East Jerusalem as well as the institutional discrimination of Israeli Palestinians. This he argues is doing untold damage to the Jewish soul and to Judaism itself. Such pro-Palestinian rhetoric does not in any way help us to find a way to the kind of negotiation that will be needed in dealing with the settlement problem.

Like you, I believe that this issue must be faced, and it will call for serious and painful compromise from both Israelis and Palestinians. As you noted, the international community considers the settlements in occupied territory to be illegal. The United Nations has repeatedly upheld the view that Israel's construction of settlements constitutes a violation of the Fourth Geneva Convention. The International Court of Justice regards these settlements as illegal. In April 2012 UN Secretary General Ban Ki-Moon, in response to moves by Israel to legalize Israeli outposts, reiterated that all settlement activity runs contrary to Israel's obligations under the Road Map and repeated calls for the parties to refrain from provocations.

These criticisms must be taken seriously. As you noted in the last chapter, as of July 2012, 350,150 Jewish settlers live in the 121 officially-recognized settlements in the West Bank, 300,000 Israelis live in settlements in East Jerusalem and over 20,000 live in settlements in the Golan Heights. These settlements range from farming communities and frontier villages to urban suburbs and neighbourhoods. Three of these settlements have achieved city status, with over 30,000 residents in each. If a Palestinian state is to be created in the West Bank, there will need to be the same policy of resettlement that took place in 1982 when, as part of the Egypt–Israel Peace Treaty, Israel was required to evacuate its settlers from the 18 Sinai settlements, and in 2005 when settlers were evacuated from settlements in the Gaza Strip and part of the West Bank. Negotiators on both sides will need to agree to the scale of such resettlement, the nature of a rehousing programme of Israelis and an accompanying resettlement of Arabs living in Israel to these settlements. Here painful compromise will be called for from both Palestinians and Israelis. Again, I want to reiterate that hysterical outbursts from either side are a hindrance to peaceful reconciliation.

The Struggle for Jerusalem

Mary Grey

I think we (almost) agree on the settlement issue! But I cannot allow you to dismiss Robert Cohen's remarks as hysteria.

Remember he is a Jewish Rabbi deeply concerned – as you are – for reconciliation. I think you should take more seriously his stance that *that the Occupation of the West Bank, the blockade of Gaza, the ethnic cleansing of East Jerusalem* (that is, the driving out of the Palestinians and the destruction of their homes) *and the institutional discrimination of Israeli Palestinians is doing untold damage to the Jewish soul and to Judaism itself.* You are only too aware that the Occupation, blockade of Gaza and the settlements are illegal. If it is the term 'ethnic cleansing' you object to, remember that this is the very term used in 1948 Israeli documents that Benny Morris cited from his research into the archives (Morris in Chapman 2004, p. 217). Such historic decisions and the continuing harshness of the Occupation cannot fail to have an effect on the core Jewish faith itself and its commitment to prophetic justice, as violent conflict on the past and present has affected the integrity of Christian faith.

But another blockage to peace is the status of Jerusalem, a Sacred City to all three faiths. As you know, because of the Occupation, Christians and Muslims from the occupied territories are frequently prevented from travelling to Jerusalem for the great feasts. Some have given up the attempt to go, such is the humiliation experienced at the check points.

The *status of Jerusalem* remains one of the core issues in the *Israeli–Palestinian conflict* we are discussing. Some would say that it is a microcosm of the whole conflict. Indeed, Benjamin Disraeli said that

> The view of Jerusalem is the history of the world; it is more, it is the history of earth and heaven.
> (Cited in Chapman 2004, preface)

Unsurprisingly, then, that it has become a source of great conflict: during the *1948 Arab–Israeli War*, *West Jerusalem* was among the areas captured and later annexed by Israel while *East Jerusalem*, including the Old City, was captured and later annexed by *Jordan*. Israel captured East Jerusalem from Jordan during the 1967 *Six-Day War* and subsequently annexed it. Currently, Israel's *Basic Law* refers to Jerusalem as the country's 'undivided capital'. The international community has rejected the latter annexation as illegal and treats East Jerusalem as *Palestinian territory occupied* by Israel (http://www.en.wikipedia.org/wiki/Jerusalem). The international community does not recognize Jerusalem as Israel's capital, and the city hosts no foreign embassies. According to the *Palestinian Central Bureau of Statistics*, 208,000 *Palestinians* live in East Jerusalem, which is sought by the *Palestinian Authority* as the capital of Palestine.

This, in a nutshell, is the issue. I should make it clear that when we speak about Jerusalem we mean first, the Old City, then East Jerusalem (outside the Old City) and thirdly West Jerusalem, controlled by Israel since 1948. Many believe that the only solution (within the Two-State Solution we are discussing) is that the Holy City should be shared by Jews and Palestinians, given its global significance as a sacred site for pilgrims around the world. Naim Ateek proposes an international charter

> which would protect the special holy zone of the Old City and guarantee the rights of the three religious traditions.
> (Ateek 2008, p. 175)

He wants the Old City to become gradually a model for peace and coexistence between the three communities. Many authorities write in this way. Michael Dumper in *The Politics of Sacred Space* (Dumper 2002, p. 148), analyses carefully what is involved. He is in no doubt that negotiations will be complex:

> To some extent that Oslo Accords are an indication of a softening of the Israeli position on Jerusalem as 'the eternal, undivided capital of Israel' . . . There is no doubt that peace will occur only when tough decision concerning military security and resource control are made . . . A negotiated Israeli–Palestinian peace will need to involved the religious and historical concerns surrounding the holy sites.
> (Dumper 2002, p. 148)

But is there sufficient goodwill for such an agreement? Simon Sebag Montefiore in his biography of Jerusalem writes that

> The history of the negotiations since 1993, and the difference in spirit between noble words and distrustful, violent acts, suggests unwillingness on both sides the make the necessary compromised to share Jerusalem.
>
> (Montefiore 2011, p. 514)

He also makes an interesting remark – one that I have been articulating throughout, that legal agreements are all very well, but will be futile and meaningless without 'the historic, the mystical and emotional'. (Montefiore 2011, p. 515) If you remember, in my last exchange (section 'What Chance for Peace?') I cited Uri Avnery who stressed the importance of the emotional dimension something that Robert Cohen was hinting at. And this emotional dimension must involve each party respecting the sacred heritage of the other.

As the Psalmist sang:

> O pray for the peace of Jerusalem:
>
> May those who love you be secure.
>
> May there be peace within your walls
>
> And security within your citadels.
>
> (Psalm 122)

And as Jesus cried, as he came near and saw the city, wept over it, saying:

> If you, even you, had only recognized on this day, the things that make for peace . . .
>
> (Luke 19, pp. 41–42)

Jerusalem and Borders

Dan Cohn-Sherbok

The fact that Robert Cohen is a rabbi does not mean that his remarks are acceptable; in my view they are deliberately inflammatory and unhelpful. You clearly applaud these sentiments, but they give a simplistic picture of the complex historical developments that we have been exploring throughout our discussion. I believe we have been anxious to demonstrate the power of two distinct narratives – the Palestinian and the Israeli – of the tragic modern history of the Holy Land. This is not simply an academic exercise, but the investigation of deeply held convictions by both sides. There is pro-Israeli rhetoric (similar to Robert Cohen's) which gives a very different caricature of the Palestinians as anti-Semitic terrorists. In my view such extremist positions do untold harm to the peace process. Such remarks should be ignored.

You are right that the status of Jerusalem is a key issue. For all three faiths – Judaism, Christianity and Islam – it is of sacred significance. Jewry today is insistent that it is the capital of Israel. Palestinians similarly contend that must be the capital of Palestine. For Christians, it is a holy city, the place where Jesus was crucified outside its walls. It is critical that the city becomes a focus for all three religions. Despite the logistic difficulties, the aspirations of Jews and Palestinians must be reconciled. As you note, hundreds of thousands Palestinians live there as do Jews. It will be a difficult task for negotiators to find a way forward, but they can and must if there is to be peace in the region.

This leads on to the question of borders themselves. As you will remember this was a central topic at the Camp David summit. The Palestinian negotiators demanded that there should be full Palestinian sovereignty over the entire West Bank and the Gaza Strip. In their view, Resolution 242 called for Israeli withdrawal from those areas which were captured in the Six-Day War. In the 1993 Oslo Accords, the Palestinians had accepted the Green Line borders for the West Bank, but the Israelis had rejected this proposal. Instead, they wished to annex numerous settlement blocks on the Palestinian side of the Green Line, fearing that a return to the 1967 borders could constitute a threat to Israeli security.

Prime Minister Barak offered to create a Palestinian state on 73 per cent of the West Bank (27 per cent less than the Green Line Borders), and 100 per cent of the Gaza Strip. It was envisaged that in 10–25 years the Palestinian state would expand to a maximum of 90–91 per cent of the West Bank. As a consequence, Israel would have withdrawn from 63 settlements; Israel would keep only the settlements with large populations. All others would be dismantled with the exception of Kiryat Arba, which would serve as an Israeli enclave inside the Palestinian state. The West Bank would be split in the middle by an Israeli controlled road from Jerusalem to the Dead Sea with free passage to the Palestinians. Israel would permit the Palestinians to use a highway in the Negev to connect the West Bank with Gaza. According to this proposal, the West Bank and Gaza would be linked by an elevated highway and an elevated railroad, under the sovereignty of Israel, which could be closed in the case of emergency. The Palestinians, however, rejected this proposal on the grounds that Israel did not offer land in return for the land it wished to annex. Further, the settlements that Israel wished to keep separated the West Bank into cantons. For the Palestinians it was unacceptable that Israel could control freedom of movement inside a Palestinian state. It is clear that these negotiations were inadequate, yet they serve as a starting point for the future.

A *Kairos* Moment for Peace?

Mary Grey

Your remarks on borders are helpful, but like other areas we have discussed this remains highly contentious, and another area where painful compromises are called for.

I am conscious that this is my last exchange with you in this book and very aware of areas we have not discussed in sufficient depth as well as the way I have failed to convince you of many points. I do not dismiss Robert Cohen's words as hysterical but take with great seriousness his words – which I have heard other Jewish thinkers express:

> *The Jewish Kairos moment will come when we rediscover our Hebrew prophetic theology of justice and choose to take it seriously. Isaiah, Jeremiah, Amos and Micah were talking to us . . . and they still are.*

I think the traditions of prophetic theologies of justice are surely what will keep alive the desire for just peace. I think what underlies some of our exchanges are your conviction that there are two narratives, Israeli and Palestinian, with injustice on both sides, and a sense that to blame Israel for all the conflict is to be guilty of anti-Semitism. You also from time to time accuse me of lacking sympathy for Israeli suffering. I have repeatedly asserted that I have boundless compassion for what the Jewish people have suffered throughout 2,000 years from anti-Semitism **globally**, and from the horror of the Holocaust. But the Holocaust is now remembered in a spirit of repentance by many nations, in a way that the Palestinian Nakba is not. I think you have found it hard to accept the argument that the Palestinians did not cause Jewish suffering, but are being made to lose their homeland so that Israel may have one. If the concept of homeland is now crucial to the Israeli people, after many years of being without one, why should it be different for the Palestinians?

You may know the Palestinian poet, Mahmoud Darwish, who died in 2008, and to many represents the soul of the Palestinian people. He articulated this love of homeland like this:

I Come From There

I come from there and I have memories

Born as mortals are, I have a mother

And a house with many windows,

I have brothers, friends,

And a prison cell with a cold window.

Mine is the wave, snatched by sea-gulls,

I have my own view,

And an extra blade of grass.

Mine is the moon at the far edge of the words,

And the bounty of birds,

And the immortal olive tree.

I walked this land before the swords

> Turned its living body into a laden table.
> I come from there. I render the sky unto her mother
> When the sky weeps for her mother.
> And I weep to make myself known
> To a returning cloud.
> I learnt all the words worthy of the court of blood
> So that I could break the rule.
> To make a single word: Homeland . . .
> (www.poemhunter.com/poem/i-come-from-there)

Yet this poet still believed that peace was possible: 'I do not despair,' he told the Israeli newspaper *Haaretz*. 'I am patient and am waiting for a profound revolution in the consciousness of the Israelis. The Arabs are ready to accept a strong Israel . . . – all it has to do is open the gates of its fortress and make peace' (www.mahmoud-darwish.com).

This is also the aspiration highlighted in the document produced by the Christian Churches and promulgated in Bethlehem, December 2009, Kairos Palestine 2009, *A Moment of Truth:*

> Our message to the Jews tells them: Even though we have fought one another in the recent past and still struggle today, we are able to love and live together. We can organize our political life, with all its complexity, according to the logic of this love and its power, after ending the occupation and establishing justice.
> (Patriarchs and heads of Christian Churches: *Kairos Palestine: A Moment of Truth: A word of faith, hope and love from the heart of Palestinian suffering*, Jerusalem, 2009, 5.4.2)

The document ends with this spirit of *kairos (now is the moment!)* and a call to the Israelis:

> This is a call to see the face of God in each one of God's creatures and overcome the barriers of fear or race in order

to establish a constructive dialogue and not remain within the cycle of never-ending manoeuvres that aim to keep the situation as it is. Our appeal is to reach a common vision, built on equality and sharing, not on superiority, negation of the other, or aggression, using the pretext of fear and. We say that love is possible and mutual trust is possible. Thus peace is possible and definitive reconciliation also.

(Kairos 2009, 9.1)

Powerful words and they emerge from the growing strategy of nonviolence that I have been describing frequently in this book. As I write, the world has been celebrating the 50 the anniversary of the 'I have a dream' speech by Martin Luther King in the United States. King left us with a dream but also a great inspiration in his method of nonviolent resistance – a strategy of hope and transformation – which has never been more relevant today as a response to this *kairos* moment. This is the vision articulated now by activists and spiritual leaders alike, from Israeli peace activists and Palestinian Christian leaders such as Elias Chacour, retiring Archbishop of Galilee (former) Patriarch Michel Sabbah and Canon Naim Ateek – among others. My own hope and dream at the end of this dialogue is that it can be a contribution joining the great cloud of witnesses yearning for peace and reconciliation. And that this kairos moment will not again disappoint those lives that are most in need of peace for their very survival.

Towards Peace

Dan Cohn-Sherbok

Our journey is nearly at an end. For twenty chapters you and I have wrestled with one another over the problem of the Palestinian–Israeli conflict. It has been a struggle, and possibly we have left our readers dazed and confused. This is inevitable, I believe, since the Palestinian and the Israeli narratives are utterly different. For the Jewish people, Israel has become a central focus of concern: in a post-Holocaust world the Jewish state is perceived by many Jews as vital to Jewish survival. For the Palestinians, the Zionists are viewed as colonial oppressors who have stolen their land. This clash of perspectives has been the cause of a century of unending suffering and bloodshed. In the past Jews and Muslims were able to live together in peace, but this is no longer so. Instead, Arab anti-Semitism and Jewish hatred of the Palestinians has poisoned both communities.

Truth is elusive – where is it to be found in this debate? As an ardent supporter of the Palestinian cause, you believe that there is a single truth to be uncovered. Throughout our book you have pressed the case for justice for the Palestinian community whom you believe has been oppressed and persecuted. By contrast, I have stated the case for Zionism, and have attempted to demonstrate the regrettable uncompromising intransigence of the Palestinian people and their determination to drive the Jews into the sea. Readers will have to decide for themselves whose cause is more just.

Despite this clash of opinion, there is one point on which we agree: the need for peaceful reconciliation. In this context, I want to go back to a speech given at the beginning of his presidency by Barack Obama in Cairo on 4 June 2009. For decades, he stated, there has been a stalemate. Two peoples with legitimate aspirations, each with a painful history that makes compromise elusive. It is easy to point fingers, he continued, for Palestinians to point to the displacement brought by Israel's founding, and for Israelis to point to the constant hostility and attacks throughout its history from within its borders as well as beyond. But if we see this conflict from only one side or the other, then we will be blind to the truth: the only resolution is for the aspirations of both sides to be met through two states.

In the preface to my book *The Palestinian State: A Jewish Justification*, my Palestinian friend and colleague, Dr. Dawoud El-Alami, was adamant that this is the only way forward. With regard to my endorsement of a two-state solution, he wrote:

> There can be no hope for peace while the Palestinians remain deprived of any recognized political identity. Dan argues that Jews worldwide should support the proposition of a two-state solution and UN recognition of Palestinian statehood in

principle. He suggests that this need not specify borders in the first instance as its importance would be an expression of good faith and commitment to a long-term, peaceful solution. At the same time, for Israel to have confidence to move forward, there would have to be a commitment to peace on the part of the Palestinians in order to ensure the security of Israel and to reassure Israelis and Israel's supporters that there will be no holocaust in the Holy Land. Both communities have deeply rooted historical, religious and cultural connections to the Holy Land and progress will only be possible when each acknowledges the validity of these connections and the equal humanity of the other. Both communities have suffered, and it is natural for this to create the determination to survive and ensure that this will never happen to us again. But suffering should also bring us to understanding and compassion and the desire to relieve the suffering of others.

(Dan Cohn-Sherbok, *A Palestinian State*, pp. xiv–xv)

This is the vision that should inspire us on the threshold of a new century.

Bibliography

Amit, Zalman and Levit, Daphna, *Israeli Rejectionism: A Hidden Agenda in the Middle East Peace Process*, London: Pluto Press, 2011.

Annan, Kofi, *Interventions: A Life in War and peace*, with Nader Mousavizadeh, London: Allen Lane, 2012.

Ateek, Naim, *Justice and Only Justice: A Palestinian Theology of Liberation*, New York, Maryknoll: Orbis, 1989.

Ateek, Naim, *A Palestinian Cry for Reconciliation*, New York: Orbis, 2008.

Avineri, S., *The Making of Modern Zionism*, New York: Basic Books, 1981.

Avnery, Uri, *In Praise of Emotion* (in Tikkun, 20 April 2013, accessed online). Available at http://zope.gush-shalom.org/en/channels/avnery/1366371319

Barr, James, *A Line in the Sand*, London: Simon and Schuster, 2011.

Ben-Gurion, David, *Ben-Gurion Looks at the Bible,* translated by Jonathan Kolatch, New York: Jonathan David publisher, 1972 (first published in Hebrew in 1969). Available at http://mailstar.net./bengur-bible.html

Buber, Martin, 1918 Essay entitled "Toward the Decision", in: Paul R. Mendes-Flohr (ed.), *A Land of Two Peoples: Martin Buber on Jews and Arabs*, New York: Oxford University Press, 1983, p. 410.

Carter, Jimmy, *Keeping Faith: Memoirs of a President*, New York: Bantam, 1982.

Carter, Jimmy, *Palestine: Peace not Apartheid*, London: Pocket Books, 2006.
Chacour, Elias, *Blood Brothers*, New Jersey: Chosen Books, 1984.
Chapman, Colin, *Whose Holy City? Jerusalem and the Israeli–Palestinian Conflict*, Oxford: Lion books, 2004.
Chomsky, Noah and Pappé, Ilan, *Gaza in Crisis: Reflections on Israel's War against the Palestinians*, London: Penguin, 2011.
CO 733/58 C.P. 60 (23), *History of the Negotiations Leading up to the Balfour Declaration*, December 1922.
Cohn-Sherbok, Lavinia and Dan, *A Short Reader of Judaism*, Oxford: Oneworld, 1997.
Cohn-Sherbok, Dan, *Introduction to Zionism and Israel*, London: Continuum, 2012.
Cohn-Sherbok, Dan, *Judaism: History, Belief and Practice*, London: Routledge, 2003.
Cohn-Sherbok, Dan and El-Alami, Dawoud, *The Palestine–Israeli Conflict*, Oxford: Oneworld, 2003.
Cohn-Sherbok, Dan, *The Palestinian State: A Jewish Justification*, Exeter: Impress Books, 2012.
Docker, John, Instrumentalising the Holocaust, in: *Holy Land Studies*, Vol. 11, 2012, pp. 1–32.
Dumper, Michael, *The Politics of Sacred Space: The Old City of Jerusalem in the Middle-East Conflict*, London: Lynne Rienner Publishers, 2002.
Eliot, George, *Daniel Deronda*, London: Penguin Books, 1995.
Finkelstein, Norman G., *Image and Reality of the Israel–Palestine Conflict*, 2nd edition. London: Verso, 2003.
Flapan, *Zionism and the Palestinians*, London: Croom Helm, 1979.
Fromkin, David, *A Peace to End all Peace – the Fall of the Ottoman empire and the Creation of the Middle East*, New York: Henry Holt and Co., 1989, pp. 317–318.
Fleischmann, Ellen L. The emergence of the Palestinian Women's Movement, 1929–1939. *Journal of Palestine Studies* 29, 3 (2000): 16–32.
Gandhi, *Notes in Young India*, April 6, 1921.
Gandhi, *Extracts from letters by*, to Hermann Kallenbach, July 20, August 16 and August 28, 1937.
Gelber, Yoav, *Palestine 1948: War, Escape and the Emergence of the Palestinian Refugee Problem*, Sussex: Sussex Academic Press, 2006.
Gilbert, Martin, *Israel: A History*, New York: Black Swan, 2008.
Grey, Mary, *To Rwanda and Back – Liberation, Reconciliation and Spirituality*, London: Darton, Longman and Todd, 2007.

Grey, Mary, *The Advent of Peace: A Gospel Journey to Christmas*, London: SPCK, 2010.
Hass, Amira, *Drinking the Sea at Gaza: Days and Nights in a Land under Siege*, New York: Holt Paperbacks, 1996
Hertzberg, A. (ed.), *The Zionist Idea: A Historical Analysis and Reader*, New York: Atheneum, 1959.
Herzl, T., *Protokoll des I. ZionistenKongressen in Basel*, Prague: Selbstverlag, 1911.
Huneidi, Sahar, *The Balfour Declaration in British Archives, 1922–1923: New Insights into Old Controversies* , Monograph No. 136 Annals of the Faculty of Arts, Volume XIX, 1999, Part 1 (pp. 1–39), Part 11 (1–45).
Ingrams, Doreen. *Palestine Papers. 1917–1922: Seeds of Conflict*, London: Eland, 1972.
Johnson, Paul, *A History of the Jews*, London: Weidenfeld and Nicolson, 1987.
Jürgensmeyer, Mark. *Gandhi's Way*, Berkeley, CA: University of California Press, pp. 63–64.
Khalidi, Rashid, *Brokers of Deceit: How the US has undermined Peace in the Middle East,* Boston: Beacon, 2013.
Khalidi, Walid, *All that Remains: The Palestinian Villages Occupied and Depopulated by Israel in 1948*, Beirut: Institute for Palestinian Studies, 1948.
Klug, Brian, *Being Jewish and Doing Justice: Bringing Argument to Life,* London: Vallentine Mitchell, 2011.
Klug, Tony, *Will the Arab Peace Initiative Rescue the Two-State Imperative?* in: *Conference on Promoting the Arab Peace Initiative*, Amman, Jordan, June 2013, with participation from Jordan, Palestine.
Laqueur, Walter, *A History of Zionism*, London: Weidenfeld & Nicholson, 1972.
Laqueur, W. and Rubin, B. (eds.), *The Israel–Arab Reader*, London: Penguin, 1995.
Legum, Colin and Shaked, Haim (eds.), *Middle East Contemporary Survey*, Vol 2. New York: Holme and Meier, 1976–1977 (published subsequently annually).
Lemkin, Raphael, *Axis Rule in Occupied Europe: Laws of Occupation, Analysis of Government, Proposals or Redress*, New York: Columbia University Press, 1944.
Lerner, Rabbi Michael, *Healing Israel/Palestine: A Path to Peace and Reconciliation*, Berkeley, CA: Tikkun Books, 2003, p. 60.
Levy, Gideon, *The Punishment of Gaza*, London and New York: Verso, 2010.

Lilienthal, Alfred M., *The Zionist Connection: What Price Peace?* New York: Dodd, Mead, 1978.

Macpherson, Duncan (ed.), *A Living Stone: Selected Essays and Addresses by Michael Prior CM*, London: Living Stones of the Holy Land, 2006.

Masalha, Nur, *The Bible and Zionism: Invented Traditions, Archeology and Post-colonialism in Palestine–Israel*, London: Zed Books, 2007.

Mendes-Flohr, Paul. R. (ed.), *A Land of Two Peoples: Martin Buber on Jews and Arabs,* Oxford: Oxford University Press, 1984.

Mendes-Flohr, Reinharz (ed.), *The Jew in the Modern World*, Oxford: Oxford University Press, 1995.

Morris, Benny, *Righteous Victims: A History of the Zionist–Arab Conflict, 1881–1999*, New York: Random House Inc., 2001, p. 301.

Naor, A, *Begin in Power* (in Hebrew), Tel Aviv: Yediot Aharonot, 1993, p. 220.

Nouwen, Henri, *Bread for the Journey: Reflections for Every Day of the Year*, London: Darton, Longman and Todd, 1996.

O'Brien, Conor Cruise, *The Siege*, London: Paladin, 1988.

Pappé, Ilan, *The Ethnic Cleansing of Palestine*, Oxford: Oneworld Publications, 2006.

Peled, Miko, *The General's Son: Journey of an Israeli in Palestine*, Charlottesville, Virginia: Just World Books, 2012.

Pinsker, Leo, *Autoemancipation*, London: Federation of Zionist Youth, 1932.

Qumsiyeh, Mazin, *Popular Resistance in Palestine: A History of Hope and Empowerment*, London: Pluto Press, 2011.

Qumsiyeh, Mazin B., *Sharing the Land of Canaan,* London: Pluto, 2004.

Rittner, Carol et al (eds.), *Genocide in Rwanda: Complicity of the Churches*, St Paul MN: Paragon House, 2004.

Ross, Dennis, *The Missing Peace: The Inside Story of the Fight for the Middle East,* New York: Farrar, Straus and Giroux, 2004.

Ross, Stewart, *The Israeli–Palestinian Conflict*, Abingdon, Oxon: Bookpoint Ltd., 2007.

Roy, Sara, *Failing Peace: Gaza and the Palestinian–Israeli Conflict*, London: Pluto, 2007.

Rubin, Barry, *Israel*, New Haven: Yale University Press, 2012.

Sachar, Howard M., *A History of Israel from the Rise of Zionism to Our Time*, New York: Alfred A. Knopf, 2007.

Schneer, Jonathan, *The Balfour Declaration,* London: Bloomsbury, 2010.

Shaftesbury, *Quarterly Review*, 1838, Vol. 64, pp. 104–108.

Shlaim, Avi, The Balfour Declaration and its consequences, in: *Israel and Palestine*, London: Verso, 2009, pp. 3–24.

Sand, Shlomo, *The Invention of the Jewish People*, Brooklyn, NY: Verso, 2010.

Sebag-Montefiore, Simon, *Jerusalem: The Biography*, London: Weidenfeld & Nicholson, 2011, p. 415.

Segev, Tom, *One Palestine Complete: Jews and Arabs under the British Mandate*, New York: Henry Holt and Co., 1999.

Shuckburgh, CO 733/35, 21 December 1922.

Sizer, Stephen, *Christian Zionism: Road Map to Armageddon*, London: Intervarsity Press, 2005.

Sizer, Stephen, *Zion's Christian Soldiers: The Bible, Israel and the Church*, Nottingham: InterVarsity Press, 2007.

Stein, Kenneth W., *Heroic Diplomacy: Sadat, Kissinger, Carter, Begin, and the Quest for Arab-Israeli Peace*, New York: Routledge, 1999.

Tal, David, *War in Palestine 1948: Strategy and Diplomacy*, London: Routledge, 2004.

Tuchman, Barbara W, *Bible and Sword: England and Palestine from the Bronze Age to Balfour*, New York: Funk and Wagnalls, 1956.

Vital, David, *Zionism: The Formative Years*, Oxford: Clarendon Press, 1982.

Wavell, Sir Archibald, *Allenby*, London: Harrap and Co., 1940.

Zaru, Jean, *Occupied with Non-Violence: A Palestinian Woman Speaks*, Minneapolis: Fortress, 2008.

Websites

www.en.wikipedia.org/wiki/McMahon–Hussein_Correspondence

www.en.wikipedia.org/King_David_Hotel_bombing

http://en.wikipedia.org/wiki/Benny_Morris

www.gandhiserve.org/information/writings_online/articles/gandhi_jews_palestine.html

www.hist.net/kieser/aghet/Essays/EssayWien.html

https://www.jewishvirtuallibrary.org/jsource/History/muftihit.html

www.jewishvirtuallibrary.org/jsource/Peace/fence.html

https://www.jewishvirtuallibrary.org/jsource/.../defensiveshield.html

www.mideastweb.org

www.mythsandfacts.org/conflict.asp

BIBLIOGRAPHY

www.web.israelinsider.com

www.palestinehistory.com/issues/refugee/ref1967

www.palestinefacts.org/pf-1991 to-now-defenseshield_2003.php

www.thejerusalemfund.org

www.peaceandPalestine.com/intoseamyth

http://www.wikipedia.org/wiki/Exodus_(ship)

http://en.wikipedia.org/wiki/1948_Palestine_war

http://en.wikipedia.org/wiki/camp_David_Accords

http://www.en.wikipedia.org/wiki/Yasser_Arafat

www.palestineremembered.com/.../Story420.html

http://truth-out.org/opinion/item/12635-noam-chomsky-my-visit-to-gaza-the-worlds-largest-open-air-prison

Index

Abbas, Mahmoud – successor of Arafat 244, 251 and US 25; and recognition of Palestinian statehood 261, 269; and talks in Sharm-el-Sheikh (2009) 264; and plea for independent state 269–270; March 2001 – refusal of peace deal and determination to declare unilateral independence 283

Abdullah, King 142

Abuelish, Dr Izzeldin – and death of daughters through Israeli shells 259; and refusal to hate 260

AIPAC (American–Israel Public Affairs committee) 215

Al Qaeda terrorists, attack on World Trade Centre 234

Allenby, General – and entry to Jerusalem 46–7; 53; 63; and Arab Women's Association

Annan, Kofi – and assessment of Arafat 161; and Wall; and speech at Yad Vashem 239; and Ariel Sharon; reaction to massacre at Jenin 239–240; 241

Arab delegation to London 1921 63

Arab League 128–129

Arab Women's Association 76–77

Arab Women and Patriarchy 80–81; and increased status in war context 81

Arafat, Yasser(Yasir)130, 141; elected Chairman of the PLO 145; rise to power 152; and Battle of Karameh 158–159, 163; and First Intifada 197–198; and Saddam Hussein 198–199, 201–202; and Oslo talks, and handshake with Rabin 204; and Cairo Agreement 205; 207; 211; and Camp David summit II 214,

217; meeting with Netanyahu 219, 220; Paris meeting 221; under siege at Ramallah 235; and Kofi Annan 239; and Nobel Peace prize 1994 244; 249; and Basic Constitution of the Palestinian transitional state- death of 251

Archaeological discoveries – of the Temple 26; the Black Obelisk 26

Ateek, Canon Naim xviii; and Nakba 108; and six Day War 147; and First Intifada 189–190, 193; and Oslo Accords 207–207; 214–215; 218–219, 221, 234, 237and six principles for lasting peace 273; and status of Jerusalem as model for peace and coexistence 286, 292

Attlee, Clement – and critique of King David Hotel bombing 94

Avnery, Uri – and Six Day War 147–148; and Two State solution 266–267; and emotional component of peace 281, 287

Awad, Mubarak – and founding of Palestinian Centre for Non-Violence 194–195

Baader-Meinhof terrorists 164
Baghdad Conferences, First and Second 184
Baker, James, US Secretary of State 202, 203
Balfour, Arthur 30; and the Balfour Declaration 30–31; 35, 36; memo to Lord Curzon 37–38, 55–56; letter to Lloyd George 39; 40; and aftermath 45–60; and attitude to Jews 51; 55, 64, 65–66

Balfour Declaration 13, 29–44; and Avi Shlaim 45–46; 49; 61, 63; and impact in Palestine 63–65; and motion to scrap in 1922 65; 68, and *passim*

Ban Ki-Moon, UN Secretary General – and settlements 284

Baron Edmund de Rothschild 29

Barak, Ehud – elected 1999 220; proposes idea of Separation Fence 220; calls for election 221

Begin, Menachem 98, and *The Revolt* 111; 113; 170–171; and Camp David Accords 176–180, 184, 185; 186

Begin Plan 173–174, 175

Bell, Bishop George 97

Ben-Eleazar, Joseph 108

Ben-Gurion, David – and the Bible 20–22; 24–25, 157; and land of Israel 23–24; 46, 89; 104; as first prime minister 117, 120–122; 130; raid on Egyptian camp in Gaza 133; law of return 134–135; and Palestinian Right of Return 136; 137; 139, 153; and Declaration of Independence 155–156; 206; and partition 267

Bernadotte, Count Folke – assassination of 118, 151–152; and plan submitted to UN 134;

Bethlehem, situation at checkpoints 223; siege of Church of the Nativity 2002 240–241

Black March 2002, and Palestinian suicide bombing attacks 238

INDEX

Borders, question of, for Peace Agreement 288–289
British Mandate in Palestine 58, 61–74; approval of 73; 82; ending of 117
Brit Shalom, 69–71; 87
B'*Tselem* 196, 198; and violence of 2nd Intifada 218
Buber, Martin 13; and bi-national state 68–69; 70–71, 82, 92–93; 266
Bush, President – and challenge to Israel 250

Camp David Accords 175–180; 181–182, 184, 201; Summit 2000 212, 217
Carter, President Jimmy – and Sadat 174; 184; and Begin 185; 191; as broker of peace with President Clinton 214; comments on the Wall 228; 234; and Nobel Peace Prize 244
Chacour, Elias, Archbishop of Galilee 108, 141, 143, 164, 292
Chamberlain, Joseph 19; 23
Churchill, Winston – and Balfour declaration 47; 52, 57, 59, 68, 73; and White Paper 35–36; and critique of King David bombing 91; 110
Chief Rabbi 13; the Rabbis Kook 16;
Chomsky, Noah – and report on visit to Gaza 252–253, 254
Christian Peacemaker teams – and work in Hebron 278
Clayton, Sir Gilbert 47–48
Clinton, President and Nobel Peace Prize 244
Clinton, President and Barak, Ehud, Peace Proposal 2000 191

Clinton, Hillary Rodham, US Secretary of State 262
Cohen, Robert – and need for prophetic justice 282, 283, 284–285, 287, 288, 289
Cohn-Sherbok, Dan xii–xiii; xx; and background 27; and article in *Western Mail* 255–256, 260; and *The Palestinian State: a Jewish Justification* 274, 293–294
Combatants for Peace 244, 280
Congreve, General W.N. 57
Contribution of Women to Zionism in Palestine 79–80
Curzon, Lord – and memo from Balfour 37–38

Darwish, Mahmoud "*I come from there*" 290–291
Dayan, Moshe 141, 143, 148, 175
Declaration of Independence 117, 153
Deir Yassin Massacre 107–108, 111–113
Dohm, Wilhelm Christian 53
Dreyfus, Captain Alfred 3

EAPPI (Ecumenical Accompaniment Programme) 278
El-Alami, Dawoud 66–67, 84, 293–294
Eliot, George (Mary Ann Evans) 9, 10, 13, 20
Eshkol, Lev 161
Exodus SS 97–98

Fackenheim, Emil xvi
Fatah 139, 144–145, 149, 152; founding of 159; and battle

of Karameh 159–160; 163; Constitution of – and armed struggle 142; and Battle of Gaza 248

Fedayeen 152; and PLO 163; and raid 174–175

First, Second and Third Aliya 29; 41; 123; and women 78; Third Aliyah and women 78

Gaillard, Philippe – and memory 165

Gandhi – and partition 10, 115; and Zionism 84–88, 92–93; 194; and 10 rules for peace (Jürgensmeyer) 281

Gaza strip – and Israeli attacks 228; 246–261; and history of 246–248; and international reaction 248; attack on Gaza and besieging of Ramallah 250; and report of Noah Chomsky 252–253; and Gideon Levy 254–255

Gaza flotilla raid 264

Grand Mufti 50; and election 1921; as Haj Amin Al-Husseini 62; instigating riots 71;133 82–83, 87, 89, 92, 94–95, 96– 97, 99, 100, 127

Grey, Mary xiii–xiv; xx; and Rwanda 56

Goldman, Felix 2

Goldstein, Baruch – and Hebron massacre 205, 206

Goldstone, Senator – and report on violations in Gaza, commissioned by UNHRC 257–259

Gush Shalom Peace Movement 266

Ha-Am, Ahad 10–11; 16, 70

Hadi, Tarab Abdul 76–77

Haganah 90, 91, 106–107, 129, 164

Haj Amin Al-Husseini 62, instigating riots 71

Hamas xvii; and Charter 67; 68; and Covenant 116; and deportation of 415 militants 202; 204; and retaliation for Hebron massacre 205; history of 208–209, extremism 209, 211; and Kofi Annan 239; and commitment to armed struggle 243; firing rockets from Gaza 244, 252; taking power as ruling party in Gaza 247, 251; and Battle of Gaza 248; tensions with Fatah 251–252; branded terrorist organisation by the west 251; and Gaza policy 257; with Hezbollah–determination to stop the Peace process 264; condemnation of 266

Haniyeh, Palestinian president 251

Hass, Amira – and Gaza 246, 248

Hebron massacre 205, 206

Hechler, William 6–7; 18

Herzl, Theodor xv; 3; 5; and *The Jewish State* 6; 7, 8, 15 18–19, 54; 20, 22, 23, 25, 28, 29, 41, 99, 125, 129

Hess, Moses – *Rome and Jerusalem* 2; 7

Hobeike, Elie – and Sabra/Shatila massacre 182–182

Holocaust xvi; xviii; 1; 8, 12, 14, 100, 101–102, 290

Hotline: Centre for the Defence of the Individual 196

INDEX

Hussein, King of Jordan 150; and Camp David Accords 177–180; 184, 208

Hussein, Sharif of Mecca – and McMahon correspondence 33–36; 37, 40

Hussein, Saddam 195, 197, 201, and overthrow by Britain 250

Husseini, Faisal Al 199–200

IDF (Israeli Defence force) – and war crimes at Jenin massacre 236; and Church of the Nativity siege 240; and Operation Rainbow 247–248, 251; and Operation Days of Penitence 248, 251; and withdrawal from Gaza strip 251

Ingrams, Doreen 36–39, 56

Intifada, First 188–202; 213; and Oslo talks 204, 206; 211, 217

Intifada, Second 216–218; and Palestinian violence 238; effect on Gazans 247

Irgun 90, 91, 108

Islamic Resistance Movement 243

Israel – admitted to UN 118

Jabotinsky, Vladimir 16; 30, 61, 90, 99

Jenin, Massacre at 236–238, 239

Jerusalem – and peace process 285–287; and suggestion of sharing – Simon Sebag Montefiori 287; 288

Jewish kairos moment 289

John Paul II, Pope, 241

Johnson, President 149

Jürgensmeyer, Mark 10 Gandhian principles for peace

Just War theory – with relevance to Gaza 252

Kairos Palestine 291–292
Kairos UK 282
Karameh, Battle of 152
Kautsky, Karl 11
Kellenbach, Katherina von xvii
Kerry, John 228
Khartoum Conference 1967 161
King David Hotel, bombing of 90–91
King-Crane commission 65
King, Martin Luther 292
Kissinger, Henry 162
Kitchener, Lord 33
Kook, Rabbis 157

Lausanne Conference (1949) 126, 127–128
Lawrence T.E. 34, 35, 47, 73
Lemkin, Raphael – and genocide definition 104
Lerner, Rabbi Michael – and post-traumatic stress disorder 69; 71, 84; and Deir Yassin 113; and Six Day War 146–147; 207, 214, 222; and support to Senator Goldstone 59
Levy, Gideon – and critique of Israel's action in Gaza 254–255
Lindsay, Hal 7
Lloyd George, David 30, 39; 46–7, 68, 73

Madrid conference 1991 197
Major, John, Prime Minister 203
Masalha, Nur 81; on Deir Yassin massacre 107–108; critiqued by Avi Shaim 124–25
Meighen, Arthur 59

INDEX

Meir, Golda 163, 194
Memoricide 165, 166–167
Mendelssohn, Moses 49, 53
Mitchell, Senator George 262
Mitchell Report 2001, terms of 231–233; 234–235
Montagu, Edwin 30; and Memorandum 42–44 55; 48–49
Morris, Benny – and change of heart 190–193, 196; and archival research 285
Morsi, President 185
Motzkin, Leo 125
McMahon, Sir Henry – and correspondence with Sharif Hussein 32–36; 39–40
Munich bombing 1972 and Black September Group 164, 166, 168
Mussawi, Sheikh Abbas, death of 202

Nakba, Al xviii, 107–109, 110; and aftermath 155; 165 *and passim*
Nasser, Gamal Abdal 131,132; and Voice of Palestine radio station 138; and PLO 138; 143, 148–150; weakening of influence 152; and Six Day War; and obtaining of Russian missiles 162
Nazis 22; and Grand Mufti 95–96; and Palestinian collaboration
Netanya, suicide bombing at – 235, 238
Netanyahu, Benjamin – wins election and forms coalition government 209; with Barak unwilling to relinquish settlements 214; 219; speech of 2009 263
Nordau, Max xv; 12, 18

Obama, President and appointment of Senator Mitchell 262; and Cairo speech 262, 293; and (2009) hosting of meeting between Netanyahu, and Mahmoud Abbas (the Palestinian authority) to establish a basis for settlement 263–264
Operation Rainbow (2004) 247–248, 251
Operation Days of Penitence (2004) 248, 251
Operation Defensive Shield 235; and Jenin Massacre 236–238; 250
Operation Cast Lead (2008–2009) 254
Osirak, Israel's destruction of nuclear plant 186
Oslo Peace Agreement 204–206; and aftermath 206–207; critique of, 208–212; 216, 217 and Wall 227; 229; and Gaza 254; and status of Jerusalem 286; Hebron massacre 205, 206

Pakistan – partition of 112–113, 119
Palestine Arab Women's congress 76
Palestine Liberation Organization PLO 116,138–139; 140; and Six Day War 150; 151; 153; denunciation with Syria – of peace process between Egypt and Israel 172; and Sabra and

Shatila massacres 181; 186; and First Intifada 197–198, 202; and Oslo talks 204, 206; 211; and commitment to armed struggle 242–243

Palestine National Council – and 10 point plan 116

Palestinian refugees and Right of Return 135–136, 137, 140, 151–15 and UN Resolution 194 154; and Resolution 242 185; failure to deal with issue at Oslo 212; 261; 272; Silvan Shalom and the waiving of the right of Return 272; and Two-State solution 272–273, 274–276

Pappé, Ilan – and ethnic cleansing 122–123; 124–126, 127, 129, 151, 155, 165

Peace Now 198

Peel Commission 20

Peled, Miko 244–245

Peres, Shimon 203; and Oslo talks 204–205; elected Prime minster 209, 211; 219, 220; and Nobel Peace Prize 244; 249–250

Phalangists 181–182, 184, 195

Piçot, Francois 32, 35 40

Pinsker, Leo *Autoemancipation* 2, 3, 7, 54

Pittsburgh Platform 49

Plan Dalet – and research of Ilan Pappé 104–105, 105–107

Prior, Revd Michael, 146

Qadaffi, Colonel 172

Qumsiyeh, Mazin – and Women's contribution 75–76; 81; and *sumud* 140, 195, 245; 187; 194; 198–199

Rabin, Yitzhak 149; and Intifada 196–198; 203; and Oslo talks 204; assassination of 207–208, 211; 220; and Wall 224–225; and Nobel Peace Prize 244, 250

Raya, Archbishop Joseph – and letter to Golda Meir 194

Robinson, Mary – and Goldstone Report 258

Rogers, William – and Peace Plan 1969 145–146; 162

Rosen, Rabbi David xviii

Ross, Dennis 189, 202; and Rabin's assassination 207

Rothberg, Ro'i 141–142, 143

Rothschild, Lord 31, 36; and Montagu Memorandum 44

Roy, Sara – and critique of Oslo Agreement 210–211, 212, 213–214; 219

Ruether, Rosemary Radford xvii; xxi

Sabbah, Patriarch (former) Michel 240–241, 292

Sabeel xviii; 108

Sabra and Shatila, massacres of 181–184, 187

Sadat, President 162, 169–170; and Knesset initiative 169–170, 171–172 ; 173–174; and Camp David Accords 176–180, 183–184

Samuel, Sir Herbert, High commissioner, 58–59, 62, 63–4

Sand, Shlomo 24–25, 27

Separation Fence/Wall/Barrier 220, 223–225, 226–228, 229–230

Settlements, The – and UN resolution 446 188; failure of Oslo to deal with issue 212;

2009 –10 month settlement freeze 263; refusal of Netanyahu to extend freeze 265; settlement expansion as obstacle to peace 277; acts of violence by settlers 277; international condemnation 284; call for compromise on both sides 284

Shaftesbury, Lord – and the restoration of the Jews 4–6; 25

Shamir, Yitzak 113, 197

Sharon, Ariel 132; and attacks of Unit 101 137; and Sabra and Shatila Massacres 181–183, 184; 186; and visit to Temple Mount 216–217, 220–221; events leading up to this 219–220; and Operation Defensive Shield 237–238; and Kofi Annan 239; and siege of Church of the Nativity 241; re-election (2003); proposal to waive Right of Return 274

Sharrett, Moshe 133, 137, 139

Shlaim, Avi 34, 45–46; 49; critique of Masalha 124–125; 198–199

Shuckburgh, Sir John Evelyn 64–65

Shukayri, Ahmad – and PLO 138, 144

Six Day War, The 144–157

Sizer, Stephen 4; 5

Stern, Avraham – and Mussolini 101

Stern Gang 101, 151–152

Suez Crisis 131–143

Sumud 140, 195; and Jean Zaru 245

Sykes, Sir Mark – and Anglo-French–Russian Agreement 32, 35, 40, 64, 82

Tantura, Al, Massacre 108–109

Tent of Nations – and efforts for peace 278–279

Two-State Solution 261; proposal of Yasser Abed Rabbo (PLO) 265; and four different options 268–271; and essential components 271–272

United Nations Committee on Palestine (UNSCOP) 103–104, 105, 107; and ending of Mandate 110–111

Vance, Cyrus 175

War of Independence (see Nakba) 117–119

Wavell, General 64–65

Weizmann, Chaim 30, 32, 38, 46; letter to Balfour 47; and Faisal 47; and Paris Peace Conference 50; 58, 73, 75, 90, 100

White, Canon Andrew 241

White Paper (1939) 97–98

Woodrow Wilson, President 30

Yom Kippur War 163, 167, 168–170, 201

Young, William 5

Zangwill, Israel 5

Zaru, Jean – and non-violence 245

Zionism, types of 15–17; 99

Zionist Congress, First, xv; 10, 15, 18; and Isaac Mayer Wise 48–49; and women 78

Zochrot 114